ONE DAY
SHE'LL
DARKEN

THE INSPIRATION FOR THE TNT SERIES *I AM THE NIGHT*

ONE DAY SHE'LL DARKEN

The Mysterious Beginnings of Fauna Hodel

FAUNA HODEL

with J.R. BRIAMONTE

Published by Graymalkin Media, LLC

www.graymalkin.com

Copyright © 2008 Fauna Hodel with J.R. Briamonte

ISBN: 978-1-63168-247-6

Printed in the United States of America

1   3   5   7   9   10   8   6   4   2

In loving memory

Linda Howard

and

Mary Sherrill Chidiac

ACKNOWLEDGMENTS

I'd like to thank the countless individuals who assisted and supported me during the writing of this book. Their contributions made this book possible.

To the many professionals all over the world who took the time to read the manuscript in its developing stages whose feedback and encouragement kept me going.

To my family, Yvette and Gino Gentile and Rasha and Vanna Pecoraro and my "through thick and thin" film partner Liliane S. Tsuha, and Jan Hewitt, Joyce Kimble, Rev. Don Butler, Rev. Michael Beckwith, and my Reno family.

To my wonderful Elvis Kawahara who proves . . . that ELVIS LIVES . . . his mother, Peace Tan Kawahara and his brother, Wendell Kawahara. Without Elvis I could not have kept going. . . .

I would like to also thank Papa and Mama Tokuda, Jacqueline Higa, Dayna Mari, Jennifer Crites, Judy Hevenly, Bill Paredes, Rev. Helen Street, Corinne Galardo, and Gerry Stober.

Please know all the ANGELS . . . here and beyond . . . I THANK YOU for the love and encouragement . . . and . . .

I would also like to thank my precious Luanne Rucker who gave me the important link I had been searching for, not knowing it would lead to my own Pandora's box.

I wish to thank James Walton.

I wish to thank my editors, Claudio Martinez, Lisa McBride Azuma, and Heidi Mulligan who helped improve the book.

AUTHOR'S NOTE

The following events are true, chronicled from the people who lived them. Both of my mothers were great storytellers, often adding plenty of colorful detail. Other accounts were verified from documented materials taken from the original sources that included diaries, letters, newspaper accounts, and official records. Some of the taped interviews were reproduced in their entirety in order to offer the reader the same sense of awe that created this extraordinary story.

The sequence of events confirms the earlier events in the book about George Hodel titled *The Black Dahlia Avenger*, by Steve Hodel, George's son, and my uncle. In his younger years, before he became a doctor who was involved with the Hollywood elite, before he became a prime suspect in the murder investigation of Elizabeth Short, and long before his acquittal in a sensational incest trial in 1948 after which he left the country, my grandfather made a living as a chauffeur. Perhaps that was a way for him to pry into the private lives of people he encountered. The decisions he made and the events in his life directly affected my entire world, even though we were separated by two generations.

—Fauna Hodel
— Rick Briamonte

ONE DAY SHE'LL DARKEN

CHAPTER 1

A female figure in a creamy white uniform hurriedly glided past the cashier's cage. But it wasn't the tempo that made this beauty conspicuous, it was her rich black skin. The woman didn't belong on the casino floor mingling among the guests—that was understood. She worked in the ladies' room as an attendant, but from her attitude and tight fitting uniform none of the onlookers seemed to mind. As she glided by, each in turn would cast a lustful gaze that only fueled her conceit. Her collar was neatly starched and finished with pale green piping at the edges, and small epaulets on the shoulders that widened her frame at the top. On other employees the same uniform hung like an old chamois waiting to dry, but on Jimmie it underscored her curves from the shoulders to the double-stitched hem just below the knee. Her shoes matched the color of the dress and highlighted her dark brown calves that shimmered through the nylons. On top of her thick, wavy black hair she wore a small white tricorne with green trim. Her rich red lipstick, flawlessly painted on as if by the hands of an artist, contrasted sharply against her ebony skin. At thirty-two years old Jimmie Lee Stokes' shapely contours still quivered when she walked. Everyone within sight noticed, and that's the way she wanted it. It made her feel confident.

Jimmie peered to the right, beyond the bar with hawk-like focus, checking to see if Chris made it to work yet. Her pace slowed to a deliberate saunter, passing the slot machines, stopping momentarily to

1

take notice of an old woman collecting a jackpot of nickels. It was 1951 and the Riverside Hotel & Casino in Reno was off limits to non-gaming employees and coloreds. Jimmie was indeed both, but she was too livid this morning to be concerned about rules.

The shoeshine stand had been spruced up as part of the hotel renovation. Three new leather chairs were bolted to the top with footrests of polished brass. As Jimmie Lee approached, she recognized the old man with short, curly gray hair. She watched him pack his satchel preparing to leave at the end of his graveyard shift. She stood squarely, arms crossed as he turned to remove his cotton apron. "Oh, Jimmie Lee," he said, "don't be sneakin' up on people like that. What's you tryin' to do, stop my heart?"

"Where's Chris?" She asked as her eyes searched about the casino.

"He didn't get here yet. Called earlier, about seven, said he'd be late. He asked me to stay until he comes in, but I can't wait no more. I got to get my grandchild to school . . . he knows that."

"Were yo'all busy last night?" she asked.

"We was early, till about 2:30, than it just got quiet. Only started pickin' up in maybe the last half hour or so."

Jimmie cautiously moved to the side of the raised shoeshine stand, out of the way, on guard for a floor boss. Within seconds, her eyes locked on to the strapping figure with the thin mustache coming from the restroom. His hands were behind his back tying his work apron, his head bowed down, emphasizing his receding hairline. His gait was quick, purposeful. Jimmie felt his presence as she turned to her left and came face to face with Chris. "Blessie," he said. She noted his surprised and somewhat annoyed stare. "What's you doing over here?" He glanced toward the old man and gave a thank you nod.

Jimmie's hands snapped to her hips. She cocked her head and glared, but spoke softly. "What am I doin' over here? What did ya think?! I come to see if ya'll was dead or not. Since ya didn't come home last night and you told me ya were gonna do some work at the church, I figured that God must of decided that He couldn't do without ya and took ya away from your poor little Blessie."

Chris chuckled, "No I ain't dead . . . see." She watched his eyes open wide and his brow lift. "But I am tired. I've been up all night with Miss Eisley, she. . . ."

"I knew it!" Jimmie erupted as she saw Chris' square face flush with blood. Quickly, she was nose to nose. "That damn little bitch's been trying to grab your ass ever since she moved here. And now you admit it! I knew I'd catch ya screwing around on me one of these days! You been doing it for a long time. Well I'm not putting up with no more a ya damn bull!" Jimmie didn't hold back her loud scolding as the veins in her neck began to protrude.

"Now Blessie, please wait a minute," said Chris, "let me explain. . . ." She felt his embarrassment, and knew she got through to him.

"I heard ya damn explanations, and ya damn sweet talkin', and your holier-than-thou preachin', and I ain't putting up with you makin' me look like no damn fool!"

The audience of two gave her power, but she didn't care who heard her rant. Her fiery eyes darted toward the stunned old man who backed away melting into the furniture.

She noticed the tiny beads of sweat glistening on Chris's furrowed brow. His eyes flicked back and forth between Jimmie and the nameless faces gathering about. She felt his nervous strength as he grabbed her arms to calm her down. His soothing voice usually worked. As he pulled her close to his chest she smelled her own breath laced with the odor of liquor.

"Now please! Blessie, listen to me, It's not what you think. I wasn't out with no . . ."

She cut him off while trying to escape his powerful grip. "Ah! Don't you touch me, you slimy dog! I don't want ya damn hands near me after you been with a filthy whore!"

"Blessie!" He said.

She was aware customers were now watching, but she let him squirm as his face oozed embarrassment.

"Blessie, please, ease up. Security is on his way over and we're gonna get written up or thrown out of here—then what are we going to do? You got to calm down woman, please!"

Suddenly she relaxed her muscles, slyly grinned without showing her teeth, pointed her nose sharply in the air and then gently placed her hands back to her sides. Jimmie sensed that Chris knew he was caught again. Her point made, she tossed her wavy black hair back with one quick motion and slowly strutted away, confident of her triumph. From across the casino floor, Jimmie glanced to the spot where Chris was standing. Their eyes met briefly, then Jimmie turned away and headed toward her work area, leaving her Daddy, as she called him at more affectionate moments, to patch up the mess she had created.

As she made her way to the entrance of the ladies' lounge where she worked, her friend Yvonne, another attendant several years older, stood cleaning her eyeglasses with a tissue. Yvonne was as much a confidante as a co-worker. They often unloaded the day's gossip on each other and on rare occasions met for a hi-ball after work. Yvonne was a single mother with three children in school, all of who were born before her eighteenth birthday.

"You lookin' kinda bad this morning. What's got you so ticked?" Yvonne asked,

"Nothing . . . you know . . . same ol' shit," she said, "I'm getting mighty tired of it."

"What's you mean, the good reverend being an asshole again?"

"No, jus' his usual self. He's done this shit a few times over the last seven years. I should know better. Zebras don't change their stripes, and he ain't changin' his ways. Shit, that's how I got him in the first place—I stole him away from his first wife back in Canton, Mississippi."

"You mean he was married before? You never told me that." Yvonne said.

"Honey, there's a truckload I ain't told you." Jimmie said as she motioned for them to step into the ladies' room. Jimmie marched right to the lighted vanity mirror and began primping her hair, with Yvonne right behind.

"Oh yeah, he was married to this prissy little thing, a preacher's wife who acted 'high sadity' and all," Jimmie said bobbing her head and pouting her lips in mocking gesture. "That's when he first came to the church," she said as she lit a cigarette.

"What's you doin' lighting up in here, one of these days you're gonna get caught." Yvonne said. Jimmie just brushed it off.

"He was the new minister, and it seemed like every girl in Canton was at his sermons. I mean everyone. He caused a big stir when he came into town. Not that he's a good-looking hunk or anything; it wasn't that. He was a young, strong, man with that boomin' voice that just made every gal wet as a watermelon." She paused a moment to reflect then said, "It was more of what his sermons were about that got me, though. He always preached about how we needed to 'unshackle ourselves from the chains of bondage' that whiteys kept locked down tight. He'd always preach like he was talking directly at me.

"Growing up in Mississippi, we was sharecroppers and my papa always told me that I was special and didn't have to take up pickin' cotton like he was for those white owners. The white landowners was the real problem." With her head down she raised her eyes at Yvonne and continued. "O'course, I ain't had to pick no cotton when my papa was alive, that was a job fo' my brothers and sisters. I was special. So I got to do the house cleanin'."

"So you mean to tell me he knew he was talkin' to you?" Yvonne asked.

"No, he didn't know nothin'. But everybody respected him and I knew that I had somethin' in common with him that nobody else did."

"What's that?"

"We felt the same way about whiteys. Hell, they're doin' the same thing now—look who owns this hotel, who do we work for? Honkies. We can't even gamble here. We just have to stay out a the way and do the dirty work."

"That's the way it's always been." Yvonne stated, "You ain't tellin' me nothing new. But at least there's one good thing."

"What's that?"

"Well, we ain't dirty Indians, are we?" Yvonne said while raising her hand to her face feigning privacy.

"No, we surely ain't." Jimmie agreed.

"What I'm trying to find out is how you got such a fine preacher to go after you in the first place?"

"The very next Sunday I jus' dressed up in my most outrageous red dress with a wide brimmed white hat with red trim—to match the dress, and white gloves. I pushed my breasts up and put on red lipstick, white pumps. I was set," Jimmie said.

"What's you tryin' to be, a candy cane?"

"Yeah, a candy cane that was gonna make him wanna lick me from head to toe!" They both giggled and she continued, "He couldn't take his eyes off me. I was innocent and pure, and in his eyes I was ripe, ready to be picked. So I jus' wiggled my way in between that Miss Prissy wife of his. He didn't have a chance."

"Innocent and pure! Who you tryin' to fool girl?"

"Hey, I'm a good actress. Besides they didn't call me Pretty Jimmie for nothing! Shit, when I was back home I was the prettiest girl in Canton, and the sexiest, and the most outspoken, and the most popular. All the men wanted me, and," she added half-heartily, "most of them had me."

"But what kind of preacher would drop everything for a pretty piece of ass?" Yvonne asked, and then shook her head. "Never mind—that's the dumbest question I ever asked."

Jimmie Lee just glanced at her and smiled. "He didn't just drop everything. It took a while for all that to happen. Hey, he did some serious Bible thumping."

A few years earlier, from the very first service that Jimmie attended, as she watched Chris preach from the pulpit, she felt the warmth and love expressed by his powerful voice burn inside her. As Reverend Chris Greenwade eloquently moralized the teachings of the Gospel, she noticed men also followed his spiritual leadership and women were captivated by his every word. Jimmie saw that as his hallmark, his attraction; to project his soft tone and resolute manner to each and every one as if they alone were the focus of his attention.

Jimmie realized then that this natural sermonizer believed in the Gospel and viewed himself as an instrument of God. She also realized that he was ambitious and conscious of his own magnetism. But she also was aware of his practical side as he cautiously kept the women of his ministry at a safe distance. Nevertheless, throughout the community she heard of many rumors of his indiscretions with the sisters of the church.

Chris straightened up as the security guard approached him at the shoe stand. "What's going on over here?" he asked.

"Oh, nothing," Chris answered with a smile. "One of my parishioners has a serious problem and we'd been discussing it."

"You're the preacher . . . I heard about you," said the young, white guard who looked more like a boy in his father's baggy uniform. He looked up at Chris with contempt in his eyes and a high pitch in his voice. "You have a church?"

"Sure, well . . . it's not mine, but I use it for my ministry."

"You have a lot of your people in the congregation?" He asked.

"My people?" Chris hesitated then added, "Not as many as I had when I was back in the South where I came from."

"Well, Mr. Preacher, this ain't no church, and you ain't preachin' in here, so keep your parishioners away."

"Yeah, sure," said Chris as the guard turned and walked off, "whatever you say." He picked up a small can of Shinola and stared into it as he thought about his life with Jimmie.

From their first meeting in Mississippi, he realized Jimmie was pursuing him, unashamedly, without regard to the consequences. Chris visualized this young temptress as a "blessing from Heaven" and affectionately called her "Blessie," a name only she understood. No matter what he did, he always succumbed to her sensuality, and that's why he stayed with her so long.

"And I wasn't interested in no one-night stand either," Jimmie said emphatically. I let everyone know that we were going to live together. Cause everyone thought it was just a scandal! The good preacher chasin' after that young girl."

"You mean everyone thought that he was after you?" Yvonne asked.

"I told you I was a good actress. Everyone knows that!" Jimmie boasted. "Besides, I convinced him to leave his wife so that we could live together—which we did. But it got so crazy with all the gossip and all, that he couldn't even preach his sermons anymore. And . . . and he was even foolin' around on me, 'cept I couldn't prove it. We'd fight like cats and dogs and then I'd get drunk. Finally, he just moved off to LA."

"You mean he left you?"

"Yeah, he left," she said sorrowfully. "But then . . . he came back." She added with a coquettish grin. "He forgot the fighting. All he could remember was my hot, delightfully sensual body. I convinced him that if we were in a different place, away from Canton, everything would be OK. So we took off together for Los Angeles."

Yvonne breathed a sigh; her shoulders sank. "I gotta go. All this horny talk makin' me flush."

Jimmy giggled as she put out her cigarette and emptied the ashtray.

Life in a big city was not a cure-all. They were more comfortable in a smaller town and the casinos in Reno provided an opportunity for them to change their fortune. Within six months after starting a new life together they were earning well over a hundred dollars a week, with Chris in charge of the money. Somewhere along the way Jimmie Lee Stokes stopped using her family name and became Jimmie Lee Greenwade.

Spending each day in the ladies' lounge, located near the casino cashier, Jimmie attended to the women patrons and kept the restroom spotless. She provided a towel for their hands, a splash of assorted fragrance and an open ear for whatever was on their mind. Jimmie could easily pick out distinctive personality types and mimic them with the sole purpose of extracting as much of a tip as possible. It was her way of pretending to be an actress. She wasn't always accurate, sometimes she'd falter. Instead of a tip, she learned a little more about their lives and their romances. From Jimmie Lee's limited viewpoint, white women only knew one thing—how to cheat on their man.

When her thoughts weren't on Chris, Jimmie sometimes tried to enhance her self-directed acting skills by shamelessly feigning a Jamaican accent to the women. "You jus' never know who's gonna be watching," she'd say, "got to be ready in case the wife of some Hollywood producer needs to pee."

As the morning hours slid into noon, the casino came alive with a small three-piece band playing country-western music, a regularly scheduled occurrence. Like obedient children the players complied while enjoying the action of rolling dice, stacking chips, or filling the slots with coins, each waiting for the free drinks from scantily clad cocktail waitresses in cowgirl outfits. The floor men hovered nearby like birds of prey keeping one eye on the tables and the other on conventioneers sporting white and blue nametags. Every few hours a busload of tourists from Sacramento or San Francisco herded in through the doors. For the hotel and casino, each customer helped pay for the new renovation, but for Jimmie, the strangers offered her the best opportunity to show off her talents.

One regular caught her eye however, a woman in her late thirties. Jimmie remembered her because on a previous occasion, she brought along a little girl and asked Jimmie to watch her for a generous tip. Jimmie liked the little tot.

But this time the woman was alone. Her appearance was different from most of the local gamblers. She had a pyramid-shaped nest of strawberry blond hair perched neatly atop her head with a long, gold chain wrapped gracefully around her neck and attached to the white frames of her cat-eye shaped glasses. She wore a bright red blouse with ruffled sleeves and a large, gold-colored monogram with the letter "L" in script pinned just below the collar. Black linen slacks revealed a straight waist and wide, flat hips.

When the restroom finally cleared out, the woman removed her glasses revealing small, piercing brown eyes. Routinely, she fixed her makeup, glanced through the mirror at Jimmie and politely asked, "How long have you been working here?"

Jimmie turned toward the woman, paused a few moments, and then responded, "Excuse me?"

"I asked, how long have you worked here?"

"Oh, about four or five years."

"Are you married?"

"Why you asking?"

"Just curious, that's all."

"Where's ya little girl?" Jimmie asked.

"Oh, you remembered," the woman said, "she's not mine, she's with her mother. You like children don't you?" She didn't wait for an answer. "I can tell by the way you treat little Abby. So, are you married?"

Jimmie became suspicious, placing her hands on the back of her hips and cocking her head in her standard defensive position. "I'm the wife of a minister . . . who can't live without me."

"A minister! That's wonderful, you should be very proud of him. Do you have any children?"

"No, God knows we tried, but the Lord didn't bless us that way," Jimmie said.

"Oh, that's a shame." She turned toward Jimmie with a quizzical look. "That is an unusual accent you have. Where are you from?"

"I'm from Jamaica," Jimmie said.

"Jamaica! How charming. My name is Louise, I'm from San Francisco," she said, slowly and deliberately as if she was speaking to a foreigner who had never heard of the city. "I own an exclusive hair salon that overlooks the Golden Gate Bridge. I have some very important and influential clients who refuse to have anyone else style their hair."

Jimmie sat down in the stool nearby and smiled attentively, suddenly becoming very conscious of her hair.

Louise continued, "One of my dearest friends, Dorothy, who is a wonderful mother, has had some serious problems with her teenage daughter. She's just a child, but really uncontrollable. My dear sweet friend, Dorothy, had one heartache after another and I'm afraid now she is about to have a complete breakdown."

"I'm sorry to hear about that," Jimmie sighed.

"Why thank you, it's very kind of you to say," Louise said. Jimmie watched the woman stand up and slowly walk toward the door and then glance back at Jimmie Lee through the mirror. She took a deep breath and said, "This rebel daughter of Dorothy's has really got herself into big trouble this time." Jimmie didn't react even when Louise turned toward her. "Somehow, she managed to get herself pregnant—and she's only fifteen! It's impossible for her to care for a baby; she's just a child herself. And my dear friend, Dorothy, I feel so sorry for her. She's done everything possible to raise this child the right way, but somehow it all seems so hopeless.

"Why, she practically begged me to see if there was anything I could do to help," Louise continued while looking directly at Jimmie, still waiting for a response. "The worst part of this unwanted pregnancy is that the father is a colored boy. I mean . . . there's nothing wrong with being colored. I hope you understand; I'm not prejudiced mind you, but how could anyone expect a fifteen-year-old white girl to raise a half-colored baby? It would be so unfair to that child; everyone would snub her. The people in her crowd would never understand, and it would be impossible for my poor friend too. That's why she asked me . . . no, pleaded with me to see if there was anything I could do to help. And I promised her, that no matter what, I would find a good home for the baby when it's born."

Jimmie raised her hand to her lips and shook her head sympathetically and said, "My, oh my, such an awful thing for a momma to go through, uuh, uuh. Same thing happened to my cousin Lily's girl. Got herself pregnant by some white boy, no offense mind you, but they had the awfulest time trying get money to raise that baby. Her momma was never the same after that." It was nearing time for lunch and she was getting thirsty.

"So you know," Louise said. "Why didn't you take the baby?"

"Me, take the baby?" Jimmie said as her head snapped straight, "it was long ago, I was too young to be lookin' after a baby. Besides, that whole family looked after the baby, was no need for anyone else. It was just the money."

Suddenly, Louise stopped what she was doing, her eyes opened wide. Enthusiastically, she said to Jimmie, "Oh, what a wonderful idea! I just thought of something that would solve both our problems."

Jimmie began tidying up while thinking of her performance, not fully in the moment.

Louise continued, "Since you and your wonderful husband, the minister, want to have children so badly, why don't I arrange for you two to adopt this mixed baby when it's born! It's perfect."

Jimmie mimicked Louise's exhilaration and nodded her head in agreement without taking the woman seriously. She anticipated a generous tip. "My man Chris would love to adopt a newborn baby. Why we'd be the proudest parents you ever seen!" she said.

"That's great!" Louise continued, "When the baby is born, I'll let you know . . . and don't worry . . . I'll take care of all the details."

"Sure, you do that," Jimmie smiled.

"Let me just get a pencil and write down your name. By the way, what is your name?"

"Jimmie Lee Greenwade."

Louise wrote the name on a small piece of paper and started to return her makeup and lipstick back into her purse. "My dear friend, Dorothy, will be so happy, and I know you will be overjoyed at having your first child. You don't know how wonderful this will be for everyone. Now remember, you will be hearing from me soon. Bye, Bye." Louise smiled politely, left a $50 tip, and walked out the door.

Jimmie shook her head and mumbled to herself, "Goddog, 50 bucks. These crazy, damn white women, where in the hell do they come from? They believe any kinda shit you tell them. Adopt a baby—humph!"

As other patrons wandered in and out, Jimmie dismissed Louise as just another rich white woman with too much time on her hands.

That evening while Chris dressed for work at the church, Jimmie walked into the bedroom, folded her arms, and leaned in the doorway. "Hey Daddy," she called, "You going to go to the church tonight?"

"Yeah, you know I've got the children's choir practice on Wednesdays."

"Is that Miss Celia woman gonna be there?"

"No, Blessie, she's not gonna be there . . . she's sick, remember?"

"She was there with you last night, wasn't she?"

Chris stood up straight, priming himself for one of her temper tantrums.

"No! Now what you going to say things like that for? Sister Eisley is a fine, married woman, who happens to be very sick . . . and I spent the night with her . . . AND her husband . . . AND the doctor, which if you didn't shoot your mouth off this morning, I would of explained it to you.

"You're just looking to start an argument with that sinful jealousy. If it wasn't Celia Eisley, it'd be somebody else. Between your drinking and the jealousy, you're going to either kill yourself or drive me crazy! So you just better stop. . . ."

"Don't tell me I got to stop drinking. It's the only way I got to put up with this damn bullshit of you running around with these women!"

Chris knew it was pointless to argue with her. "Well, what did you do today? Who'd you meet?"

Jimmie looked down at the floor, she was tired and languid, too much so to argue. "Well . . . not much . . . some crazy white woman gave me a $50 tip."

"Wow, what did you have to do for that?"

"Nothing . . . she jus' was in trying to get me to adopt her friend's baby."

Chris, startled, turned to her and asked, "You mean she brought a baby into the casino?"

"Hell, no! The baby ain't even born yet. It's some mixed baby they got in San Francisco."

"What did you tell her?"

"I told her sure, I'd love to adopt a baby."

"What!" He said.

"Don't let your hair curl, the fool was drunk. I paid her no mind," Jimmie said.

Chris accepted Jimmie's explanation and dismissed the thought of adopting a baby. He stepped forward, took her chin in his hand, and planted a kiss gently on her cheek. "I have to go. I'll be home early," he whispered.

"Yeah, sure." She dropped her head somberly as Chris walked out the door.

About two months later, on a hot afternoon in August, a knock on the door of the ladies' lounge stopped Jimmie from daydreaming. Thinking it was a maintenance man, she yelled, "Come on in, nobody's here." But no one answered and a second knock forced her to the open the door. "What are you, deaf? I told you . . . ," she said. There, standing in the doorway was a frail looking boy in a green uniform. "Who are you?" she asked.

He was holding a small book in his hand. "I'm looking for Jimmie Greenwade," he said.

"That's me, I'm Jimmie Greenwade."

"I have a telegram for you. Just sign here, please."

"Telegram? Who'd send me a telegram?" She looked at the address and it was made out to:

JIMMIE LEE GREENWADE
RIVERSIDE HOTEL
C/O LADIES' LOUNGE
RENO, NEVEADA

She signed the book and gave the messenger a casino chip for his effort. She never received a telegram at the hotel before, nor was she expecting one. Jimmie walked to the vanity and tore open the envelope and read the address again; it hadn't changed, still addressed to her in care of the Ladies' Lounge. The message was short:

"Baby girl arrived today Stop
Please come to St. Elizabeth's Hospital San Francisco Stop
Louise."

Jimmie did not know anyone named Louise, nor anyone in San Francisco. She re-read the message again, "This don't make no sense at all! I ain't got no baby!"

Over and over she read the message hoping that something would click in her mind, but it was hopeless. Part of her instinct believed the telegram was in error, while the other half didn't want to know. The last thing she needed in her life was a baby. Jimmie crunched the telegram into a ball and flushed it down the toilet and continued about with her chores, never mentioning the incident to anyone.

Three weeks later when she spotted a woman in a bright pink blouse walking briskly toward her, the meaning of the contents hit her hard. Jimmie immediately recognized the woman who gave her a big tip a couple months earlier. As she got closer Jimmie felt the fire darting from Louise's eyes. Within seconds she stood directly in front of Jimmie and said, "Didn't you get my telegram? That poor baby is sitting in a crib in San Francisco waiting for you to come and pick her up. I thought you were a decent, God-fearing woman. You told me your husband was a man of the cloth. Now you just let the little baby lie there without anyone to take care of her! What kind of person are you!"

Jimmie gasped as she held her hand to her mouth. "Oh, My Lordy!" she exclaimed, "You're the one who sent me that telegram—you're that Louise!"

"Of course I am the one who sent the message. I told you quite clearly that I would be in touch. I always keep my word and do exactly what I say I'm going to do—not like some people!" she said, "Now . . . when are you going to get the baby?"

Louise's outburst drew a few onlookers. It wasn't the first time Jimmie put herself into a ticklish situation, that was her nature, but dealing with a baby left her bewildered. Now she began to understand how Chris felt each time she put pressure on him, and she reacted as he does. Her first instinct was to calm Louise down by gently clutching the enraged woman's arm and looking directly into her eyes.

"Come with me," she said, "We'll go talk to my man."

"That's fine with me," replied Louise indignantly, "I'd like to see just what kind of a man he is!"

They walked together toward the shoeshine stand. Louise with her head held high, peering down her nose at the assortment of gamblers and locals while Jimmie strutted in her usual manner.

Chris just finished up a pair of boots that someone had left off earlier. He turned quickly when he heard Jimmie's say in a fearful tone, "Daddy, I got to talk wit' you—something important—real important!"

The sight of Jimmie with an angry looking white woman put Chris' instincts on the defensive. His shoulders went back and his neck stiffened. "What is it, Blessie? What's the matter? Who is this?"

Chris knew Jimmie well enough to realize that her exasperation meant whatever predicament she was in it was serious. She struggled with her words, "Well a . . . this is . . . uh. . . ."

Louise's impatience didn't allow Jimmie the slightest courtesy.

"I'm the woman who went through a lot of trouble to arrange to have the both of you adopt a baby in San Francisco. Your wife agreed to the arrangement and now the baby is waiting for her new parents to take home. I sent a telegram for you to come to pick her up at St. Elizabeth's over three weeks ago, and I haven't heard a word since. Now tell me, Reverend Greenwade, just what kind of people would leave an innocent child to fend for herself in this world?"

Chris didn't like to feel threatened, particularly by a well-dressed white woman who seemed to believe everything she was saying.

"Baby! What Baby? We don't have no baby," he snapped.

"Yeah, Daddy," Jimmie interrupted, "it's a poor white woman's baby with the Negro father I told you 'bout a few months ago. Don't you remember? I told you 'bout the crazy white woman who asked me to adopt a mixed baby when it got born."

Chris saw Louise raise her eyebrow at Jimmie's reference to the description of their first encounter.

"Yeah, I remember. But you told me the woman was . . . well, who's baby is it?" asked Chris.

"I know what I told you, least that's the way it looked to me," Jimmie added.

"That information is strictly confidential, and neither you nor the child must ever try to contact the mother—a child herself," replied Louise.

"You can't just adopt a baby like that," said Chris.

"Oh yes you can and you'd better! All the arrangements have been made, and the details taken care of. You must go to San Francisco, sign a few papers, and pick up the beautiful little girl—her name is Fauna. The baby is in excellent health, ready to be cared for and loved. The bills have been paid—including the cost of the private adoption. The parents cannot keep it . . . but I told you all that when I was here last time speaking to your wife, who, by the way, agreed to the entire arrangement. And now the baby is alone in a hospital crib, waiting for some lucky people to love and keep her. It's your responsibility now—there is no one else who can take care of her. It's much too late to try and find suitable parents especially with all the paperwork and such. You have no choice!"

"I was not aware of any of the details of this . . . this. . . ." he was somewhat at a loss for words.

"Parenthood?" Louise interrupted.

"Ah, yes, parenthood. I need to speak with my wife for a few moments . . . in private . . . if you don't mind."

Louise stood firm, contemptuously nodding her head in agreement. Chris led his wife to the side of the shoeshine stand far enough away to be out of earshot of Louise. Before he could say one word Jimmie started ranting in a guilt-ridden manner.

"Daddy, I had no idea this crazy white woman was for real. When I talked with her a few months ago, I thought she was drunk. You know how many of these crazies come in. . . ."

"That's OK, that's OK," Chris whispered.

"No it ain't OK! I can't take care a no baby."

"Listen Blessie, this woman came all the way down here . . . from San Francisco . . . just to meet us for the second time. She's taken care of all the paperwork. Now she could have just as easily picked out anyone up there . . . but she came to us! Now God must have wanted us to have this baby for some special reason. I don't know what it is yet, but if it's His will . . . and He wants us to do this . . . then we got to think of the baby."

Chris watched Jimmie roll her eyes. He knew she was trying to get through to him.

"But what if this Louise is really crazy, like I think she is?"

"Well, I don't think so, I may be wrong, but she seems too legit. And I know people. I deal with white people all the time. She seems serious. Besides we'll find that out when we get to San Francisco and all we'd have wasted is a short vacation . . . besides I wanted to try our new car on a trip anyway."

Jimmie remained silent with her arms folded and her lips taut.

"This is a good sign that this baby is coming into our lives at this time. Don't you realize that? We need to have something more important than just ourselves. It'll make us a family, a real family, just like we planned years ago." Chris knew that changing Jimmie's focus to a baby meant less time for gossip, and more importantly, the responsibility would keep her from drinking. It seemed like the best course of action, even though he still wasn't convinced it was legitimate.

He continued, "We could raise the little girl as if it were our own. It's a baby, just a baby . . . something we always wanted."

Jimmie continued her silence, but he saw that the look in her eyes was softening, and he continued, "You love children!"

"I hate children," she snapped back.

"You love children!"

"I won't have no baby named Fauna," she said, "sounds like some fairy-tale."

"So we'll change the name."

"But I got to go to work. How I'm gonna take care of a baby while I'm working?"

"Don't be foolish, woman! You don't have to work. We got plenty of money. I make enough here plus with the church growing all the time, you won't have to work at all. Besides, people do it all the time."

Chris knew that he was finally getting through to Jimmie. He saw hope and trust in her eyes.

"Blessie, we just got to adopt this baby, or at least find out more about it—God has put her in our hands."

Between Louise's insistence and forceful guilt, and Chris's divine logic, it was more than Jimmie could understand. She reluctantly agreed by nodding her head to Chris saying, "Let's see what we can do."

Chris put his arm around Jimmie and walked back to where Louise was standing and waiting impatiently.

"Well," demanded Louise, "when are you going to San Francisco?"

Chris smiled and said, "First thing in the morning."

CHAPTER 2

O n the following morning, the sound of sparrows chirping in the crisp air broke the silence as Jimmie wobbled into the kitchen. She noticed two tweed travel bags near the screen door. She frowned at the sight of the luggage, poured a cup of coffee, sat down at the gray Formica-topped table, and began to grasp the profoundness of the situation. The predicament she created made her anxious and afraid—another excuse to drink to excess. She was only hours away from potentially accepting the unending responsibility for another human being—something that she had successfully avoided for many years. In her mind it wasn't a question of capabilities, but more of adjustment. Within the span of only twenty-four hours, her life was forever altered.

Jimmie Lee glanced through the kitchen window and noticed Chris fiddling under the hood of their new Cadillac—a well-deserved reward for years of hard work and frugal living. Jimmie understood why Chris avoided using it to transport himself back and forth to work, concealing it from the jealous white bosses at the hotel. If they suspected that a Negro who shined shoes was able to afford a new Cadillac, the job would go to a white person. As she watched, she noticed Chris' energy and enthusiasm come alive. Something she hadn't seen in a long time.

Jimmie felt Chris enter through the door before she could see him, just as she felt the warmth of the sun on her arm before noticing it burst forth from behind the clouds. He wore a yellow polo and brown slacks and he was ready to go.

"Mornin' Blessie!" He opened the small icebox and then asked, "I wasn't going to wake you until breakfast was ready. Want some bacon? Or how 'bout some nice, hot oatmeal with toast?"

"Oatmeal! I can't eat no mushy shit in the middle uh the night. What in hell ya doin' out there making a racket anyway?"

Chris paused and looked at her bloodshot eyes, mussed hair, and shabby form.

"What do you mean? I was checking out the car, making sure that it's safe to take on a long trip. Today, Blessie, is the day we go to San Francisco and get our new baby. The bags are packed and I'm ready to go."

"You can go by yourself. I'm exhausted."

"Nonsense! We're both going. Besides, you're the one who got us into this in the first place. Didn't you sleep well last night?"

"Sleep? Sleep! Huh. I feel like some spooks dragged my ass out a bed in the middle of the night and beat me up."

Chris chuckled, "You'll feel better after a shower and some fixing up."

A big day was ahead of her with many uncertainties and the only way to get through it was by being relaxed. While Chris sat in the car with the motor running, Jimmie retrieved a pint of gin stashed away in the linen drawer. Within minutes they were on the road heading toward California. She sat quietly in the passenger seat staring blankly at the road ahead, without enthusiasm for the trip, or the potential obligation of raising a baby that seemed to come out of nowhere. It irked Jimmie to watch Chris and his eagerness. He was at the prime of life, in good health, with a little money in the bank, and now about to get a baby.

"Ya know Blessie, God sure has a strange way of throwing the knuckle ball. It seems like only a short time ago we were struggling with those folks down in Canton. Yeah, those people used to gossip about us a whole lot—spreading rumors and making up stories. It's a wonder we lasted as long as we did.

"Now things are a whole lot different. Everything is going nice and smooth; we've made a new life, in a new town, with new friends. Sure is

great. But the best thing of all is that we are going to have a baby! And
you didn't have one day of morning sickness—or labor pains! Ha! Ain't
that great!" he laughed as he sat up taller behind the wheel, pouring out
giddiness.

Jimmie turned toward Chris with a sardonic glance and then let
her eyes wander out the window. As she watched the familiar sights just
outside of town quickly turn from desert into tall pines, she turned to
Chris and said, "I gotta pee."

"What? We've only been driving half an hour."

"Well, that's long enough for me."

"Didn't you go before we left?"

"Whats that gotta do with it? I gotta-go now."

Jimmie knew that Chris pushed his luck about as far as she'd let
him, convincing her to go to San Francisco; she knew there would be no
argument. Within minutes Chris pulled into a general store with Texaco
pumps and a sign in front with an arrow pointing to restrooms. Before
she made it to the restroom, she wandered into the store and hurriedly
bought a pint of Gordon's gin and a few bottles of 7-Up. She hid the
liquor in her satchel, went into the ladies' restroom and emptied half
of each soda into the sink, refilling the bottles with the gin. She gulped
down the remainder of the liquor and went back to the car.

"You feeling any better?" Chris asked as Jimmie closed the car door.

"Fine, I'm fine," she said, "Now let's get this buggy going. I ain't got
all day."

By midmorning, Chris' lighthearted eagerness turned into a lesson
in etiquette on how to deal with the Catholic nuns at St. Elizabeth's.
"You just got to be polite, that's all," Chris said as he concentrated on his
driving, "and if they ask you anything about your job, just say you're a
housewife, but don't get into any other details."

"What details?" Jimmie asked, "I don't know no details."

"That's okay, just don't go there. And be respectful, no cussing and
no swearing either."

"Do I got to bow?"

"No, you don't bow."

"Do I got to curtsy?"

"No, you don't curtsy, they're nuns, not royalty. Just act yourself." Chris hesitated, "No, on second thought, just follow my lead. Let me do all the talking."

"Sure, you do all the talking." Jimmie said as she turned toward the window again. "And the diaper changing, and the getting up in the middle of the night. Yeah, you do all the talking."

As the Cadillac sped along the open highway at 70 miles per hour Chris continued his lecture. Jimmie drowned out his incessant chatter by pickling herself with the contents of the 7-Up bottle. The routine nudged her thoughts away from Chris' idea of family life and brought it to the present—staring at the boundless vistas of the picturesque California countryside. The gin alleviated her monotony. By the time they reached San Francisco, Jimmie had forced Chris to pull over five times in as many hours and she was totally soused.

Upon arriving in the Bay City, they headed toward the Jack Tarr Hotel, the only first-class lodging available to coloreds in San Francisco in 1951. Chris confirmed their reservations and prepaid their bill with cash. He was anxious to see his new daughter, so he allowed Jimmie barely enough time to freshen up before making the short trip to the hospital.

As Chris entered St. Elizabeth's, he held Jimmie firmly with both hands, trying to steady her walk. Her eyes were glassy and bloodshot, and she maneuvered about awkwardly, weaving from side to side as if these were her first moments on dry land after months at sea. Her head bobbed while Chris walked proudly. In the quiet atmosphere of the waiting room, Chris approached the receptionist, a pregnant girl of about sixteen.

"Good afternoon," he said, "I'm Chris Greenwade, and this is my wife, Jimmie Lee."

Startled, the naive teenager took one glance at Jimmie and politely interrupted. "Oh, I'm sorry, we haven't any emergency facilities here. This is a Maternity Hospital."

"What?" replied Chris.

"Isn't she sick? What's the matter with her?"

Chris looked at the girl and then glanced at Jimmie, plastered to the core. "No. Well, yes, she is. We drove a long way and, uh, she gets carsick. She'll be all right. My name is Greenwade, Reverend Greenwade."

"Oh, yes, Reverend Greenwade, Sister Teresa is expecting you. Please sit down and I'll get her right away."

He helped Jimmie over to the oaken bench opposite the receptionist's desk. With a firm tone he said to Jimmie, "Now Blessie, let me do all the talking. I'm sure they're gonna ask a lot of questions, probably a lot of forms to fill out. They don't give away babies just to anyone, you know! They'll probably have to check us out first, so I'll answer all the questions."

He raised his eyebrows, looked straight at her and then continued, "All I want you to do is just smile, and use your charm—the way you do with those white folks at the casino."

Jimmie Lee sat silently with her eyes half-opened, grinning stiffly, as if her face was frozen. Chris glanced at her blank expression, shook his head, and hoped for the best.

The receptionist returned with a tall, thin nun in her fifties with horn-rimmed glasses that rested gently on her shiny soft white cheeks. She dressed in a dark blue habit trimmed in white with the customary rosary beads draped around one side. She stood silently with her hands gently touching each other at the waist, patiently waiting to be introduced. Nervously, the teenager fumbled with the words, but the nun interrupted and introduced herself. "Hello, I'm Sister Teresa. You must be Reverend and Mrs. Greenwade. I'm so glad to finally meet you both."

"Same here, Sister Teresa," replied Chris.

"I've heard so much about you. How was your trip from Reno?"

"Oh fine, just fine. It took us a little longer than expected. We just bought a new Cadillac and I took it nice and easy."

"Well, that's wonderful!"

Jimmie burped loudly, interrupting Sister Teresa's thoughts. Chris tightened his fist nervously waiting for time to erase the moment of awkwardness that sliced through the delicate meeting.

The nun finally spoke, "Well. I'm sure you're both very anxious to meet your new daughter. So, why don't you come with me and I'll take you to our family room."

Before Chris could answer, Jimmie blurted out, "Where's da bathroom?"

"I'll show you," replied the young girl.

To his chagrin, the nun never acknowledged his wife's obvious condition, but instead, began to exchange some information concerning the care and feeding of an infant, which Chris found quite boring. He was far more interested in the legal adoption process and its obvious ramifications. Sister Teresa briefly apprised him of the situation from an experienced layman's vantage point and provided the name of the attorney who would handle the arrangements.

Upon Jimmie's return, the affable nun led them into a labyrinth of corridors and stairways that eventually led to a small area near the maternity ward.

"Please, make yourselves comfortable while I go and prepare your daughter for her first glimpse of her new parents."

"Ah, wait a minute, Sister. We're not her parents yet," said Jimmie. "We just come to look her over . . . to see . . . uh . . . to see."

"To see what?"

"Well, uh, we're not sure." Chris took over and stammered to find the right words. "Well, we were under the impression that we . . . could. . . ." It was evident to him that the nun was unaware of how all this began.

"The arrangements have been made, I can assure you. Just wait until you see her. You'll see."

Chris looked at Jimmie as Sister Teresa quietly slipped out of sight. He noticed the expression in her face change from semi-consciousness to curiosity. The pungent odors of newborn babies mixed with the requisite, yet peculiar, hospital smells, intensified the experience and reality began to set in. Chris bit his lip and smiled nervously, ambling back and forth while clutching his hands. The few minutes wait seemed to go on forever.

When Sister Teresa came into view, her bright smile lit up the room. She stepped lively and stood before Chris and Jimmie holding a tiny bundle of pink blankets in her arms. "Reverend and Mrs. Greenwade, let me be the first to introduce you to your new daughter, Fauna Hodel," she said, carefully raising the tip of the cotton coverlet, revealing a seven-pound, white-skinned baby girl with sleepy blue eyes and thin blond hair. "Hi, Fauna, this is your new Mommy and Daddy."

Chris' broad, natural smile radiated white teeth, his eyes widened and his brown face glowed. Instinctively, he raised his hand to affectionately stroke the infant with his finger. His first impression was that she was a gift from heaven and it reminded him of Mary handing over the baby Jesus. But before he could comment, Jimmie jerked away as if Sister Teresa had unveiled a voodoo doll and exploded into a fury.

"That ain't no colored baby!" she screamed. "What kind a fool ya think I am? You white folks is all alike, tryin' to con us simple, God-fearin' coloreds into takin' care of ya rejects! We drove all the way from Reno across mountains to get ah'selves a new mixed baby. A mixed baby is always brown skin, with brown hair, and brown eyes. Everybody knows dat!"

The baby began to cry, but Jimmie continued.

"Ya come out here with that—that pinky skinned, blue-eyed, white patty, and expect us to be jumpin' wit joy! Well, I got a news flash for you, Sistah: we don't want no white baby and we ain't gettin' no white baby!"

Chris felt a cold chill fill his body, his knees weakened. The baby began to cry. Sister Teresa held the howling infant closer to her breast, trying to shield her from the rage of what appeared to be a possession.

Jimmie pushed her finger into Chris' face while she continued her tirade. "I knew there was something fishy about this damn deal right from the beginning. This son-of-a bitch is tryin' to dump this white baby on us—and we ain't takin' it!"

Chris turned his back on Sister Teresa, grabbed his wife's shoulders, forcing her back toward the wall. His body went hot with embarrassment, enough to make him spit steam. His brow rose below his tightened forehead and his voice exhaled a deep vibrating tone powerful enough to drown out Jimmie's hysterics. "Blessie, please. This is a woman of God you're talking to. Calm down! This must be some mistake. She probably has the wrong baby, that's all. Now control yourself. We'll just get it straightened out."

"I'll tell ya what the mistake is," she screeched as she struggled to free herself from his grip, "We come up here to get a mixed baby, and that baby ain't mixed!"

Chris, his face sweating, turned to Sister Teresa in a panic and said, "My wife didn't mean what she said; she's just very upset. You see, Sister Teresa, we were told that this was supposed to be a mixed baby, and . . ."

"This is a mixed baby," interrupted the nun. "The mother's name is Tamar Nais Hodel and the father is Negro. It says so on the birth certificate and the mother attested as to who the father is and his race. There is no mix-up!"

"That baby sure don't look like it has no Negro blood to me," said Jimmie, "and I don't want nothin' to do with it. How I'm gonna explain a damn white baby to my family? To my friends—to anybody?"

She stomped out of the room, gibbering about all the trouble she was in, and tossing her arms about like a disjointed puppet.

"Blessie, wait a minute," snarled Chris, starting after her. But he hesitated as he quickly realized that Sister Teresa tried to compose herself while simultaneously rocking the baby in an attempt to abate the infant's howling.

"Blessie, wait a minute!" he shouted. Then, to Sister Teresa, he said nervously, "I'll talk with my wife when she calms down and gets over the shock. She's very upset, but I'll make her understand. Don't worry, everything will be all right."

"Well, if you do, Reverend Greenwade, and right now it looks quite doubtful, and you still want to adopt this baby, then it will be necessary for both of you to go to the office of Cyrus Waters. He's the attorney who is handling all the legal documents. He'll explain to you what papers must be signed. And, Reverend Greenwade, let me remind you that you cannot go through with this adoption without proving your worth, not only financially, but also emotionally.

"You can pick up the baby when all of the documents are returned to us at the Administrator's Office," she said.

"Thank you, Sister Teresa, thank you very much. I appreciate what you've done." Chris hurried away.

"Oh, Reverend Greenwade, good luck with your wife. I think you're going to need it!"

CHAPTER 3

Chris met up with Jimmie near where they had parked the car. As he fumbled with the keys, his anger became evident. "I thought I told you to let me do all the talking."

With a hateful look, she glared at him. They endured the short drive back to the hotel in silence. Chris entered the hotel room and plopped his tired body into a stuffed chair at the far corner of the room. He stretched back, crossed his legs, folded his hands and stared at the ceiling. He was confused. He tried to sort out the calamitous events that had just occurred. In the quiet of his mind he prayed for guidance, going over the sacred Scriptures, hoping for an answer to resolve this awkward predicament.

As the late afternoon passed into early evening, Jimmie spent time soaking herself in the bathtub and fussing with her hair, allowing Chris to relax and compose himself.

The sign from God that he had been waiting for was far different from the one that called him to the ministry years earlier. At that time he felt that he had been "touched" by God, to help spread the Word of Jesus Christ. As with other Pentecostal ministers, his spiritual revelation came directly from God, who outlined his mission here on earth.

Chris had an unshakable belief in the Gospel and the teachings of Jesus Christ. Chris felt that, through him, God wanted to create a sense of "family" among the people of the earth. His moral responsibility as a minister was to unite the people of this planet and to bring them out of bondage. He believed that his noble race was not meant to be the mere slaves of white people, but their brothers and sisters. Now here was this white-looking child—a true test of his faith and moral beliefs.

If indeed faith could move mountains, as Chris believed, then it should be a simple task to help rid the world of a prejudice that was well understood. It was time to take a stand, time to put the core of his sermons—"We are one from One"—into practical use. Gladly he accepted this subtle sign from God that was innocently thrust upon him—a sign that would test his faith, a sign that was too powerful to ignore. This little, innocent "angel from God" would be part of their family. After all, this was not a white child; this was a human child—a child from God.

What better way to begin to break down the color barrier separating the races than to start with his Blessie, who had been prejudiced all of her life. If he could begin with her and show her the light, just think what a testimonial he would have for the rest of the world!

Chris rose from the chair with a renewed sense of purpose. His eyes penetrated Jimmie as if he could see through to her soul.

He found her lying on the bed. She looked worn out from the long trip, the scene at the hospital, and her drinking. He knew that she was unprepared for the little sermon he was about to unleash. Chris, in a deep and powerful tone, let the words flow anyway.

"Blessie, I know you are right; this little baby could very well be a lot of trouble. But I didn't see her that way. When I first laid my eyes on her, all I could see was the glow of an angel from heaven. I didn't think of her as being a white baby, although I admit, she is lighter than most mixed children; I thought of her as being our baby. God has finally given us a child after being barren for so many years.

"Now I know it's gonna be difficult to raise a white-looking baby— at least initially, anyway. But you know as well as I do that most little Negro babies are born lighter, and darken as they grow older; one day this baby, too, will darken. After all, it is a mixed baby; the father is Negro. The baby just looks white, prematurely white." He stepped back and slowly walked toward the window. Jimmie's eyes followed him as he turned and continued, "The road ahead is going to be tough on both of us, but that's only temporary. Even if the baby doesn't darken as much as we expect, we still know that it's a mulatto; and there aren't any laws against it, either. Still today there are some states that have laws on the books prohibiting Negroes and whites from marrying each other. Having a white looking baby in our midst could very well open up the doors of hell, but if it's God's will, then we should educate the ignorant. I don't know what lies ahead for us, but we are in it together, and I'm putting my faith in God. For it is His will that provided us with this opportunity, an opportunity similar to the one He provided the Pharaoh's daughter in Exodus, chapter two. Here, let me read it to you."

Chris noticed Jimmie sit up on the bed. He knew she was paying attention. He could sense her excitement, and that encouraged him. Chris reached for his Bible, quickly flipped through the thin pages and began to recite.

> "'And there went a man of the house of Levi. And the woman conceived, and bore a son; and when she saw him that he was a goodly child, she hid him three months. And when she could not longer hide him, she took for him an ark of bulrushes, and daubed it with slime and with pitch, and put the child therein; and she laid it in the flags by the river's brink.
>
> "'And his sister stood afar off, to wit what would be done to him. And the daughter of Pharaoh came down to wash herself at the river; and her maidens walked along by the river's side; and when she saw the ark among the flags, she sent her maid to fetch it. And when she opened it, she saw the child; and, behold, the babe wept. And she had compassion on him and said, This is one of the Hebrews' children. Then said his sister to Pharaoh's daughter, Shall I go and Call to thee a nurse of the Hebrew women, that she may nurse the child for thee?
>
> "'And the Pharaoh's daughter said to her, Go. And the maid went and called the child's mother. And the Pharaoh's daughter

*said unto her, Take this child away, and nurse it for me, and I will
give thee thy wages. And the woman took the child, and nursed it.*

*'And the child grew, and she brought him unto Pharaoh's
daughter, and he became her son. And she called his name Moses;
and she said, Because I drew him out of the water'."*

Chris closed his well-worn book and continued in his own words,
"Just as the Pharaoh's daughter was chosen by God to save Moses from
sure death, so, too, are we chosen to save this little baby, but not from
her death at the hands of the Pharaoh, but from an emotional death just
as sure as a death from not being loved and nourished. The love that we
give her will show the world that we are all children of God and we can
live in harmony. We were chosen to let our brothers and sisters know
that we can all be free from the bondage that plagues our people—the
bondage of white hypocrisy and slavery.

"Now listen," he said, again opening the book. He began to read
from the same book of Exodus.

*"'God called unto him out of the midst of the bush, and said,
Moses, Moses. And he said, Here am I. And he said, Draw not night
hither; put off thy shoes from off thy feet, for the place whereon thou
standest is holy ground. Moreover he said, I am the God of thy
father, the God of Abraham, the God of Isaac, and the God of
Jacob. And Moses hid his face; for he was afraid to look upon God.*

*'And the Lord said, I have surely seen the affliction of my
people which are in Egypt, and have heard their cries by reason of
their taskmasters; for I know their sorrow; and I am come down
to deliver them out of the hand of the Egyptians, and to bring
them up out of that land unto a good land flowing with milk and
honey; unto the place of the Canaanites, and the Hittites, and the
Amorites, and the Perizzites, and the Hivites, and the Jebusites.*

*'Now therefore, behold, the cry of the children of Israel is
come unto me; and I have also seen the oppression wherewith the
Egyptians oppress them.*

*'Come now therefore, and I will send these unto Pharaoh,
that thou mayest bring forth my people the children of Israel out
of Egypt.*

*'And Moses said unto God, Who am I, that I should bring
forth the children of Israel out of Egypt? And he said, Certainly I
will be with thee; and this shall be a token unto thee, that I have
sent thee: When thou hast brought forth the people out of Egypt, ye
shall serve God upon this mountain.'"*

"And so as God is with Moses as he is chosen to deliver his people
from the Egyptians, so too is God with us to raise this little white-
looking baby and deliver our people from the 'reason of our taskmaster'.
She is a sign from God, and His will must be done!"

Although Jimmie had listened to the story of Moses many times
before, she had never heard anyone interpret it quite like Chris, nor was
she going to let him get away with it that easily.

"What's ya tryin' to tell me? That I'm the Pharaoh's daughter and
that little pinky-skinned white-patty is Moses? Huh? You silly ass fool.
I don't wanna be the one to blow out your candle, but it seems like you
got nothin' but space between your ears! Don't you let no one else hear
ya talk like that. Huh! They'll lock your black ass up!"

"Now wait a minute, Blessie, I'm serious!"

"I knows you is serious, that's the problem."

Chris looked at his wife sitting on the bed unconvinced. Quickly, he
picked up his Bible and flipped through the pages trying to find another
approach. "Here. Here, listen to this."

*"'For God so loved the world, that he gave his only begotten
Son, that whosoever believeth in him should not perish, but have
everlasting life. For God sent not his Son into the world to condemn
the world; but that the world through him might be saved. He that
believeth on him is not condemned; but he that believeth not is
condemned already, because he had not believed in the name of the
only begotten Son of God'".*

Chris laid down his book and sat opposite Jimmie on the bed. He began to speak with a sincerity and softness as a father would speak to his daughter. "Listen, God did not send his only Son to a hell on earth to save just a single race of people, but to save all the people of the world. After all, Jesus was color-blind."

Jimmie's eyes rolled in disbelief.

"He never knew who was white or black or yellow. We're all God's children and we must all live together on this planet. We're not categorized by the color of our skin. And just as Jesus was color-blind, so, too, is love. Our love for each other, for our brothers and sisters, and now for this baby is also color-blind. The only reason we see different color is because of a self-inflicted disease we call racism."

Jimmie Lee still wasn't convinced, but Chris could see in her eyes that she was trying. He still hadn't pushed the right buttons, nor was he about to give up.

"Maybe you'll understand it this way," he continued. "Many people, especially in this day and age, have contracted this contagious disease, this prejudice. You saw what this just did to Europe, didn't you? Hitler cultivated this dormant virus that lay within thousands of people and spread the dreaded disease throughout the continent of Europe, eventually setting the whole world on fire. Through this little baby, we have the opportunity and the support of God Almighty to show the world that this disease need never plague the world again!"

Chris continued, alternating his reading of Scriptures with a soft, gentle tone and a powerful, vibrating voice, thundering to a crescendo when so inspired by a particular parable sympathetic to his argument. He was tireless, almost driven. His preaching went on for almost four hours before Jimmie, sober, exhausted, and sexually aroused, could no longer absorb any more of Chris' incessant pounding and preaching.

Finally, she gave in, agreeing to accept this new baby into their lives if only Chris would just shut up, and get to bed. He did, and they spent a most memorable night together in each other's arms.

The following morning they were both awake very early. There was a renewed spirit between them. For the first time in many years they were both in agreement and equally determined to pursue their united goal of raising this new found "joy" in their lives. Each, however, had very different reasons.

After breakfast, Chris phoned the attorney as instructed by Sister Teresa. He was surprised when the secretary informed him that he could come in right away, but instead of doing so, he decided to make the appointment for eleven o'clock, which would give him enough time to do some necessary shopping and plan the mechanics of taking on a newborn baby girl.

When Chris got off the phone, Jimmie sat down next to him on the bed and placed her hand on his leg very gently and said, "Daddy, I know that this baby means a lot to you. It means as much to me, too! You're probably gonna need to take some time away from the church and spend it with us, cause a daughter takes a lot a work from both parents."

"I know that, Blessie," he replied. "This also means that you'll have to quit your job at the casino."

"What? Quit my job? What for? I was thinkin' to let Rosie watch the baby while I was working."

"Rosie, your sister-in-law, Rosie? You can't let someone else watch a brand new baby. What's the matter with you?"

Jimmie jumped from the bed and put her hands up to her cheek as if a bolt of lightning had struck. "Rosie! Oh Shit! In all the excitement, I ain't never told anyone. They sure as hell gonna be surprised when I tell them we're gonna have us a baby!"

They glimpsed at each other and ruptured into laughter until they were out of breath with tears blurring their vision. It was the first time in a very intense twenty-four hours that they realized the irony of their situation. After ten minutes they felt relieved and calmed down, Jimmie picked up the telephone receiver and asked for the long distance operator. "I'm sure she'll be home at this time of the day," she said to Chris.

He sat up and watched Jimmie. She was on stage now, trying to act calm and sophisticated. A transformation was taking place. Chris put his head in his hands trying not to giggle, only imagining Rosie's reaction.

"Hello, Rosie?" Jimmie chuckled loudly and held her hand over the mouthpiece.

"Who is this? Is that you, Jimmie?"

"Yeah, it's me."

"Are you drunk again?" Rosie asked.

"No, I'm sober as a . . . a nun! A nun!" She could barely talk.

"Well, then what you giggling at?"

"We're gonna have us a baby. A little girl."

"You gonna have a what? Now I know you're drunk. When all this happen?"

"Just yesterday."

"Yesterday! A girl! Don't you dally wit' me, Sistah, I ain't got no time for your foolishness. Every time you get drinking too much of that poison, you start running off at the mouth about some half-witted thing or another. Now where you at, and what you want?"

"No Rosie, damn it. It's true. We're in San Francisco, and we're gonna adopt a newborn baby—a girl!"

"San Francisco? Is Chris with you?" Rosie asked.

"Yeah, right here," Jimmie said.

"Let me talk to him."

Jimmie began chuckling again and handed the phone to Chris. "Rosie don't believe me. You tell her."

"Hello, Rosie? This is Chris. Now listen. You are the first to know. It's all true. We're in San Francisco to adopt a little mixed baby. A girl."

"Have you been drinkin' too? How'd all this happen?"

"It's a long story. No time to explain," he said.

"Before you do something you gonna regret, you better tell me what this is all about!" said Rosie.

"Okay, okay, but briefly. Some woman stopped in the ladies' lounge a few months ago and asked Jimmie if she'd adopt a little baby. Jimmie said yes and that's that."

"That's that? That's what?" Rosie asked.

"It's God's will, Rosie. We're going to pick her up at the hospital this afternoon and we should be back in Reno about eight tonight. It's a long story. I'll explain it when I see you tonight."

Chris hung up the phone, turned to Jimmie and said, "You're right, she don't believe you."

Chris and Jimmie checked out of the hotel and drove to the downtown shopping area in search of clothing and other paraphernalia for the infant. They picked out the best baby carriage and loaded the new Cadillac with baby clothes, toys, dolls, bottles, diapers, and rattles. When the shopping spree ended the next stop was to sign the adoption papers at the attorney's office. They arrived at the address fifteen minutes ahead of the scheduled appointment. Without waiting, the secretary ushered Jimmie and Chris into an inner office where a stocky, rosy-cheeked man of about sixty sat with his feet up on the radiator, and the phone to his ear. They seated themselves on the hard oak chairs in front of an old desk strewn with papers, books, files, and the like. The room was in disarray. Chris couldn't help but notice a large Confederate flag trimmed in gold fringe, pinned against one wall. There were stained black-framed photographs on another wall of Mr. Waters, perhaps in his younger days, shaking hands with what appeared to be a few not-so-memorable politicians. Chris recognized only one character among the half-dozen pictures. It was larger than the rest and displayed proudly in the center of the others—a black and white etching of General Robert E. Lee in full dress uniform.

Cyrus Waters hung up the phone and stared at the couple from over the top of his glasses long enough to make them uncomfortable. He opened the folder lying on the desk in front of him and slowly read to himself, occasionally glancing up in a suspicious manner. Finally, he looked up again and spoke.

"Are you Jimmie Lee Greenwade?"

"Yes, sir," she answered politely.

"And I am Reverend Greenwade," Chris interjected.

The lawyer sat back in his chair, placed his hands firmly on the armrests, and looked down past the tip of his nose at the young couple. "I see here that you are the colored couple who want to adopt that little nigger lover's baby."

Chris sprang to his feet, squarely placing his big hands on the front edge of the desk. He leaned over, face to face with Waters. Just as quick, he felt a jolting stab to the back of his leg. It was Jimmie who reacted swiftly, kicking him hard enough to make Mr. Waters notice. Chris realized that Jimmie was well aware of the manner in which black people were supposed to act in the presence of whites. He saw how she would sometimes kowtow to get what she wanted, then denigrate them when their backs were turned. It was the only satisfaction in an otherwise hopeless situation. From her simple reaction, Chris understood that nothing would be accomplished by a confrontation with this white bigot.

"Now, Mr. Greenwade," said Waters slowly and deliberately, as if to provoke the gentle giant, "did you want to say something?"

"It's Reverend Greenwade," Chris said firmly as he sat back down.

"Oh yes, you are a minister. I almost forgot," he said in a voice tinged with sarcasm.

Jimmie nudged her husband and whispered softly in his ear, "Losin' ya temper is not the way God intended you to spread His Word."

Chris realized that she was right and for the first time understood the trouble this little baby could cause.

After a few further unpleasant exchanges, Waters explained that this custody was merely a trial period and that it would take at least a full year before the adoption would become legal. He then allowed the Greenwades to sign the papers. They left the office hoping never to see Cyrus Waters again.

Chris and Jimmie delivered the notarized documents to St. Elizabeth's Hospital, picked up their newborn baby with some last-minute instructions from the nurses, and headed back home to Reno.

CHAPTER 4

A grin stretched across Chris' face as the joy from his sudden change of fate engulfed him. He glanced occasionally at the bundle of life sleeping peacefully on the soft blankets next to him. It was less than thirty-six hours since he first laid eyes on Louise and now the miracle baby was in the car. Only at this moment did he start to think about the practical side of his decision. He wondered how to explain the sudden appearance of a baby to the congregation? Would they believe the enlightenment that he made clear to Jimmie the night before? Can he let the hotel know? Fragmented thoughts raced about in his mind, exciting every nerve. The pride that only comes with father-hood overcame any of his imaginary obstacles. "Daddy, what are we gonna name her? I ain't calling her Fauna. That's a dumb name. Besides, she don't look like no Fauna." Jimmie's question suspended his blissful reflections.

"Yeah, you're right," Chris said, "she looks like a little star—sent from heaven. How's about we name her Esther, like Esther from the Bible?"

"Esther? Do you think I'm gonna tell everybody I got a daughter named Esther? Esther? No way!" Jimmie paused for a moment staring at the child. "The more I look at her, the more I think she's white. Are there any white-sounding names in the Bible?"

"No, but there's Ruth. Ruth stands for friendship," Chris said.

"Ruth Greenwade . . . Ruth Greenwade . . . nah," Jimmie shook her head. "Don't feel right."

"How about Miriam? She was rebellious."

"Sounds like broken glass to me. She sure looks white. Yeah! We got a white patty on our hands."

They looked at each other, neither saying a single word until Jimmie added, "We should name her Pat. Yeah. Patty—Patricia! Patricia Ann Greenwade. Yeah, that's it! Now that sounds like her!"

The birth certificate with the child's legal name given by the natural mother wasn't even a consideration. Fauna Hodel meant nothing at all. The child was to be called Patricia Ann Greenwade and that was that.

Chris' silence was his agreement. He seemed unconcerned, knowing it would be impossible to legally change her name at this time anyway. It was more important that Jimmie be satisfied. He knew that to argue over such a moot point would be more trouble than it was worth.

"Sure, that's a fine name. We'll call her Patty," he said. Jimmie smiled contentedly.

Chris noticed calmness in her. The obstinacy that plagued both their lives diminished. No longer was Jimmie argumentative and contrary. Chris hadn't heard a vile word leap from her tongue all day. But more significantly, she never reached into her purse for a ration of gin. It was as though she never even knew it was there. The message, although quite premature, was becoming evident. Jimmie was finally becoming a woman, and a mother, and a wife.

The return trip was the most enjoyable time they spent together in years. The hot, arid air during the late August drive kept their minds clear of the social hurdles that were looming because of their decision to accept this mixed-race baby. But for now, a few brief hours of peace were a welcome respite. Patricia Ann provided both curiosity and excitement. She was silent during the ride.

As they approached the Sierras, the sudden drop in temperature and the sweet smell of summer pine refreshed not only their bodies but also their hearts.

It was around 8:30 in the evening when they reached the outskirts of Reno. The sun had set. The proud new parents were anxious to show off their newfound possession. "Let's stop by Rosie's," said Chris.

"Yeah, Daddy, you promised to see her when we got back. She'd be pissed off if we didn't. There's still plenty of time."

"This'll be kind of a shock to her. After all, she didn't even know you were pregnant!" Chris said with a chuckle.

Rosie Bilbrew was a few years older than Jimmie, more stable, and much wiser. Neither had been formally educated for more than a few years, but Rosie was more independent, determined, and grounded. She read a lot, particularly in the area of psychic phenomena. Everyone in the family counted on her sensitivity and understanding. Her dark reddish-brown hair and light complexion contrasted with Jimmie's more accentuated features. She was generous—a true helper. Her manner was feisty, often argumentative, but in a loving, more amusing way.

Rosie stood on the porch, her arms folded, watching Chris glide the Cadillac into a space in front of her house while Jimmie Lee leaned on the horn announcing their arrival. Rosie ambled down the hollow wooden steps with a half smile and greeted the two most unlikely parents with suspicion.

"Let's see what you got here." She peeked her head in the open window, but Jimmie had the baby wrapped up tighter than a pot roast. "Well, I'll be damned! I didn't believe you two this morning! And I still don't. But it sure looks true now! You really went to San Francisco and adopted a baby?"

"Yeah, sister, we surely did," replied Jimmie as she stepped from the car.

In the dark, Rosie could only make out a small bundle of fluffy blankets. "Well let the Lord be praised! This is sure some kind of miracle. Come on inside, that little baby's gonna catch a cold in this night air."

Before they got to the front door, friends from the neighborhood made their way out of Rosie's on to the porch, greeting Chris and Jimmie, while anxiously waiting to see the baby.

"What's all this?" Chris asked.

"I just invited a few of friends and neighbors to see the new baby," Rosie answered, "kind of like a baby shower, without the gifts."

The atmosphere was charged with cheers and well wishing, handshakes, hugs, and congratulations. Jimmie Lee and Chris beamed, acting as any proud parents would, bringing home a newborn infant for the first time. There was constant noise and chatter, each vying for the right to see the baby first and catch every word of how this whole thing had happened. Somehow they felt this was a momentous occasion.

"Wait, wait a minute," yelled Jimmie. "The first thing that's got to be done is to change my baby's diaper."

Like the Piper, Jimmie marched into Rosie's bedroom with everyone merrily following. Jimmie could not have asked for a better spotlight to show her off. Rosie's bedroom was small and congested with furniture. There were statues of Jesus and Mary on every flat surface with photographs, odd wooden boxes, books and trinkets mixed in between.

"Let me see, let me see," someone kept yelling.

"Just a minute. Just wait. I'll show ya," Jimmie mimicked back. From all the commotion and excitement, the baby started crying. Jimmie gently placed the infant on the bed.

Over the "oohs" and "aahs" Rosie asked, "What's the baby's name?"

"Patricia Ann Greenwade," said Jimmie proudly as she unveiled the baby under the pink blanket.

Suddenly, all the chatter went quiet as though the film broke. "What kind of baby is that?" asked Julian, a friend of Rosie's.

"That's a white baby!" Shellie said.

"A white baby!" added Mrs. Rollet.

"Maybe you all got the wrong baby," Julian replied.

"What did they do, get the wrong baby? That ain't no mixed baby! Somebody made a switch," Shellie said. The silence turned to a constant murmur.

Rosie eyed Chris as he looked at the puzzled group of friends, expecting a display of emotion. "No, no, no! This is a mixed baby," he explained in an effort to arrest their obvious confusion.

Rosie gazed quizzically from the opposite side of the bed directly into Jimmie's eyes. She was astonished at her sister-in-law's acceptance of this white-looking baby in spite of Chris' remarks. She had a hundred questions on her mind, but held her tongue. Jimmie never noticed Rosie's penetrating stare. Her response to the enthusiasm was a mix between elation and embarrassment—just what Rosie expected.

Chris' powerful voice quickly drowned out all the noise and confusion. "Now, hold on to your pants, everybody. You're all making a mistake here. This is a mixed baby. You all know that. babies are born light and as they get older they darken."

"With blue eyes?" said Mrs. Rollet.

Chris ignored the remark, but the comments kept coming. "Nah, don't worry about that, her eyes will darken, too!"

Margaret and Bonnie Ulster just gazed at each other with a look of total disbelief.

"Who does she look like?" asked Julian.

"Where did you get her? How much does she weigh? Do you have to give her back?" Ellie Daniels' rapid-fire questions rolled out without waiting for a response adding to the giddy spectacle of a white-skinned baby within their midst.

Rosie leaned across the bed and finally spoke quietly to Jimmie, "Sister, you're in a heap a shit. What are you doing with this white baby?"

Jimmie completed the diaper changing ritual. She looked back at Rosie and snapped to attention with her hands planted firmly on her thin hips, her all-too-familiar stance, and her head cocked to the right. "Now you listen here, Rosie Bilbrew, we ain't in no shit at all! We did this whole deal right and legal—with the lawyer and everything. We signed the papers. This is a legal adoption, as legal as you is standing there. Everything was taken care of and we even know the people that gave us the baby. Ain't that right, Daddy?"

Chris nodded proudly, as he listened to his wife's explanation. It was the first time that he could remember them both being on the same side of an argument. Jimmie continued, "The woman who set this thing up is a dear friend of mine. She knows we didn't have no children, and she thought it'd be just the right thing for us.

"The baby is a mixed-baby. Her real mama's only sixteen, and white—too young to take care of a little one like this. Why, she's just a baby herself."

"And the father?" Rosie asked.

"He's colored," Jimmie responded, "just as colored as we is. It says so right on the birth certificate, too! She's our baby and we're gonna keep her."

While Jimmie got everyone's attention, Chris took quick advantage of the mood she created. It would be a perfect time to rest any rumors before they got started.

"Everything Jimmie is telling you is the absolute truth. I was there through the whole thing. This little baby, our Patricia Ann, is mixed, all right; we've got the papers to prove it. Besides, if the baby was white—all white, I mean who in the world would give her away; a beautiful, healthy, little girl . . . to a colored couple in this day and age?"

His logic was obvious to Rosie. Neither Chris, nor Jimmie, nor any of her friends from this small group could possibly imagine a circumstance. Rosie saw that Chris was happy, proud, and content with the knowledge that his first encounter with prejudice had been successful and far less difficult than he expected.

Rosie prepared a small potluck buffet and Mrs. Barbre made a chocolate layer cake decorated with a hastily written, "Congratulations—Mom and Dad!" Chile, a housekeeping client of Rosie, brought a white-laced infant's gown as a gift. The same gift as James and Martha—the only two gifts that were identical. Bert, Elaine, Mrs. Rollet, and Ellie Daniels, also brought something for this unusual and spontaneous occasion.

They all savored the story of how this whole situation came about. They wanted to hear as many of the details as possible. Alternately, both Jimmie and Chris enthusiastically obliged for almost two hours before calling it a night.

The following weeks were full of discovery and busyness. In addition to numerous trips to the store for supplies and baby food, there were also constant adjustment to the feeding times, washing diapers, and waking up in the middle of the night; a chore that quickly became Chris' responsibility. Jimmie did not have the patience to calm the baby when she cried at night. Chris, on the other hand, had a soothing voice with women, and baby Pat was no different.

Both knew that their lives had changed for the better. Taking care of a baby was more work than either anticipated. The focus of their life was now altered and their routine was no longer determined by their own whims but by the constant demands of the baby.

The congregation at the Pentecostal Church became aware of the little miracle at the very next service after their return from Reno. Chris Greenwade spent much of his spare time passing out cigars and shaking hands, as though he was running for mayor. His reputation as a dignified preacher was enhanced by being a proud new father of a mixed-race little girl. He told everyone of his new daughter, the angel that had come into his life.

His sermons would change dramatically too, both in tone and content. The orations moved from urging sinners to repent, to that of hope for the future of his race.

As the weeks passed by, he would bring the new infant with him as a headliner to show off to his congregation, elevating his status among the parishioners. This new spark of enthusiasm created by the baby absorbed much of the preacher's time. It left him little to spend with Jimmie, a woman who thrived on attention.

Jimmie Lee went from a life of independence, earning her own way, to that of a housekeeper, babysitter, nursemaid, and full-time attendant to the impulses of both Chris and the baby. Her entire life revolved around diapers, formulas, and the like. In addition, at the most inopportune time, sisters from the church would drop by to see "Reverend Greenwade's daughter." Jimmie made it her business to spend less time in the house and more time away with the baby in order to avoid some of their unkind comments about raising a white baby. She did not fear confrontation but chose the time and place as it suited her purpose.

Together with Rosie, her confidante and sister-in-law, and the baby, she took long walks around the neighborhood, often removing the blanket from the infant leaving Patty naked, exposed to the sun. Frustrated by the restraint the baby placed upon her own freedom, Jimmie became more insecure in her life and bored with the baby. When Rosie noticed, she would cover up the baby and mumble something about how she couldn't understand how such a little one could kick off the coverlet so quickly. Jimmie just smiled. When Rosie wasn't looking, she'd removed the blanket again.

Rosie responded in a cautious tone, "Why you keeping that baby in the sunshine all the time? You know that it's not good for her white skin to have that hot sun beating on it all the time. She's gonna get burnt!"

"Oh, she's all right. Fresh air and sunshine is always good for babies—especially this one."

"Yeah, but she's just an infant and her skin ain't used to the sun like ours; she's got that pinkish white skin, you know!" Rosie covered up the baby with the light blanket; Jimmie promptly removed it.

"You've got to keep the covering over the eyes, or that baby will never get to see the light of day. You keep this nonsense up, and you're gonna bake this baby's brains out!"

"Listen to me, Rosie Bilbrew," she snapped back, "Chris promised me that the baby would darken. All I'm doing is helping her along."

"This baby ain't gonna darken. What's wrong with you? You either colored like us or white, you can't change somebody's skin."

"Don't you tell me what I can and can't do; I'll change this baby from white to colored, even if I don't change the color of her skin. This baby is gonna grow up to be just like me!"

"Lord help us. The last thing we need is another Jimmie Lee running around."

"What do you mean? There ain't nothing wrong with me."

"Huh! Nothing that a healthy dose of the Bible won't cure, and I'm not talking about reading it. I'm talking about you eating it, page by page."

Jimmie laughed out loud as a car passed by with a couple of young white boys inside. They mimicked her laugh, and Jimmie flashed a rude gesture after they turned away.

"White trash. They all alike."

"Yeah, that's what you always say."

"Well, it's true. They use the coloreds as if they were their own property, to mess around with until they get tired. It never changes."

"What do you mean, it never changes?"

"Just what I said. We colored and they white, and to them we ain't nothing but dog shit!" Rosie peered at her with a quizzical look, waiting for Jimmie to continue.

"Jimmie Lee, you ain't never gonna change."

"I changed since me and Chris been together," Jimmie replied, "and I really changed since this baby come along. That's for sure!"

"You and Chris changed since this baby come along."

"Yeah, I'm doing all the raising, cleaning diapers, feedin', and making formulas. That's how I changed. Him—huh! All he gets to do is walk around like a big shot, tellin' everybody about his 'Little Angel that was sent by God'. Well, if his 'Little Angel' was sent by God, why didn't He send a damn babysitter instead of letting me do all the shit!"

Rosie looked over at Jimmie and said, "This don't have anything to do with God, but your niece is looking to go to college and I bet she'd jump at the chance to make a little money."

"What niece you talking about?" Jimmie asked.

"Sally." Rosie responded.

"She's in LA. She old enough to go to college?"

"Not yet, but I know she'd love to get out of that full house," Rosie said. "I talked to her mother the other night, and she kept on complaining about all the kids in the house and couldn't wait till they all grow up and get jobs."

"Yeah, she's always moaning about something. I'll tell Chris. See what he says," Jimmie said.

Since Chris' work schedule and church responsibilities forced him to spend time away from Jimmie Lee, she became more bogged down with the details of motherhood. She became frustrated at not knowing precisely where Chris was all the time, jealous at believing the worst, and angry at her ineptness in dealing with the situation. Within a short time after the baby arrived, she plotted ways to combat her confinement and Chris' freedom. Her idea of battle, however, was to drink more heavily. Her responsibilities were dramatized even more when she received the first of several letters from Dorarro, Dr. Hodel's current wife.

Dear Mrs. Greenwade,

Congratulations to you and your husband from all of us on the new addition to your family.

I know it took a lot of courage for you to accept a stranger into your home. However, I am confident that you will raise her with the warmth and love you've shown. As you know, Fauna's biological family needs to be treated with secrecy. I want you to know that you will have complete responsibility for the welfare of the baby and we will not interfere in any way. If you need help in the future, we'll do what we can.

There are certain conditions you should be aware of and that we will insist upon. First and foremost, the child's legal name cannot be changed. It must stay Fauna Hodel. This is the one request of Fauna's mother. She didn't ask for much when she gave up the baby, but that's all she wanted. Of course, you can call her anything you want, but there are some future financial circumstances that you should be aware of. Fauna's grandfather, George, is a respectable physician living in California. Some of his assets were inherited from his father. There is no doubt that he would have attained this money and power on his own. Dr. Hodel is a certified genius with an IQ that's off the scale. He is notoriously charming and persuasive, and as shrewd as he is brilliant, with some rather unusual behaviors that I don't want to write about at this time. Let's just say that he is not one to fool with—under any circumstance.

You may be aware of the adverse national publicity generated by the trial involving George and his daughter, Tamar. He was acquitted of the charges and is very sensitive toward any further scandals relating to his family. This brings me to the second request.

You must never contact my husband directly. If for some reason there is need to get in touch with us please do so by writing to me first. I will then pass on the information to George and I can assure you he will take whatever action is necessary. He cannot afford to be connected to you directly for fear of the press and their insinuations.

Finally, Fauna must never know about any of this until she is older. She needs to be raised normally, like other kids. Do not let her contact her biological mother. She is immature and cannot be trusted.

Thanks again for the courage and generosity you've shown for taking on the responsibility of raising a mulatto child. If you have any further questions, please feel free to contact me at my P.O. Box.
    Sincerely,
    Dorarro

Jimmie Lee read the letter slowly. She then fixed herself another drink, and read it again to make certain she understood everything. At first she was agreeable to the request. There was nothing demanding about it, nor did she, at the time, have any plans to contact these white folk in San Francisco anyway. This adoption deal was much too easy for her to make any waves. It would be difficult enough trying to keep a white-looking baby without complicating matters by bringing in outsiders who could very easily persuade the authorities to force the Greenwades to turn the child over to a another couple. Besides, Jimmie Lee was getting used to having Pat around. She was feeling good about the attention she was receiving and knew it would be her last hope in keeping Chris for herself. She had no intention of contacting Dorothy, no matter what problems arose. The more she thought about the letter, the more annoyed she became at the gall of this white woman.

She walked into the bedroom where the baby slept and cradled her in her arms. In the dimly lit room the contrast between her own black arms and the pinkish white flesh of this infant was remarkable, and bore a striking similarity to what Jimmie was feeling inside. She stroked the infant's thin blond hair and said to herself, "I don't know where you come from, little girl, whether you half-colored or not. It don't matter much to you now; but I'll tell you something that you can keep for the rest of your life. The half of you that's white sure ain't gonna act like these white folks who sent me this letter. No, my Lordy, you sure ain't.

"These whiteys don't look out for nobody but themselves. You may look white to a lot a folks, little girl, but you sure ain't gonna grow up like one," she said pitifully.

Jimmie folded the letter slowly, returned it to the envelope, and placed it in a lower dresser drawer. All she ever wanted was for Chris to love her as he did when they were younger. Instead, she strapped herself with someone else's baby. A baby whose skin was whiter than any mulatto she'd ever seen. The pressure threatened to sink her. She sauntered from the bedroom to the liquor cabinet and plopped down with a full bottle of gin and proceeded to wash away reality.

———————————

It was early evening when Chris returned home. While still on the doorstep, he heard the screams that could only be made from an infant in serious trouble. He shook with fright as he rushed into the bedroom and saw Patty struggling to grab her breath between howls. His little angel was bright red, alone, and afraid. He plucked her up and held her gently in his powerful arms. "Shhhh, shhhh, my baby, Daddy's here. It's OK. Everything's all right." She continued to scream as if she was in deep pain.

"Blessie, Blessie, where are you?" He shouted while walking from room to room. As he stepped into the parlor, he noticed Jimmie's limp body slumped between the couch and the floor with an empty liquor bottle by her side. He rushed over to her with his screaming daughter

in his right arm and shook her warm, clammy shoulder. Kneeling down
he shook her again, yelling in her ear. "Blessie, Blessie, are you all right?
Wake up! Wake up! Are you all right? What happened? This baby is a
mess; can't you hear her screaming? Blessie!"

Jimmie struggled to lift her head. She slowly opened one eye, glassy
and bloodshot and zeroed in on the crying baby. "What's a matter, baby?
You hungry?"

"Hungry?" answered Chris, "What do you mean hungry? How long
you been like this?"

"I must of fell asleep."

"Asleep! You're dead drunk. What's the matter with you? Something
could have happened to the baby and you wouldn't have known a damn
thing!"

"Don't you give me none a your shit." Jimmie sat upright. Her body
stiffened. The attitude quickly changed from that of a sleepy lamb to an
angry wolf.

"You're never here to take care of this baby." She said indignantly.
"I'm the one who does all the pickin' up, cleaning, feeding, washing
clothes, all the walking outside. You never take care of this child. Then
you come home and decide that I'm not doing a good enough job. Well,
if you don't think I'm doing enough," she slurred. "Then damn you, do
it yourself! Cause there's no way this girl's sitting by taking care a this
child while your ass is out fooling with those sisters at the church, which
I know you're doing, so don't try to tell me different."

"What, Sister?" Chris snapped back still holding the screaming
infant. Jimmie's argumentative nature was coming out quick and furious.

"You been spending more time between going to work, high
stepping about town, and going to the church, and less time with me.
We was to be a family. But instead, you saddled me with a baby that does
nothing but cry and mess up herself. You go out and tell everyone how
proud you is to be a real father—which you ain't—and I get stuck doing
the work. Now you give me that damn kid, she needs to be changed."

Chris was visibly upset by his wife's remarks. Disappointment
etched his face as he watched this strange woman take the baby into

the bedroom. Not quite herself yet, she staggered most of the way. He followed her to make sure that she would not fall with his precious angel.

"Little Patta, my white little Patta. You sure are white," she whispered as she placed the infant on the bed and began the routine of washing, changing, and feeding. "You belong to me, too. Yeah, you do. He doesn't really want anything to do with you. Just wants to show you off like a new suit. You such a helpless little thing, but that's cause you're so tiny. But you'll get bigger and grow up, and you'll still be white. That ain't never gonna change. Don't matter what that piece of paper says. You're my baby, and I'm never gonna let anything bad happen to you."

Chris stomped out the back door into the yard and took a few deep breaths of fresh air to calm down. He overwhelmed his wife with the time-consuming duties of being a mother and homemaker, leaving time for himself to work with his congregation. He now knew that Jimmie wanted to use the child to bind them together. It was difficult to conceive of either fulfilling their goals: neither wholesome nor compassionate as Chris had hoped, nor romantic as Jimmie wished. From that moment on, only Chris knew the outcome of this perilous arrangement.

Jimmie Lee went back to work part-time at the hotel, forcing Chris to spend more time with the baby, a diversion he found rewarding but frustrating. Patty Ann learned to walk early, and she was talking up a storm at fourteen months. But the baby cried frequently, leaving Chris to comfort her.

"Aaah, calm down little angel, try to be a little patient. What do you want? Your Momma's not here and I can't understand you at all." Chris left the baby to cry while he gathered up the gear that always accompanied little Patta for the short journey to Rosie's.

When Rosie came to the front door and saw Chris with the baby, she braced for another imposition from him. "What's the problem this time?" she said stiffly.

"I can't get her to stop crying and I got to get over to town to get some things done before it's too late."

She gently held the baby in her arms and looked down with a smile. "What kind of things?"

"You know, church things."

"Church things! Church things! Well, I told you before and I'll say it again, I just can't stop everything I'm doing just because you can't take care of this baby."

"No, it's not that. I really need to get this stuff done."

Rosie looked with suspicion at Chris, then down at the baby. A puzzled look came over her face. "What's ever gonna happen to you, child?" She turned and walked with the baby into the house. "What's ever gonna happen to you?"

Chris finally got the message, and hired a babysitter, rather than listen to Rosie's scolding.

As the months went by, each week brought a new problem and a new babysitter. The common-law marriage began to unravel. Jimmie Lee was suspicious of her suave preacher. Chris responded by appeasement and agreed to provide room and board to her teenage niece, Sally.

"Hey, Lil' Patta." Jimmie Lee had the twenty-month-old baby on her knee. "We gonna even out the sides a little. You gonna get a good babysitter."

"Baaaaaaaabysitter," said Patty. "A babysitter. I a babysitter."

Jimmie Lee laughed, "No, no, no, you the baby. Sally's the *babysitter.*"

"Sally a babysitter?"

"Yeah, that's it! She is Sally, and she is beautiful! You're gonna love her. She's just graduated from high school. And she'll be going to college too. How 'bout that?"

"How 'bout that!" The baby mimicked Jimmie.

"You talking just like me. You sound like one of my own—that's if I had any, which I ain't. If I closed my eyes and just listened to you, I'd know you anywhere. You sound like me. You smell like me. But you sure don't look like me." Jimmie put herself nose to nose with Patta and gave her a big kiss. "You ain't mine, and you are white, but I surely do love you. I surely do."

CHAPTER 5

In keeping with the latest style, Sally wore her blouse with the collar upturned, letting her wavy, black hair dangle just below. Her slacks were always skin tight and pegged at the ankle. She was energetic, charismatic, and colorfully dressed, accentuating her well-proportioned features—soft, slender arms, full breasts, and shapely hips. Each crack of her contagious smile coerced the only mar in an otherwise flawless, brown complexion—elusive dimples that surfaced on each side of her soft lips. When anyone retreated after a glance, her glistening brown eyes invited another look. Her disarming innocence and bubbly personality brought her to the center of attention at almost any gathering. She made everyone feel at ease.

Jimmie, however, noticed that Sally treaded lightly the first few days at her the house, cautiously staying out of Jimmie's way and performing each assigned chore with the minimum of instruction. The addition of a family member living under her roof boosted Jimmie Lee's confidence while relieving the routine of raising a baby. Jimmie now had a live-in housekeeper, babysitter, and a built-in audience of one.

Within a few weeks, Jimmie's enthusiasm for the ingénue began to wane as she noticed Chris' charm soar to a new high. One evening, after Sally fell asleep early in the baby's room, Jimmie sat with her head in her hand at the kitchen table, drinking 7-Up, while waiting for Chris to come home. He arrived with a small bag that he laid on the countertop and said, "Where's Sally?"

"She went to bed early, said she was tired." Jimmie responded while keeping an eye on his movements.

"Patty too?"

"Yeah, they both asleep," she said, looking up at Chris as he pulled a colorful plaything from the sack.

"What's you got there?" Jimmie asked.

"I picked this up for the baby, at that new department store. Sally said Patty needs some more stimulation," Chris responded.

"Sally said, Sally said, who the fuck is Sally? So now you taken orders from a teenager?"

"She didn't give me an order," Chris said with a chuckle.

"Seems like the only thing that stimulatin' you is my niece," Jimmie snapped back.

"Sounds to me like you're a little jealous," Chris said.

"I ain't jealous. What do I got to be jealous of? Cause she's so young and sweet? Or cause you two are always off talking together. What do you yak about anyway?"

"We yak about your family mostly. There's a lot of stories she never knew about," Chris said.

"Yeah, and don't think you know them all either," Jimmie responded.

"It's good to find out what they're teachin' in school today. Like what they say about this McCarthy business or politics, you know—current events. Or sometimes we talk about books, like *The Invisible Man*. I wanted to know if they were discussing that in her class, and other stuff too. She's curious and interested in learning new things."

"I know what you up to. You ain't the one who's gonna be teachin' her anything either. And don't even think about trying nothing with my niece," Jimmie shot back.

"What's the matter with you woman? What do you think I am? Your jealousy is like a dog with a bone . . . never lets go." Chris said while shaking his head on the way to the bedroom.

The tension between Jimmie Lee and Chris increased with each passing week. Allowing Sally to take care of Patty provided Jimmie with some well-earned freedom, but it also created as much of a temptation for Chris as did the sisters from the church. Sally was caught in the middle of Jimmie's crosshairs.

Each Thursday Chris plied his trade polishing out boots made of soft calfskin, alligator, or engraved leather, or buffing out exotic snakeskin, a few custom designed with etched silver toe-tips, for high rollers at the Riverside. While he worked, Jimmie now had the luxury to slip off in her most conspicuous outfit spending the afternoon in the New China Club, a casino owned by Asians and the only one that permitted Negroes to play. The other casinos barred the few free-spending Negroes that had money because the white owners didn't want to alienate the white clientele. The New China Club needed money and catered to everyone, and Jimmie knew many of the regular customers. She rarely gambled, mostly drank. For Jimmie it was a place to be seen in her efforts to become part of the local color. It was her way of becoming famous.

Chris always met her there after he finished work at the hotel, but on this day he was more than an hour late. When he finally arrived, Jimmie's irritation was evident in her gaze; she suspected the worst. "Where you been?" she asked.

"What do you mean? I had some things to take care of."

"What kind of things? Things that wiggle their ass?"

Chris gave a calculating glance. "I don't know where you get your ideas from, and at this point, I really don't care." He motioned for her to follow him as he headed out of the casino and into the parking lot for the drive home.

"I get my ideas from what I see with my own eyes," she continued, following along for just a moment, then took the lead and let Chris follow. "I been watching you with my niece, how you two been carryin' on."

"Carryin' on? There ain't no carrying on. Oh, woman, what's with you?"

"Yeah, you think I don't know what you been doing behind my back! That girl's been going out of her way to keep it from me. Always ironing your clothes, picking up after you, following you around likes a little puppy dog."

"That's why she's here," Chris snapped back.

"And you. You can't keep your eyes off of her breasts, staring her up and down every time she walks with that ass of hers shakin' like jelly."

"That's nonsense! Why, that girl is only trying to keep out of your way by helping to keep the house straight and taking care of Patta. Now you accusing me of messing with her. What the hell do you think I am?"

"I think you're a damn snake—that's what I think!"

Jimmie saw the veins rising from his neck as he slammed the car door shut and firmly took control of the wheel. "You're drunk," he said.

"I ain't no such thing. I know that girl since she was born," said Jimmie, "and in all her years she had boys chasin' her because she's so pretty and that ain't never changed and she knows it, too!"

When the car stopped in front of the house, Jimmie noticed the front lights go off in the dining room, replaced by candlelight flickering in the window. "Now what she up to. She must got one of her boyfriends in there."

As Chris entered the front door, with Jimmie a step behind, Sally met them wearing a light blue dress. An old recording by the Ink Spots was scratching away on the phonograph in the background. The table was set perfectly for two, with Jimmie's best satin tablecloth and fine china. Two candles on the table cast the only light in the room that made the silverware, glasses and Sally's big brown eyes sparkle in harmony.

Chris grinned. "Blessie, look at the beautiful table Sally's set here," he said, "And what is it that smells so good?"

"It's about time you two got home," said Sally. "I made dinner and been keeping it warm for the last half-hour. I expected you a little earlier. Come, sit down. And wait till you see what I made for dessert!"

"Dessert!" said Chris, "Well . . . what's the occasion?"

"I'll tell you what the occasion is," growled Jimmie in a slow, deliberate, and strained voice that froze everything but the candles.

Chris quickly tried to make light of her tone. "Well, it must be something very special."

Before Chris uttered another word, Jimmie reached for the end of the tablecloth and violently yanked it from the table propelling silverware and glasses in every direction. In an instant, Sally's romantic setting that she so meticulously prepared was now garbage littering the floor. Jimmie charged after her niece, knocking over the chair, yelling incoherently, only to be stopped by Chris blocking her way. Jimmie knew her wrath hit its mark as she gloated over Sally's tears.

"I know what you've been up to, you damn little whore! Ever since you come into my house you been trying to get your little hands wrapped around my man. I'm watching you all the time. Don't think I don't know what the fuck's going on between you two. The only reason I let you stay is cause you're my niece, and I feel sorry for your Momma!"

"Blessie!" yelled Chris. "What the hell are you saying! Are you insane? How could you even think that about your own niece after all she's been doing around here to help you?"

Sally pushed herself from the protection of Chris and charged through door into the night. Jimmie turned to Chris and saw contempt in his eyes. "If this is what you believe in your twisted, drunken mind," Chris said, "then there is nothing I can say to make you believe anything else. I can't be bothered with you and your stupid jealousies any longer. I got my own life to live."

Jimmie began to speak, but Chris steadied his broad hand in her face, stopping her cold. She watched him stomp into the bedroom to return with only a small suitcase. That would be the last Jimmie would see of the only man she had ever cared for; he was gone forever.

CHAPTER 6

Chris left with all of the assets: the car, the bank account and the real estate, leaving Jimmie Lee with the liabilities, including Patta, who she now had to raise on her own. Keeping regular hours at the Riverside Hotel and taking care of a baby proved impossible. She quit her job, to the delight of her employers, and began cleaning houses a few days each week. Her work was sporadic, never earning quite enough to get by and always spending more than she made. Bills piled up and Jimmie borrowed from her family and close friends, but that sliced deeply into her pride, particularly after having been the center of attention for most of her life. Her dream of celebrity slowly dissipated with the weight of responsibility. But her generosity and impulsiveness never waned. At times she tossed silver dollars to neighborhood kids to let them know she was alive. She was poor and generous, an unfortunate combination.

Always under the threat of repossessing the few things she bought on time, Jimmie tried charm to fend off the repo man, but her excuses only made them more aggressive, often cornering her on the street. To keep them at bay, Jimmie sometimes returned home with an admirer from the New China Club, deliberately showing off Patta. She told most of them that she was babysitting for some white folks. However, to those she trusted, she told the truth. The sight of a little white girl calling Jimmie, "Momma," easily persuaded even her most down-and-out suitors to kick in a deuce to help her cause.

Jimmie Lee sat on an old wooden stool on the porch drinking gin and 7-Up out of a mug while watching Pat play in front of the house. Jimmie fixed her gaze on the baby; her eyes began to swell with tears. "How I'm gonna keep you?" Jimmie murmured. "You're my whole life. I can't let them take you away from me."

"What's the matter, Momma? You ain't feeling good?"

"No baby, I'm just worried about you. I don't want anyone to take you away from me."

"Who's gonna take me away? You're my momma. I stay with you."

"I want you to stay. But I ain't your real momma. She's someone else."

Pat looked up again with a puzzled and curious expression; she wasn't too young to grasp the concept.

Jimmie Lee continued, "You're three and a half years old now. You're old enough now to understand some things," Jimmie Lee said as she shuffled down and sat face to face with her daughter.

"What kinda things, Momma? Like why you walk funny sometimes?"

"No, not that. That's something you shouldn't be worried or even thinking about. I drink cause Chris walked out on me and you. He left me alone with nothing. No money, no car, no job, and you."

"Me?"

"Yeah, you," she gazed sternly. "He left me and you. And he left without getting any adoption papers signed, so you don't even belong to me."

"Yes I do. I belong to you, Momma."

"Well, how do I know that? I ain't got no papers that say you belong to me."

Pat looked uncomfortable. Jimmie knew the baby didn't understand, but continued anyway, "Are you gonna just up and leave me just like your daddy? Huh? You can, you know. You could just walk out that door anytime you want. I ain't your real momma. Do you want to leave? Do you want to leave me?"

Pat grabbed hold of her momma and held on tightly. "No, no, I don't want to leave you. I'm never gonna leave. You're my momma."

"If your daddy, Chris—and he's ain't your real daddy—hadn't left us with no money, and if he did what he was supposed to do with the paperwork, then no one in the world would be able to take you away from me. But he didn't. So we got to be careful about who we tell what to. I've got to protect you from those white people who would take you away in a flash."

Pat stood back and stared at Jimmie. "Tell me who's my real momma," she said.

"Well, she's something else." Just then she noticed a car driving slowly down the street. "And someday, I'll tell you all about her. But right now we got to go inside." She swooped the child up and fled inside, locking the door behind her. She peered out the window and realized the car drove by the house without stopping.

Later that afternoon, Hemphill, a boyfriend of Jimmie's stopped by for his occasional visit. Jimmie was in no mood for a romp this day and let her feelings be known. That led to an argument. As the commotion intensified, Jimmie filled a pot of water, placed it on the stove, and brought it to a boil. In between her turns at hurling high-pitched epithets, she began humming an eerie, inharmonious tune. Jimmie eyed Pat who was hiding her head, and visibly distressed. Jimmie knew that her bad-temper was useful for controlling any situation. As the argument reached a peak, she grabbed the pot and flung the scalding water into Hemphill's face.

His wild screams crashed through Pat's protected world. Shocked by Hemphill's expression of agony, shocked by the extremity of Jimmie's action, Pat froze in horror when a few minutes later the police were outside the door ready to investigate the screaming. When Jimmie heard the banging at the door, she hid Pat in the closet, avoiding any explanation of her presence to the officers.

She congratulated herself for talking her way out of being arrested by sloughing the incident off as an accident. But the police didn't much care anyway. They saw it as just two coloreds trying to kill each other—and to them that wasn't such a bad thing.

It was later that evening that Jimmie realized it would be better if Pat stayed with her mother for a while. "Patta, we're gonna take a trip to see my momma. Would you like that?"

"Who's your momma?" Pat asked.

"Who's my momma? My momma is my momma. Everybody's got a momma." She paused and look at Pat. "Yeah, we'll take the bus and you could watch out the window. Maybe if you're real good, I'll let you stay there with Big Momma, too. Sound good?"

"Where's her house?" Pat asked.

"Oh, it's far from here, Los Angeles. That's where they make all of the movies," Jimmie said.

"Does Big Momma make movies?"

"No, you silly thing," Jimmie giggled. "If Big Momma made movies then I'd be a star already. I'd be on TV and mixin' with all the other stars. I'm a good actress, too. You know that?" She looked down at the baby and made her eyes open wide. "Why I'm as good as any of them. I can sing just as good as Lena Horne. And I'm prettier than all of them. And someday I'm gonna be famous and rich, too. I woulda been on my way already if you didn't come along."

To the child the Greyhound Bus was big and bright—an adventure. Yet, to Jimmie it was a place to be cautious, a holdover from her days in Mississippi. They sat in the back. Pat stood on the seat near the window watching the mountains and desert pass by. The trip still seemed to take forever.

When they arrived at the bus depot in Los Angeles, Pat saw the woman that Jimmie called Big Momma standing with a warm, glowing smile and arms open wide. Pat knew she would be safe.

"Oh my, my, what a big girl you getting to be!" Big Momma said as she swooped the child off of her feet and into her arms. "You are about the most beautiful child I'd ever seen. And look at that blond hair, all curly and such."

Pat returned the smile and quickly gave Big Momma a kiss on the cheek. "You Momma's momma?"

"Yes I am, child, but let me put you down cause you are just a bit too big to be holding on to."

Together they took a cab to Big Momma's house on East Fifty-sixth. It was a home more refined than the dwelling that Pat was accustomed to in Sparks. With two bedrooms and a big kitchen and a large parlor, it had more than enough space for a three year old. She enjoyed the conveniences too: a front porch closed in with screens and glass, a brick stoop with big planters at each end, and a small front yard with lots of colorful flowers. Inside, Big Momma kept dozens of interesting objects in a massive glass china closet: small statues, pictures of saints, souvenirs, candles, black-and-white photographs of her family, and odd curios that endlessly amused Pat.

As the two women watched her enjoy her new surroundings, Big Momma motioned for Jimmie to come into the kitchen out of earshot. "What are going to do with that child?" Pat overheard Big Momma say. "When she's a baby that's one thing, but she's getting big and she sure isn't getting any darker, no matter what you tried to do."

Pat stepped closer toward the voices, but out of view.

"I know, I know. She's such a sweet child and I love her like she was my own, and I'm gonna do what I said I was gonna do. I'm gonna keep her, except right now I need to get some things straightened out at home and I need to leave her with you for a while," Jimmie said.

"You're gonna keep her? Do you have any idea what kinda problems you in for trying to raise a white child?" Big Momma said.

"Momma, this ain't Mississippi. You living in the past, this is modern times. They don't hang you from the nearest branch no more. They don't run you off with tar and feathers. . . ."

"Now you listen to me," Big Momma interrupted, "nothing has changed. I'm as God fearing as anyone and I've seen what they can do without hanging you from a tree. And you, as spunky as you are, ain't gonna be able to deal with what they do to you when they find you holding on to a white child that you don't have adoption papers for. Even if you did get the papers, it still wouldn't matter. That child belongs with her own people. You know that."

"Well she's mine and I'm not gonna let anyone take her away from me," Jimmie said.

"But she's white! And you hate them."

"Her birth certificate says otherwise and I'm gonna teach her to be black like me."

Jimmie Lee returned to Sparks the following day. Pat was so busy with all the new things to do that she didn't notice until after supper that evening that her momma wasn't there, "Where's Momma and when's Momma coming to put me in bed?" she asked.

"Your momma hasn't been feeling very well since Chris went away, so she had to go back to Sparks and she wanted you to stay here with me."

"Is she coming back?"

"Oh she'll be back, don't you worry about that."

The child just sat in thought. Then Big Momma added, "Are you afraid of Jimmie . . . I mean your momma?"

"She scares me sometimes, but I'm never gonna leave her."

"You love your momma, don't you?"

"Oh yeah, she's my momma.

"Listen, Pat," Big Momma got up close to her, "if your momma does something that seems crazy, or gets angry or starts trouble of some kind and you get scared, here is what I want you to do. Fold your hands together like this and pray to God and He'll send His angels to protect you and you'll have nothing to worry about."

"Pray to God, who's God?"

"God is the One who'll keep you safe, He is the One who made you and He is always lookin' out for His little girls to make sure nothing can happen to them. So when you need help of any kind, just say, 'Dear God, it's me, little Pat, and I need Your help to protect me from the bad thing that may happen to me."

"And you know what? He'll send His angels around just to watch over you. It works all the time. You just got to believe it."

Pat smiled and let out a sigh as if the weight was lifted from her tiny shoulders. Big Momma gave her a big hug and put her to bed.

For the first few days, Pat slept in the bed with Big Momma, but then she moved Pat into a room with Big Momma's nephew. Johnny was about ten and watched over her like a big brother.

Big Momma took Pat and Big Johnny all over the city with her— to shop at the grocers, to the church, to pay some bills, or to the bank. Sometimes she took Pat to work with her at the different homes where she worked as a cleaning woman. Mrs. Rolstadt was one she respected and admired.

"Well, who's this lovely little lady?" the woman asked as Pat stood by the couch fiddling with her hands.

Big Momma quickly replied, "I'm babysitting while her mother is up in Reno. She hasn't been feeling very well and she asked if I'd take care of her. And it's been a delight."

"Oh, lovely." The woman knelt down near the child and looked right into her eyes. "You are a cutie. What's your name?"

Pat looked up at Big Momma as if to ask for approval. She didn't answer. "Her name is Pat," said Big Momma.

"Well, Pat, would you like some cookies and milk?" Pat nodded and followed the woman into the kitchen. Within moments, Pat was chatting away with Mrs. Rolstadt. They hit it off very well.

Pat spent all of her time with Big Momma, shopping, or running errands. Four or five nights a week, she took Pat and Johnny to church, attending services or helping the minister. On Sundays, from nine o'clock in the morning until late at night, they were at the church.

Pat thought that going to church was exciting, watching all the people jump up and down and scream "hallelujah" and "the Lord be praised, I'm saved." After a few visits she knew who the sinners were; they were the ones who always sat up front and faced the congregation, confessing their wicked ways. Pat never got bored with any of it, even though the same people were saved each week.

Each day was the same routine, Big Momma would wake the child up with a big hug and kiss and then make her breakfast, help her get dressed and then they'd be off either to someone's house that needed cleaning or to church.

When they returned home, Big Momma would work in the garden with Pat at her side.

"What's you puttin' in the ground?" Pat asked.

"Planting seeds. When you want something to grow, you just plant them in the ground and give them a little water and a little sunshine and they come up real, just like these." Big Momma pointed to her gardenias.

"What can I put in?"

"You can put anything you want child, even your wishes. If you put your wishes on a little piece of paper and place it into God's earth, He will hear you. And His angels will make the wish come true." She smiled at Pat with eyes of love and tenderness, and then gave her a big hug.

Pat was the happiest she had ever been. They had a special feeling for each other. She would sit Pat on her lap and tell her stories, sometimes about the Bible, but mostly about her own family. She'd tell some of the foolish things that Jimmie Lee did when she was a youngster and how everyone thought she was the prettiest girl in Canton, Mississippi. She told Pat that Jimmie Lee always wanted to be famous and she was always showing herself off. Pat felt secure within her care.

Pat was in the parlor coloring in her book, as she did many times before. She wasn't paying much attention to Big Momma who sat on her favorite chair knitting a doily for the upcoming church bazaar.

"Ohhh, Lord," Big Momma moaned, "I'm not feeling so right, I feel a little dizzy."

Pat looked up to see Big Momma's ashen face in pain, her movements were slow and she was holding her arm. Pat grimaced as Big Momma painfully wiggled herself to the edge of the chair.

"Why you makin' them funny faces?" Pat asked.

Pat noticed tears roll slowly down the woman's cheeks as she said, "Big Momma don't feel well, Pat. I think I'd better call Aunt Lucille to take care of. . . ." She stopped in mid-sentence, stood up and reached out in front of her with one hand, gasped and then fell into the glass doors that led onto the porch, shattering splinters of wood and glass.

Pat began to whimper. "Big Momma, Big Momma, stop it! You're scaring me." Pat shook her hands and backed away from her fallen guardian. She tried to get out of the house as quickly as possible, but part of the door was lying on Big Momma's leg, blocking her way. Pat stepped over her large body, looked back at her as the woman grasped for a breath of air, with a painful moan. "You okay? Big Momma? Big Momma? You okay?"

When there was no answer from the considerable body lying awkwardly on the floor, with blood now forming a small puddle, Pat carefully stepped passed the debris and rushed down the steps to the house next door, beating on the screen door.

A short middle-age black woman suddenly appeared at the screen. "Little child, what's all this noise about?"

"Big Momma's on the floor. She won't get up!" Pat said.

"What's this? Oh dear!" She said as she rushed to the aid of the stricken woman, the child in tow.

Within a few minutes, the ambulance arrived on the scene and took Big Momma away. Jimmie's sister, Lucille came to stay with Johnny and Pat while her mother was in the hospital. Pat missed her Big Momma and prayed to God for her angels to help.

Although Big Momma recovered within a few days, she remained bedridden for a few weeks. But for Pat, that was great news. Not only was her Big Momma saved, but she now knew that when she prayed to her angels, her prayers worked, just like she was taught.

Little Johnny and Pat did what they could to make it easier for Big Momma, trying not to make as much of a mess as usual. Pat overheard Lucille say that she had a stroke. At the time Pat didn't know what that meant, but knew it was serious. She knew that Big Momma was too sick to spend as much time with her as before she fell down. She wondered what would become of her now.

Jimmie came down again from Sparks to check on Pat and Big Momma. She made the trip often over the next few months. Sometimes her brother Willie, who had a car, offered to drive to Sparks and pick her up because he liked to gamble. All the family—Willie, Lucille, Jesse,

Jimmie, and Dolly—helped out with the expenses of Big Momma whenever they had a little extra cash. Jimmie would leave Pat with Big Momma on and off, sometimes for a few days, sometimes for a week at a time. Jimmie liked to have fun with her friends in LA just like she did in Reno.

Among the many cousins that were part of the family in Los Angeles, Pat's favorite was Poochie, Dolly's daughter, a girl twice Pat's age, just old enough to be a real idol.

"I'm goin' outside, Mom," Poochie said.

"I'm going, too," Pat added.

"No you're not," Poochie shouted back.

Pat put on her sad and rejected face long enough for her aunt to notice. Dolly fixed the sadness quickly, "Oh yes she is, girl, or you ain't going nowhere."

So off they went, Poochie, who had a reputation of being tough among the other kids, with Pat in tow, off to see her black friends from the neighborhood. They were no more than a block or two away when Poochie's friends, all older than she, between eight and eleven years old, started making noise about the little white Patty. Two of the friends wanted to get Pat and Poochie to fight each other. "What's you doin' with that whitey? You know they don't belong in this neighborhood," asked a girl who was about eleven years old.

"Oh, she says she's mixed, got colored blood in her," Poochie responded.

"She's too white. Hair is white, eyes is white. She's all white, ain't no color in that girl," said another.

"Colored blood! She don't have no colored blood. If she did she'd be that color all the way through."

"How she know she got colored blood?" Another asked.

Poochie just stared at Pat and shrugged her shoulders. "My Aunt Jimmie is her momma and she says her daddy's Negro."

"Your Aunt Jimmie ain't her momma," said the girl again, "your Aunt Jimmie is as black as black, so that means her Daddy must be whiter than white for this white Patty to be as white as she is."

Pat stepped up and shouted, "My momma says I'm white on the outside and black on the inside."

"Then we jus' got to open her up and see for ourselves, if she's got the blood. She either has or she hasn't." Said another boy. "You brought her Pooch, you cut her and see what she bleeds."

"Yeah, Poochie, cut her throat to see what color she's got," said the boy again. "Here, use this." He handed her a small pocketknife.

One of the older girls grabbed Pat by the arm and pulled her over to Poochie. She squirmed free, but for just a moment. Poochie grabbed the knife and held it in her hand while trying to hold onto Pat's arm, but Pat kept wiggling. The other kids were all trying to get Poochie to cut her and continued yelling. "Cut her Poochie, see what she bleeds." Pat finally broke free and started to run. Poochie started to take chase but then stopped. Pat made it home by herself.

When Pat made it back to the house, her cheeks were streaked with tears. She tried to tell Big Momma what happened, but her incoherent cries and sniffles made everyone uneasy. She was used to most blacks outside of her immediate family looking at her with disapproval because she was a different color. But this was the first incident that forced her to feel the hatred. This time it was very personal and it scared and confused her.

Dolly was furious at her daughter for not taking care of Pat, and when confronted with the incident, Poochie denied that she was involved. "It wasn't me who tried to see her blood, it was the other girls. I tried to get them to stop. I told them that Aunt Jimmie said she was half and half, but they didn't believe me. They wanted to see for themselves. I tried to grab her away from them."

Dolly didn't buy into Poochie's account and punished her accordingly. No one in the family was prepared to explain Patty's whiteness, except Jimmie.

CHAPTER 7

"Pat, I'm having a rough time watching out for you," Big Momma said softly to her. "With things the way they are in the world, and you looking so much whiter than you're supposed to, I think you'd be better off with your own people."

Pat's scrunched-up nose and puzzled expression said it all, "Who's my own people?"

"Someday you'll know . . . someday." Big Momma knew that Jimmie was not capable of raising Pat. Even if she was, she still didn't think it was safe for a little white-skinned child with blue eyes to be living among the Negroes, particularly during the mid-fifties. The Supreme Court had just ruled against segregation and the reaction in the ghetto was more hostility and anger than fear. But the old woman was uneasy about the child's safety.

When Big Momma was well enough to get around, she thought more seriously about what to do with Pat. A foster parent or adoption by a white family was the only answer, and Mrs. Rolstadt, a married woman with no children, was her first and only choice. Pat got along with her each time they met. She asked the woman if she and her husband would be interested in adopting a light skinned baby of mixed race. When Mrs. Rolstadt discovered who the child was, she quickly consented and began arrangements for an adoption.

The very next day Big Momma's other daughter Lucille, and her son Jesse's former wife, Isoli, were visiting.

"I don't think I'm going to be able to take care of this child much longer," Big Momma said while sitting at her kitchen table.

"Oh, Momma, don't be silly, you're gonna be fine," Isoli said.

"Well, that may be, but this child is getting bigger and she's going to need some schooling. How am I supposed to get her into school? It would be much better if she was with her own people."

Lucille asked, "Only Jimmie knows who her own people are, and she sure ain't about to tell anyone."

"No, I don't mean her real mother," Big Momma said, "I mean her own people, white people. She'd be better off with them. And besides, I already made the arrangements."

"You made arrangements with who?" asked Lucille.

Big Momma hesitated for a moment and then said, "They're are some nice white folks that I do cleaning for. They're God-fearing people. The husband has a good job, they're stable and mature, and most importantly, they already met Pat and they get along real good. So it's all settled. I just wanted to let you know what was going on. Cause I don't want anything to happen to this child."

Lucille held on to Big Momma's hand, "You sure you know what you're doing? Did you tell Jimmie about this?"

"No, I'll tell her when the time is right, after all the legal stuff is done," Big Momma responded.

Isoli raised her eyebrows, walked out of the room and wasted no time in calling Jimmie in Sparks to let her know that Big Momma was planning to have a white family adopt Pat.

The very next day as Dolly was just putting the finishing touches on Pat's sandwich for lunch, Big Momma heard someone pounding on the front door. "What's all that noise?" she asked. "Who's doing all that banging?"

Dolly eyed Pat with a puzzled expression, as if the child had an answer. She walked into the parlor and opened the front door. "Jimmie! What are you doing here?" Dolly asked.

"Where's my damn baby? Where's Patta?" Jimmie yelled, pushing Dolly out of the way.

"Pat? She's in the kitchen . . . eating her lunch. Why didn't you tell us you were coming down?"

"So Big Momma could sneak my daughter out of the damn house in the middle of the night!"

"What?"

"You heard me. You think I don't know what she's up to! Ha! She has to be a whole lot damn quicker to fool me!"

Big Momma slowly got out of her bed just as Pat rushed to her side. She noticed the child's body stiffen as they listened to the shouts echo back and forth. It had been a long while since they heard Jimmie's temper and from the snarl in her voice they both knew there would be trouble.

Within moments Jimmie was in the kitchen standing beside Dolly. "Patta, where you at?" Jimmie yelled.

Pat was out of the bedroom and into the kitchen in a flash.

"Get your things, I'm takin' you back to Sparks with me!"

"Just hold on here. . . ." Dolly began to say.

Big Momma hobbled out of the bedroom. "What's all the commotion about . . . did you come down here just to make trouble?" she said in a weakened voice.

"Oh! Here's the one that's trying to give my baby to some damn whiteys," Jimmie snapped back. "Who do you think you are, anyway? I asked you to watch my Patta . . . my own daughter . . . and before ya know it, and behind my back no less, you're trying to pawn'er off. You didn't think I'd let ya get away with that shit, do ya?"

"Pawn her off! What do you mean? I just had a stroke. Don't make me get upset. You know I can't give that little baby all the love and attention she got to have! God knows you ain't fit to take care of her. The family that wants to adopt her is a good Christian family . . . that's a whole lot more than you could give her. Who told you about this anyway?"

"Never ya mind who told me. I got my sources," Jimmie said angrily,

Big Momma and Dolly returned glances, but Jimmie didn't let up.

"And thank God for that!" Jimmie said. "To think you'd give my baby away . . . to a damn white family no less . . . knowing that the white bastards gave her away in the first place! Well let me tell you something . . . I'll see you dead first before I let you give my baby away!"

Big Momma was shaking. The skin on her soft, brown face hardened as the tears trotted down her cheeks; her eyes filled with sorrow. She never imagined that her own daughter would turn on her. Without a word, Big Momma held her chest and gasped for air. Pat began to cry. Dolly put her arms around Big Momma and led her off into her bedroom to rest, with Jimmie and Pat in tow. Dolly turned to her sister and said, "How can you do this to your mother? You know how sick she is . . . don't you have any feelings whatsoever? If anything happens. . . ."

"You mind your damn business. Just get my baby's things and let me get the hell out of here!"

Pat, her face flush, stood by out of the line of fire, shivering, as she watched Dolly pack a small satchel and place it near the front door. As the tears swelled in her eyes, she kissed her Big Momma good-bye. "Don't worry, little child, everything's going to be all right. Big Momma will always be here when you need me."

"You promise?" Pat asked.

"I promise," said Big Momma as she hugged Pat and tapped her on the head.

Jimmie grabbed Pat by the hand and pulled her out the door.

That afternoon they boarded the Greyhound Bus. Pat wasn't looking forward to the long, hard journey back to Sparks. She remembered how unpleasant it was last time when she was anxious to visit Big Momma, and that was under more favorable circumstances. She hated the way strangers stared at her when she called Jimmie "Momma." It seemed as though Pat had awakened from a long, charm-filled dream. The only thing that changed was that she was a little older and more aware of what was going on.

The twelve-hour ride through the California countryside was difficult for Pat. Jimmie let her stand on the seat to watch endless rows of small trees and bushes that stretched from the mountains to the roadside,

filling the small valleys, and covering each hilltop as if God had laid
down a massive brown and green carpet. For a while, it kept her thoughts
occupied, postponing the sadness of being absent from Big Momma. But
the noisy hum from the bus and the foul smell of fumes brought Pat back
to reality. Each time she sat back down, tears came to her eyes.

"What's the matter, my little queen? I missed you. I missed the
prettiest girl in the whole world. Are you just gonna cry all the way
home? I hope not, cause I was gonna tell you a story about your real
momma." Jimmie looked away, then glanced back just long enough to
see that she got Pat's attention. "And I know lots a things about her."

Through her tears Pat could see that Momma was very nervous.
Jimmie sipped from the flask she brought with her, then turned to Pat
and said, "Patta, I know you miss Big Momma. You were very happy
there . . . wasn't you?" Pat looked up at her bloodshot eyes, sniffled, and
nodded yes. "There's lot's of things you just don't understand. It's not
that I want to be mean to Big Momma, after all, she's my momma, too!
Just like your real momma loves you. Even though she's not with you,
she still wants you to be taken care of—by me. And it's important that
you know that."

"Where's my real momma?" The child asked.

"Don't you worry, your momma is fine. She's just real young . . . too
young to take care of you. And she's beautiful, too. Got big blue eyes and
long blond hair, just like you."

"Am I ever gonna see her?"

"Oh yeah! Someday you'll meet her. In fact, I can get a hold of your
granddaddy anytime I want," she said smugly. "All I got to do is pick up
the phone and call. He's a very powerful man . . . your granddaddy is.
One day, when you's older, I'll tell you all about your real momma and
your whole family, too."

As she spoke, the child only imagined what her real mother looked
like and how her granddaddy acted.

Jimmie continued, "Your real momma wanted me to raise you . . .
raise you to be black. But you already knew that. I told you that before.
So I couldn't let Big Momma give you away to some white folks. That

would ruin everything. What would your real momma say if she knew I let somebody take you away from me? She be spittin' chickens." Pat began to giggle. "You're a very special child and someday you're gonna be very rich and live in a big house with servants and fancy cars and lots of clothes. You'll be just like a queen."

With those words, Jimmie Lee left Pat alone to daydream. After the sun went down, Pat slept the rest of the way. When they reached Sparks, the cold night air made Pat shiver. It was late and they took a cab to a small house that Pat had never seen before. It wasn't anything like the home they lived in with Chris and certainly nothing like Big Momma's. The light was on and the door was unlocked. Jimmie, carrying some paper bags with Pat's things, let the child in first. As she entered from the darkness, Pat noticed only one big room. As her eyes focused, she become aware of a small kitchen area off to the left with dirty dishes piled on a counter and half-filled beer bottles cluttering a small, painted wooden table. The room smelled old and musty in contrast to the clean, night air outside. She heard her momma's footsteps from behind, then the door slammed shut. She looked up at Jimmie who was glaring at the bed and watched her gasp momentarily.

Jimmie screeched, "what da fuck is this damn shit!" She threw the packages at the icebox across the room and fixed her hands firmly to her hips. The force knocked a small picture from the wall. Jimmie's rage stunned Pat and quickly she stepped to one side out of harm's way.

Suddenly, to the right of the doorway, a solitary figure wearing a torn, white t-shirt over slumped shoulders arose from the bed. His brown skin and bald head appearing out of nowhere startled Pat. As she focused on his face, she saw that his dark, bloodshot eyes were filled with fear.

"Oh shit!" He said, when he saw Jimmie.

It made Pat relax some.

An instant later, a woman popped up from the same bed. She was rubbing her eyes, trying to block the light with her hand. Just as suddenly, a second woman emerged, "Who da hell is this?" She asked irritatingly.

"Now, now, now Jimmie Lee, it ain't what ya think," said the man with a slight stammer.

Pat tightened her shoulders as she watched Jimmie's face stiffen, her eyes bulge, and her hands stretch out in front of her. Jimmie rushed to the bed and grabbed one of the women by the hair and dragged her out onto the floor. The woman started screaming. "Let go of me! Let go!" Pat could see the pain in her face but Jimmie didn't let go. She held onto her hair with one hand and began pounding her head with the other.

"You damn whore! I go away for one fuckin' day and you think you could jump in my bed with my man! I'll teach you who's in goddamn charge around here!"

The other woman was now wide-awake hugging the wall on the other side of the bed, clear of Jimmie. The stocky man shuffled out of the bed and tried to stop Jimmie Lee. Pat watched in horror, hiding behind the door, as the four adults screamed and grappled with each other. Jimmie let go of the woman's hair and took a swing at the man. He blocked it with his shoulder and quickly picked Jimmie up, his arms wrapped around her waist. She continued to yell and wiggle trying to get out of his grip. As he struggled with her, the veins popped from his shiny head and his brow was scrunched and wrinkled. "This isn't what you think!" he said, "We all went fishing s'afternoon."

"Fishin' my ass!" Jimmie screamed, twisting in every direction to release herself.

"We caught a whole mess of fish and fried them . . . right here . . . in the kitchen. There. . . ." He let her go and pointed to the table with all the dirty dishes filled with fish heads and bones.

"You're a damn lying nigger!" She yelled.

"No . . . No . . . it's the truth, Jimmie Lee. We ate like hogs and drank too much beer. We just fell asleep . . . that's all!"

Pat watched this older man as he spoke to Jimmie and knew from the softness in his eyes that he was telling the truth. She believed him even though her momma didn't. When he peeked down at Pat with his soft, glassy eyes, she felt a warm gentleness just like Big Momma. He smiled at Pat and said, "Is this your daughter! She's just about the most beautiful little thing I ever seen!"

Jimmie Lee began to calm down. "You see what your doing to my daughter, you good for nothing bastard!"

The man just ignored her. He struggled to kneel on one knee and then stroked Pat's face with the back of his hands; they felt soft.

"I'm Homer," he said, "you must be Pat." She nodded nervously, clearly frightened, but not of this man. She knew from that first moment that this gentle and kindly man would be her friend.

Jimmie ranted on with the two women. She stayed angry with Homer until well after they left. Pat went off to bed, still listening to them argue.

The following morning when Pat awoke, it was as if nothing had happened. The dreary image of a two-room shack disappeared with the night. Jimmie had the house spotless. Doilies were neatly placed on top of the end tables with small knickknacks perfectly arranged. The curtains appeared to be stiff with starch. There were flowers in vases atop the TV and a bouquet in the center of the table. Jimmie was ironing a pink blouse. Homer was sitting at the table drinking a big mug of coffee. The air was fresh and clean; the fishy odors from the night before had vanished. All traces of the nightmare were gone.

Homer got up from the table and limped toward Pat wearing a big smile on his face. "Good morning, Sunshine! Did ya get a good night's sleep?"

"Yeah," she answered, nodding affirmatively.

"Good! Your momma's made you some hot cakes. I got to go to work. If you were up earlier, I'd take ya with me."

"Where do ya have to go to work?"

"At the barber shop"

"You cut momma's hair?"

"No . . . I shine shoes . . . and help keep the store ship shape for the customers. But I'll tell you about that later. I got to go now." He kissed Pat on the forehead and limped out the door.

Pat turned to her momma and said, "Why's Homer walk so funny, like his shoes don't work?"

"There ain't nothing wrong with his shoes. He had a bad leg that never got fixed, so he walks funny. But don't you ever make fun of him, ya hear me?" Jimmie said.

"Now eat your breakfast while I get ready."

Jimmie came out of the bedroom wearing a soft, yellow blouse and matching pedal pushers. Pat watched her delicately trace the outline of her mouth with a bright red lipstick.

"Where we going, Momma?" Pat asked.

"Well, you been gone for such a long time, and you been wearing them same old clothes. It's time I got you some new dresses. We don't want you looking like some poor white trash when you start kindergarten, do we?"

"I don't want to look like no white trash, I want to look like you," Pat said.

Jimmie Lee picked out two new dresses, socks, and matching new shoes from the Carousel Dress Shop, to make Pat look like another version of Shirley Temple. Jimmie took the scenic route home, making sure that everyone in town feasted their eyes on the little white girl walking with the stunning black temptress. Pat reveled in the attention almost as much as Jimmie.

"You got to make sure you always look your best. After all, your real momma always wore the finest clothes and had servants and everything. She didn't need to take a bus nowhere. No baby, she had her own limousine with a chauffeur and everything—that's how she got to school."

"I want a limousine when I go to school." Pat beamed while she strutted smugly, knowing her real momma rode in fancy cars.

Jimmie Lee raised her head and puffed out her chest, feasting on the contemptuous eyes that watched the enigma step proudly down the street. "See, this is how y'all walk and strut when you get to be famous."

"I'm gonna be famous too, just like you."

"Well, a course ya are. You're the daughter of Pretty Jimmie Lee. You are the little queen."

About two weeks after they moved to Sparks, Pat was playing with clothespins in the dirt when she spotted Homer walking toward her only a couple of hours after he left for work. Affectionately, she jumped up and hugged his good leg, trying not to let him go, but something was wrong. She heard the distress in his voice, "Not now, Pat. Why don't you come into the house, your momma needs you," Homer said. Pat smiled but didn't let go. He carried Pat in anyway.

"What's you doin' here so early?" Jimmie asked.

"Dolly called me at the shop just a little while ago," he said. Jimmie stood up from the table, instinctively she knew something was wrong. "It's your momma, baby. I'm sorry. She passed on. She's with Jesus now."

He put the child down. Jimmie's mouth opened wide, but no sound emerged except that of a faint gasp while her eyes filled. Pat watched Jimmie as Homer tried to comfort her. Pat didn't understand what it meant to be dead, other than going to heaven, but from Jimmie's reaction, she knew it wasn't such a good thing. Before Pat knew it, they were back on the Greyhound, heading toward Los Angeles. For most of the trip Pat remained silent sadly watching her momma whimper.

CHAPTER 8

When they arrived at Big Momma's house, dozens of people moped about, some sobbing, others quietly murmuring, and still others eating. The kitchen table served as the main area where trays were half-filled with cheeses, rolled baloney, ham, and beans all mixed between cans of beer and soda, and salads, and cakes. Dolly lifted Pat in her arms and hugged tightly. "Oh Pat . . . oh Pat," she exclaimed. "Big Momma loved you so much." Pat felt Dolly's wet tears press against her face. She tried to feel sad emulating the gloom that choked the atmosphere and cry with her, but death had no meaning. They all thought that Big Momma was gone forever, but Pat knew she wasn't dead. The last thing she told Pat was that she'd always be there when she needed her, and her Big Momma would never lie to her.

Like a sharp blare from a foghorn, Pat heard a man's agony cut through the hum. "You killed her! You killed her!" All eyes locked on the kitchen. Pat's skin quivered when she heard Jimmie Lee screeched back. "I didn't kill nobody!"

"Yes ya did! You wished her dead," Jesse said, "all because of that white Patty you got!" He was Jimmie's brother, a man she warned Pat to stay away from. Pat worked her way through the adults to see what all the commotion was about.

"Don't you blame me for your momma's death. She died from a heart attack!"

"No . . . it's your fault . . . you rotten bitch!" Jesse continued, "You put an evil spell on her and wished her dead."

"And don't you be blamin' nothin' on that little girl, either," Jimmie said.

"It's your fault . . . who told you to take in a white baby! If you wanted a kid, why didn't you help out ya own kind . . . why didn't ya take one a mine . . . you knew how hard it was for me to take care of eleven children. No! . . . you had to adopt a 'white patty' just to be different from all the rest of us!"

"Ya dumb fuckin' fool . . . who told you to have that many kids in the first place! If you're man enough to take that thing outta ya pants, then ya should be man enough ta support eleven kids . . . that's if they all yours in the first place," she said.

"Aaahhh! You . . . you . . . filthy, shit! Somebody shoulda killed you, instead a you killin' Momma!" Jesse said.

"I didn't kill yo' momma . . . and don't ya be sayin' I did . . . that old woman tried to give my baby away."

You're a murderer, a murderer! . . . Ya killed Big Momma! . . . and if I see you at that funeral tomorrow, I'm gonna kill you!" He kept shouting louder and louder.

"Shut up! . . . Shut up! . . . ya dumb bastard!" Jimmie screamed back.

To Pat, it seemed like everyone was trying to talk at the same time, but the two siblings were louder than the rest, until a roar went out from the crowd. Pat's eyes were glued to Jimmie as she watched her momma grab a knife from the sink and go after Jesse. Quickly, a man grabbed her arm and wrestled the knife away. Jimmie was hustled out of the room. The cacophony of voices was quickly muffled when Lucille held Pat close to her side.

The next morning, as Lucille fixed breakfast for Pat, Jimmie sat down with Pat. "I want you to try and understand what's gonna happen this morning. Big Momma has passed away . . . and we're all going to the church to pay our last respects. There'll be lots of people crying and shouting, but I don't want you to be scared. Just pray for Big Momma. Tell those angels she taught you about to usher her directly to God. Oh, and stay with Aunt Lucille."

Pat didn't understand what she was talking about, but staying with her favorite Aunt Lucille was fine with her. Many times Pat watched lots of people cry out loud at church before. Why should this be any different?

As they were leaving the house Pat, holding her aunt's hand, turned to see if her Momma was following when she noticed Jimmie slip a kitchen knife into her purse. Pat pretended it didn't happen.

As they approached the block where Big Momma lived, there were black, shiny limousines parked in the middle of the street with chauffeurs standing by each door, waiting for scores of people milling about the sidewalk. Everything looked black: the people; the cars; the drivers and their clothes; everything except Jimmie. She wore a bright red sequined dress. They were the last to arrive.

The hearse carrying Big Momma's remains stopped in front of the church. Pat watched the men, including Jesse, lift the casket on their shoulders and slowly march in unison into the wood framed building. Pat held on to her aunt Lucille's hand as they entered the church. Lucille led her to a seat right in front of the large white casket passed the many parishioners already seated in the pews. Pat stood on her toes and looked up into it and saw Big Momma lying down. She looked beautiful and peaceful, dressed as Pat always remembered—in the white church uniform she always wore when it was her Sunday to be usherette. There were flowers placed all around her. She was the center of attention.

Strangers sobbed, a few wailed as if they were getting their teeth pulled out. Pat looked over at Dolly and watched her vomit into a brown paper bag. She didn't understand what was going on.

Unexpectedly, Jimmie ran up to the casket shouting, "Momma . . . Momma! . . . I didn't mean it! I didn't mean it!" Lucille rushed up and tried to make her sit down. Jimmie was no more hysterical than any of the other mourners, just more noticeable in her red dress.

Pat noticed Jesse first glare at Jimmie, then turn his head toward Pat and give her a look filled with contempt. She felt the chill rush through her tiny body. Pat knew she did nothing to invite his hostility, other than looking white. She would remember to stay out of his way.

Slowly the noise, the confusion, the crying, and shouting seemed to fade away. Everyone was moving just as before, but Pat couldn't hear it. Instead, she heard Big Momma calling her from the Sunday school room at the side of the church. *"Pat, Pat I love you . . . and I will always be with you, don't worry."* She couldn't have been there; Pat was looking right at her, right in front of her. *"I'm not dead . . ."* she continued, *"I'm just away for awhile. I'm in the Sunday school room watching everything. I'm praying my children will stop all this stuff. I am happier than I've ever been.*

"Pat, I love you. You have a special mission on earth, and I will help guide you through. I will always be with you, don't worry, keep praying, everything will be OK."

Her voice stopped, and the noise and confusion continued again . . . just as before. Pat tugged at Lucille's dress and asked, "Is Big Momma playing a trick on us?" Pat noticed the puzzled expression and continued, "Big Momma's not dead, I could hear her, she's in the Sunday school room . . . she said so!"

Lucille patted her head and held the child close to her bosom. Pat knew then that her Big Momma would always be with her. Her voice was real and she was the only one who could hear her. She realized from that moment that she was different from all the other people around her; and she was different from her real family, too. She believed that God put her on this earth for a special purpose. In time, she hoped to find out its meaning.

CHAPTER 9

The one-room shack was constructed some twenty years earlier, during the Great Depression It sat clumsily between two other shanties, about three miles from the Reno city line in Sparks. It featured a black, cast iron stove that used coal for both cooking and heating during the cold winters. In the summer, when it was too hot to use, the stove became an ideal spot for the TV. It was a rarity for Jimmie to cook and even more so when she ate. Her diet consisted of mixing gin and 7-Up. But for Pat it was different, Jimmie fed her neck bones, fried pork with fat, or sometimes just peanut butter and bread without the jelly. Homer ate out a lot, preferring a hot dog and fries to Jimmie's unique cuisine.

Together, they eked out a living. Jimmie ironing or cleaning sporadically as day labor, and Homer in front of the Esquire shining shoes, for which he charged 25 cents per shine, and the ten dollars per week he received to clean up the shop. Although the poverty was unrelenting, Jimmie made sure that Pat's clothes were of the latest styles, and always washed and neatly pressed.

On Saturday, Jimmie allowed Pat to come along with her on her weekly cleaning job on the other side of town. "Now don't you be causing no trouble, or asking no questions either. And don't be givin' no answers either, no matter what the question," Jimmie said to Pat as they walked to the back of the two-story, Victorian-style home that seemed to go around the block, "You hear me?"

"I hear ya," she replied. "Why ain't we going in the front door?"

"We the servants. Servants use the servant's entrance. Someday you'll be able to go in the front door, but right now we using in the rear." Jimmie watched Pat's eyes wander, awestruck by the size of the home and attached garage. She knew Pat was impressed.

"This is a big house," Pat said. "Who lives here?"

"Don't you worry 'bout that, they white people, that's all you got to know. And don't you be trustin' them neither. If they want to give you something, you know it ain't free. There's always a catch. May not be right away, but it'll be there, don't you worry."

A plain but comely woman in her early forties, dressed in jeans with a white riding blouse and tan boots let them in through the kitchen entrance. Jimmie noticed that she immediately focused on Pat.

"Well, who is this little ray of sunshine?" the woman asked in an authoritative voice.

"Oh, this is Pat. I'm babysittin' for Mrs. Anne. I hope you don't mind, she'll be my helper today."

"No, not at all," she said without taking her eyes off Pat. "Hi, I'm Candace."

"Hi." Pat answered.

"I want to stay longer to show you some things I need done, but I've got to run some errands and I'll be back late." She said and promptly left the house.

Before Jimmie put her supplies down, she felt Pat tugging at her dress. "What's you want?" Jimmie asked.

"Who's Mrs. Anne?" Pat whispered.

"That's our little secret."

"Why we gotta have a secret?" Pat asked.

"Cause of the Welfare people. If they find out that I was your momma, they'd take you away. Do you want them to take you away from me?"

"No, Momma," she said. "Where would they take me?"

"To the welfare home and you'd have to live with the foster parents, and you don't never want to live with no foster parents. They won't care nothing about you, they just want the money." Jimmie added.

"What about my other momma, my real momma. Where is she?"

"I know lots about your real momma, and I know lots about your real family too. I can get hold of 'em any time I want to. Right now, I know your Momma's living in Mexico . . . far away from here. And you know what?"

"What?" Pat said.

"I feel so sorry for her. She had to give you to me, because her mother couldn't live with a mixed baby. All the whiteys feel like the coloreds got bad blood—and your real grandmother is one of 'em. But someday . . . someday, you'll find her. I know that."

"If they'd of let me, I'd taken her in right along with you. She was way too young to have a baby of her own. I'd a raised the two a you myself. And when she's old enough, I'd a given you both back to your real family." Pat seemed satisfied with that and Jimmie was quiet the rest of the morning.

When they arrived home, Jimmie retrieved a small, pink envelope from her nightstand. With a worried look, she sat down with her back toward the window, noticing the daylight peek through the wooden blinds, creating a ladder of light that covered Pat's face. While Pat daydreamed, Jimmie opened the envelope and began to re-read a letter.

> *Dear Mrs. Greenwade,*
>
> *George has told me of your mother's recent illness. I am truly sorry and hope that she recovers quickly. We understand that Fauna is very fond of her, and the respect and admiration is mutual.*
>
> *Dorothy has taken Tamar to Mexico in order to help her relieve some of the pressures of her past hardships. Apparently, from what Dorothy has told me, Tamar has become intolerable with deep psychological problems stemming from the trial and subsequent adoption. She is no more capable of raising a baby then when she was fifteen. Dorothy is grateful to you for your generosity and understanding.*
>
> *She has also told me that Tamar has been telling outrageous stories, spreading rumors, and continually lying about the scandal that has so devastated her family. Everyone agrees that she is a*

beautiful girl and her looks will probably get even better with age. It's just that she goes against the grain, so to speak, and that takes away from her overall beauty. We all hope and pray that maturity will bring her into the fold.

Fauna's grandfather has also been in a sizzle over the problem with Tamar. His practice has been reduced to a shambles due to the scandal and publicity, and he will be moving out of the country to the Philippines. But I am sure he will continue to keep his eye on all that is going on here at home.

I hope that everything is well with you. If there is anything you need, you know where to contact me.

Sincerely,

Dorarro

Jimmie stared at the letter, glanced at Pat and then placed it back in the envelope.

"What's that you got, Momma?"

"Oh, nothing you need to know."

"Get up sunshine, get up sunshine," Homer said. He knew that his early morning, gravely voice wake-up call annoyed her, but at the same time he was thrilled to have his shiny, bald head be the first thing the four year old saw when her eyes opened. After breakfast, with his transistor radio in one hand and Pat in the other, Homer marched off to work, limping down the street, listening to the Giants play the Pirates with the volume turned up loud enough to hear it a block away.

"I can hear them talking on the radio, too," Pat said, "It's noisy."

"I got to keep it loud, so everybody knows I'm coming," Homer said. But in reality, he loved the Giants so much that he didn't want to miss a single word of the play-by-play action, not even the beer commercials.

"Oh no!" he yelled, "they hit a homer with two men on. Now, what they go and do some foolish thing as changin' that pitcher for?" The Giants were losing to the Pirates that day.

As they turned on to B Street, Pat mimicked Homer's limp by stiffening one leg, making it stick out to the right. He noticed right away and thought it amusing, until people he knew said hello. "Cut that shit out, Pat, you're slowin' us down. I'll be late."

"Wait," she said, "this ain't the way we go."

"We got to go to the post office first," he said.

"What for? You got to send money again?" she asked.

"Yeah, I got to send money, again," he repeated, "but remember, this is a secret only you and I know about, so you can't be telling your momma."

"Oh, I know. I ain't telling no one nothing."

Homer's first wife lived in San Francisco and didn't know that Homer was living with Jimmie Lee, and he did his best to keep it a secret. Together they had eleven children and two of them, his eldest daughters, were older than Jimmie Lee and were the only family he trusted enough to let them know about his new woman. Once in a while they came to Sparks to visit him. When he had some extra money, Homer sent his sickly wife a few dollars. If Jimmie had found out, she might have crippled his other leg.

The Esquire Barbershop was a well-known hangout for local businessmen, casino dealers, and hotel people who patronized the shop. When they first arrived at the shop, Pat noticed there was a customer getting up from her favorite leather-bound chair that had a foot pedal attached to a round white base that seemed to grow out of the hardwood floor. It reminded her of a giant, deformed mushroom. The sweet smell of colognes and shaving cream permeated the room.

"Hello Pat," Kirk said looking at her through the mirror. The short, stocky barber with thin graying hair, took two steps toward Pat and picked her up, gave her a big kiss and set her on a padded seat that he placed across the armrests of the barber's chair. Pat felt important in that big seat.

It was no more than a few minutes before Jim, the tall barber who looked like Davy Crockett, began to tease Homer. He wasn't the only one who goosed him when he least expected it, causing Homer to lose his balance and tumble to the floor, but today he was the first.

"Damn it, why don't ya pick on somebody ya own size!" Homer grumbled, then began to steady himself, rising to his feet.

"Yeah, why don't ya pick on someone your own size?" Pat balked. "Leave Homer alone. Don't be makin' him fall."

"OK, OK. Take it easy," said Jim. "It seems our little princess gets upset quite easily. Here, I've got something for you." He reached into his pocket and pulled out a crisp, new dollar bill and handed it to her. But before Pat could grasp it, he pulled it away and said, "First, you have to give me a big kiss."

Pat smiled and put her arms around his head while holding on to his soft, brown hair so she wouldn't fall off the chair. The barber's face was smooth, just like hers, and Pat gave him a big kiss right on his cheek.

"Oh, that's my girl. Now here, " he said, handing her the paper money. "Don't spend it all in one place, OK?"

"OK, thank you," Pat said.

Everyone laughed and even Homer smiled again.

"That little girl is gonna be rich someday. A dollar for a kiss, that's something," said Kirk.

Pat felt special at the Esquire and seldom left empty handed. If it wasn't a quarter, or a dollar, it was a toy, or a book, or a homemade pie. During the hunting season when Jim was lucky enough to bag a buck, he filled bags with fresh venison. For Thanksgiving, Shorty bought everyone, including Homer, a big turkey with all the trimmings.

Mrs. Atkinson owned a very spacious two-story home on C Street. At the far end of the property, about 50 yards from the back of the house were three small cottages tucked neatly together in a semi-circle court. The wood-framed structures were built long before the war at a time when the area was used as a campground. In those early days, fishermen used the cabins on weekends rather than pitch a tent near the river. Jimmie and Homer moved into the end cottage when Pat was about five years old. It was still only one big room, but with an electric stove for cooking and heating that replaced the black soot from the old coal-fired one, it kept the cottage cleaner. The furnishings were also in better condition; the move was clearly a step up.

Months later, a man everyone knew as Joe the Italian, moved into the cottage next door. He was friendly and spent some time with Jimmie Lee and her friends drinking beer. Frequently, he'd stroll off with Pat on snack runs or errands for Jimmie. As they walked together, a white man and a white child, she became almost invisible. No one called her 'nigger lover,' or made the rude comments that became routine when she was seen with Jimmie or Homer.

Mrs. Atkinson never cared much for Joe and Jimmie Lee never cared much for Mrs. Atkinson. Often Jimmie chased Pat out of the house and let her stay with Joe just to annoy the landlady.

One day when Jimmie had to leave for one of her cleaning jobs, she asked Joe to keep an eye on her six-year-old. Jimmie wasn't gone for more than a minute when Joe came into the house. "Come on, Patty, get your doll. We're going next door till Jimmie gets back. We're gonna play a game and I got somethin' for you."

"What is it? You got a prize for me?"

"Yeah, but only if you're a good girl."

"I'm always a good girl, everybody knows that," she said.

"You have to be real quiet, too. Not a word to anyone," Joe said, holding a finger close to his lips

"No noise, I'll tiptoe. What's the game?" Pat replied.

"And then I'll give you a dollar," Joe said.

In the beginning, Pat didn't understand the game. He gave her money, which she used to buy candy, but she knew that what he was doing wasn't right and prayed that he would disappear. Pat confided in no one for fear of Jimmie finding out. She isolated herself from other children and became sad and lonely. For two years, Pat lived with the guilt and shame as the sexual abuse continued when, suddenly Joe just moved away.

At about the same time, Pat began having stomach pains. When she complained to Jimmie, it was first dismissed as something she ate. But soon, everything Pat ate didn't agree with her. Jimmie wasn't much of a cook and knew even less about nutrition. Pat's diet consisted manly of chicken necks, pork fat, burnt fries, chitlins, and Pepsi. One night, a few months later, Jimmie found Pat crying in bed, looking frightfully ill.

"What's with you, Patta?" Jimmie asked. "Ya lookin' pale, don't you feel good?"

"I got pains all around here." Pat held her stomach and back.

She put her hand on her forehead. "Ya burnin' up! What's wrong with you?"

Patta shook her head, sobbed painfully and watched her Momma's expression turn to genuine concern. "I better get Aunt Rosie to take a look at ya."

Jimmie sent Homer over to fetch her sister-in-law and then fed Pat some Bayer aspirin. When Rosie arrived with her bag of magic, the one she used when anyone in the family was sick, she touched Pat's forehead, pulled her eyelids up, held her chin, opened her pajamas and began pressing on her stomach. Pat howled like a caged wildcat.

"This child's in bad shape. You better get her to the doctor's."

"What's da matter with her?" asked Jimmie.

"I dunno, but it ain't good. Might be her appendix."

"Nah. Can't be no appendix. She's been acting funny for a while now."

"For a while? How long for a while?"

"Oh, maybe three or four months."

Aunt Rosie turned her head away from Pat and stared hard at Jimmie. Softly, she asked, "What did you do for her?"

"Well, I been givin' her aspirin."

Homer shook his head and limped over to the kitchen chair.

Doctor Berger immediately put her in the hospital for tests. Pat had needles in her arms, a tube in her nose, compresses, alcohol rubs, blood tests, fluid samples, and a lot more procedures that she didn't care for.

Jimmie came in very early the next morning, waiting for the doctor. Pat wasn't afraid because she was asleep most of the time. When Doctor Berger finally arrived, he examined her again. He kept looking over some charts and shaking his head, occasionally glancing at Jimmie with a disdainful eye.

"What's the matter with her?" Jimmie asked.

"Mrs. Greenwade . . ."

"Mrs. Faison," she corrected.

"What?"

"My name is Mrs. Faison."

"Oh." Doctor Berger looked puzzled. "Didn't it used to be Mrs. Greenwade?"

"Uh, huh, but now I'm Mrs. Faison."

Although Jimmie and Homer never married, she used his name, as was customary in the neighborhood.

"OK. Mrs. Faison. What has she been eating?"

"What she been eating? The regular stuff, why?"

"The regular stuff? What's the regular stuff? Has she been eating from the basic food groups? Has she been eating plenty of vegetables, cheeses, milk, fish, breads, cereals, and red meat? I know she hasn't been getting well-balanced meals."

"She eats finicky. She likes chicken, and pork, mostly chitlins, and she just loves candy and ice cream. She lives off cookies and cakes."

Doctor Berger shook his head in disgust. "Mrs. Faison, this child is very, very sick. And it's not something that happened overnight. This condition has progressed over a period of months, maybe years."

"What she got?"

"It's called glomerulonephritis and possibly arteriolar nephrosclerosis as well, but we won't know that until further testing."

"Glomaflitiscis?"

"Not quite. It's her kidneys," He said as he glanced back at Pat. "She's been getting too much grease and fats and sugar and not enough proteins, minerals, vitamins. Her diet consists mainly of fatty foods and it's caused havoc with her system." He looked at Jimmie very sternly for a moment. Then, shaking his head, he said, "I just hope it's not too late; another hour and for sure she would have been gone."

Pat looked at Jimmie, and for the first time saw tears in the older woman's eyes that were meant for her. Jimmie's expression was unlike anything she had ever seen. The pain in her face, a blank, heartbroken and empty face showed real fear. Now Pat was afraid, too. Jimmie Lee raised her hands slowly to her cheeks and glanced over at Pat. The doctor continued to describe Pat's condition, but neither Pat nor Jimmie heard a word.

"Doctor," said Jimmie, "you can't let anything happen to my baby. No, she's got to get better. You've got to do something. Anything that will help."

The physician looked at her and said nothing.

"Can't you operate?"

"Operate, on what? This doesn't require an operation."

"Then give her a transfusion, put her in one of those iron lungs that everybody uses. Do something, you got to make her better!"

"We'll do what's necessary. Just stay with her and give her hope."

Jimmie slid to her knees at the side of her bed, praying. Pat was touched. She knew Jimmie really cared. Pat became drowsy and floated between light and dark, fading in and out. Her dreams were vivid. She envisioned a noble lady, draped in radiant blue, standing before her who said in a hollow voice *"It isn't time for you to leave earth, you have much work to do."* She parted by reassuring Pat that she would return to good health and when she became afraid to just call on her.

Each time Pat awoke, Jimmie Lee was there, sitting silently at her bed, day after day, praying to God to make her well. When she wasn't there, Homer or Aunt Rosie was vigilant. When Pat began to recover, the nurses asked her a lot of questions about living with the coloreds. Pat told them she was half-Negro, too, but somehow she felt they didn't believe her. A few times, Dr. Berger asked her how they were treating her. When Pat asked him who he meant, he said, "You know, the colored people you live with."

"Fine," Pat told him, "they're my family."

"If they treat you badly, or if anything unusual happens," the doctor told her, "you come to me."

Pat didn't understand, but she agreed anyway. And then, at the first opportunity, she told her Momma.

Before she left for home that day, Jimmie Lee intercepted Dr. Berger in the corridor. "What do you mean by askin' my baby, 'If they treat you badly, you come to me?' And just wut are you gonna do? You think I spend my whole life looking after my child, giving up everything I have for her just to treat her badly? You think cause I'm colored that I don't know what's good for my child?" Tears swelled her eyes; Dr. Berger became a blur. But she could see that he was taken by surprise.

"Well, let me tell you something, Doctor. I won't let anyone or anything get in the way of Patta. She's the only thing I got and I'd die before I let anything happen to her. So you just mind your own business and take care of her sickness, and tell them nosy body nurses the same. She's my daughter and I'll take care of her."

"Oh, Mrs. Faison," said Berger, regaining his composure. "I'm sorry if you misunderstood. I only meant to give her an option. She is malnourished and that's a fact. As a doctor, I have to look at the whole picture—not just the current illness, but what caused it. I don't want anything to happen to her, either."

Jimmie Lee stuck her nose in the air and sauntered off back to Pat.

———

Her full recovery took almost a year. Pat dropped behind in school. But the vision of that Lady in Blue gave her hope. When Pat first arrived home, she felt strange. After being in the hospital with all those white people, Pat was a little disoriented. For the first few months after they moved into the cottage, Pat's solitude remained noticeable, but the Lady in Blue stayed with her.

"Patta baby," said Jimmie Lee, "why don't you go outside and play with the other kids while I finish my ironing? You can't be mopin' around the house all the time. Are you trying to be some kind of hermit? It's not good for you."

"You always ironin' something, Momma. Besides, I don't want to, I'd rather stay here," she replied. She had been gone from the neighborhood a long time and was still shy. It wasn't that Pat was afraid of them; she was afraid of being different. After being in the hospital, and now back with her momma and her drinking, she was embarrassed. Pat picked up a glamour magazine and started flipping through it.

"Why you actin' so blue, child?"

Pat didn't look up at Jimmie, she kept flipping through the magazine. "Why ain't I Negro looking like my daddy was? Why ain't I like everybody else?"

Jimmie snickered, "You don't want to be like everybody else. If you was like everybody else nobody would notice you, and you'd wind up cleaning rooms, and ironing other people's clothes, and getting cussed at, and treated like dog shit on somebody's shoe," Jimmie was getting angrier as she spoke. "You wouldn't have people move away from you when you come into a store, or watch your every step as if you was gonna steal something, or be afraid to touch you cause they think the color's gonna rub off on them. If you was like everybody else who is Negro, you wouldn't get to do the things that you want to do, you wouldn't get to be famous. Only white people get to do what they want and get to be famous. They got all the power. They got all the money. We jus' do the work!" She continued ironing while mumbling to herself. "And you ain't gonna do the work!"

"Then what am I gonna do?"

"Well, you're always reading something, magazines, books. You're always writing something, so I guess you're gonna be a writer. You're gonna be a famous writer. And everybody's gonna know who you are.

If you was like me, then nobody would ever pay attention to you, as much as you tried to let them know who you are. It just ain't the way it is. You got to be white. So you should use that to your own good."

"But I don't want to be white. It don't do me no good. White people look at me like I'm a disease. And everybody else just laughs at me for saying I'm Negro.

"If I was really like my daddy, then nobody would make fun and I'd be like everybody else."

Jimmie just shook her head, "Child, you don't know nothing, but you'll see when you get to be famous. See if you could've done it if you was Negro. There ain't no famous Negroes—and the ones who are, got to fight every day for the fame. So you just better be grateful that you ain't like everybody else."

After her prolonged stay in the hospital, Pat enjoyed the solitude and safety of home. Homer didn't wake her up to go with him to the shop. Pat slept until noon, escaping into fantasy dreams spotted with wordless musings of another life with her real mother. She dreamed of living in a fairy-tale castle next to the ocean, staffed with servants, filled with toys, chocolate candy, and a stable of the finest white ponies. She dreamed of being a movie star, dressed up in front of the camera.

When Pat finally awoke, she spent part of the day at the Sparks library, an old facility with wide concrete steps leading to a world less stimulating than her dreams. In between browsing Nancy Drew Mysteries and other children's books, she leafed through a few biographies of famous people and then headed home to watch TV. The small black-and-white Philco stayed on from early in the morning until late at night, providing both company and a program timed clock based on the TV schedule. Both Jimmie and Pat's favorite was *Queen for a Day*, and they loved to watch it together, reflecting on who had the worst circumstances, always comparing each to their own pathos. Homer watched baseball. Sometimes Jimmie Lee would act out some of the characters on the variety shows, particularly the famous actresses. "That should be me talkin' with Milton Berle!" she said more than once. "I could've played that part with a much better accent."

Later, when Jimmie, in a jovial mood, returned home from the New China Club with one of her suitors, Pat was pasting pictures in a scrapbook while the TV blared.

"This is my daughter, Pat," Jimmie said to the older man.

"How do you do?" he said to Pat.

She didn't answer, just nodded her head and went about her business.

"Why don't you go on outside and play for a while," Jimmie said to her daughter.

Pat remained silent, picked up her cutouts and scissor and went off to her room. She overheard her momma.

"I took that child in when she was but three weeks old. Her folks didn't want her—thought she was gonna be mixed. Her momma claims her daddy was Negro." She'd laugh, and then, pointing to her own black skin. "That gal ain't no more mixed than I am," she said, "but keep it under your hat."

Pat came out of the bedroom and glared at the man as she walked toward the door. "Hey, you like ice cream?" He said.

Pat turned toward him and nodded without a word.

"Don't you talk?" He asked.

"Sure, I can talk. I just don't have nothing to say," She replied.

He reached into his pocket and handed Pat a dollar bill, "Here, why don't you head over to store and get yourself some ice cream or something." Pat took the money and started to walk away.

"Hey," Jimmie said, "don't you got something to say?"

"Thank you," Pat said and continued out the door. Her thoughts wandered to Homer, wondering if he was aware of Jimmie's other men friends. She never saw Homer upset or jealous. He worked six days a week and she knew that he loved Jimmie's sassy, sexy side, but loathed and feared her vile temper. Pat knew that her momma couldn't change.

It was a month later when another friend of Jimmie's stopped by for a visit. She sent Pat out to play as usual, but dark clouds covered most of the early afternoon sky. As Pat wandered about trying to entertain herself, finally setting down on a rock in the back yard forming faces in the dirt with a stick, a few droplets of rain sprinkled on her arm. She left the stick in a hole, hoping the images would be there when she returned after the drizzle stopped. She brushed the dirt from her hands and walked toward the cottage.

When Pat entered the house, a muscular built man named Blackie was sitting naked on the bed with his wide back glistening like a sweaty prizefighter. Jimmie was leaning up against the headboard with the white cotton sheets pulled up to her waist. She had on a yellow blouse, unbuttoned, draped about her shoulders with the collar turned under on one side. In that afternoon light, the contrast of their skin against the white and yellow fabrics fixed Pat's eyes into a blank stare.

"Thought I told you to stay outside," Jimmie said.

"It's rainin'." Pat jumped at the sound of Jimmie's voice and then closed the door.

"Rainin' my damn ass. You just wanna sneak up on me to see what's goin' on. All you whiteys wanna see is black meat—even when they's a little shit, like you! Y'all the same, thinking 'are they as big as they say? Are they as big as they say?'" She mimicked a bobbing head and her eyes opened wide. "Well, ya wanna see?" she said, stretching open her blouse. "I'll show ya." She thrust forth her naked black breasts. "See how big they are?! Ya wanna suck on them?" Jimmie screeched while flouncing up and down on the bed, making her breasts bounce up and down in unison. "Are you happy now?"

Pat shook with fear and embarrassment. Her eyes locked on Blackie, who returned the stare. He studied her for a moment and then turned to Jimmie. "Wut da fuck are you doin'?" he asked.

Jimmie ignored his question and peered contemptuously at Pat. "Now get your ass outta here," she growled, "and don't come back till I say so!"

Pat dashed out the door into the rain and then quickly ran to the side of the house, shivering under the overhang trying to stay dry. She heard the screen open and Blackie calling her name.

Pat stepped from the side of the cottage and peeked up at Blackie. He returned the look with a big smile. "You momma is drunk. Don't pay her no mind. You know how she gets. It's got nothing to do with you, just remember that." He patted her head, gave her a dollar and headed off into the rain. Pat watched him jog along the dirt road and out of sight.

Three weeks later, Pat and Homer were at the kitchen table on a rare occasion when Jimmie Lee was on the wagon and calmness prevailed. Pat never attributed her momma's erratic behavior to bouts of drinking; she blamed herself for Jimmie's unpredictability. But she always noticed when Homer was around, her momma relaxed. And now she watched Jimmie fussed about cleaning up after dinner. "How come Momma's so calm when she's around you?" Pat asked Homer.

"I'm always calm," Jimmie said, "he ain't got nothing to do with it."

Homer chuckled and said, "I'm the spike in the track, I keep everything tied down so the train rides smooth."

"Huh, you keep talking nonsense like that, this trains gonna run you over," Jimmie said.

Pat giggled and then asked Homer, "When did you two meet? I mean, like how did it happen?"

"Why you want to know that for?" Jimmie asked.

"I dunno, just because."

"Well, just cause there ain't no reason to be snoopin' into anybody's business," Jimmie said.

"You want to know?" Homer said, "Well I'll tell you. When I first met your momma, she was in the China Club all looking fine and chattin' up with some Orientals. Neither one knew what the other was talking about, till I come along. I tried to do the intrepretin' for those nice men. But it seems they didn't want to pay the freight. They kept asking for a discount."

"You lying," Jimmie chuckled, "that ain't the truth."

"Well, I kept bargaining with her and finally got it down to as low as she was gonna go. I turned to those Oriental fellows and they just shook their heads and walked away."

"What did they say?" Pat asked.

"How was I supposed to know? I don't speak no Chinese." He said as Pat laughed and Jimmie snickered. "So I took the deal for myself. I never guessed that a two-dollar trick would get me a whole family."

Two nights later, while Homer moonlighted at the Nugget for a few extra dollars, Pat played alone at the cottage, listening to the radio and coloring in her book. Homer called on the phone. "Pat, are you all right?" he asked.

"Yeah, when ya comin' home?"

"I'll be there in a little while. Ya Jimmie's in trouble, and we got to help her," he said.

"Wut kinda trouble? Did she get hurt? Was she in a accident?" Pat asked.

"She's in jail. We got ta bail her out."

CHAPTER 10

Pat was perched on a bench by the front window as the taxi stopped in front of the cottage. Homer motioned from the back seat for her to get in. "What happened?" Pat asked.

"Don't know, but we're off to the rescue."

The police station was intimidating. In the darkness the building looked old. They made their way through a heavy door that led through a vestibule and into a larger room, bare except for one wooden bench. The musty smell reminded her of an old school that Homer took her to a year earlier. There were "Wanted" posters and official-looking notices on the wall. A tall counter extended from one end of the room to the other. The eight-year-old child barely reached the top, let alone be able to see what was on the other side. Pat held on to Homer's hand as she heard a faceless voice from beyond the cage. "Homer! What brings you down here?"

"I come to get my old lady outta jail," Homer said. His voice yielding and placid.

"I didn't know you even had an old lady," replied the officer.

"Sometimes she don't know it either."

"What's her name?"

"Jimmie. Jimmie Lee Faison."

"Faison. Faison. Now why does that sound familiar? Let me see." He shuffled through a few papers. "Oh shit!" he chuckled and then burst into a high-pitched giggle. His laughter was contagious. Pat began to snicker herself, not knowing why, or at what.

"Wutcha laughing' at? My woman's in jail, and you's cacklin' like a barn full of hens."

"Sorry, Homer, it's not funny. It's serious, but, well, never mind."

"Wut she do, anyway?"

"Well," said the officer, "it says here in the report that while leaving the parking lot of a liquor store, she struck a telephone pole."

"Struck a telephone pole? Struck it with what?"

"She was driving a vehicle."

"Jimmie don't drive no vehicle. That's crazy!" said Homer.

"A man . . ." the officer stifled a giggle, "a little man, no, a *very* little man was seriously injured and he's in the hospital. She's been charged with disorderly conduct."

"I don't believe that shit!" objected Homer. "I'm tellin' ya, she don't drive no vehicle. We don't even got a vehicle!"

"Apparently she was driving the vehicle," said the officer. "It was a Cadillac that belonged to the victim in the hospital. There was a witness; a woman in the liquor store saw her drive out of the parking lot in the vehicle, where she collided into a pole. The car was totaled, and she was arrested."

"Damn that woman! Wut she doin' drivin' some car when she don't know how to?" Homer thought a moment. "Wut I gotta do to get her out?" he asked.

"You need to go and find out how much the bail is going to be. Now you can wait here until the paperwork comes back, or you can go over to Night Court." He pointed toward the big clock on the wall and said, "It's already started, so you might be able to say something to the judge."

Homer turned and yanked Pat by the hand and they started out the door.

"Good luck, Homer," the officer yelled. "Hey, who's the little girl?"

Homer glanced back and mumbled, "Jimmie's daughter."

Pat glanced over her shoulder to see the face that belonged to the voice that laughed so heartily and saw a young man with thick glasses scratching his head.

They rushed over to the courthouse. Homer made Pat sit in the last seat while he limped up to the front. She could see Jimmie easily. The judge's chin rested heavily in one hand. Pat thought he looked bored. She noticed his eye wander toward Homer who was tiptoeing respectfully to a seat just behind Jimmie. Pat watched, but couldn't hear Homer and Jimmie as they exchanged a few words. She quickly became fascinated by what was going on with the two men standing before the judge. Suddenly Pat heard the crack of the gavel hit the wooden surface and the Judge bellowed, "Next case!"

Another man, who Pat couldn't see, called Jimmie's name and she stood up and swaggered toward the Judge. Homer limped up beside her. The judge acknowledged Homer with a grin, and then turned his attention to Jimmie.

"Do you have an attorney representing you?"

"No, sir. I don't need no attorney."

"OK. The charge before you is disorderly conduct. If you are guilty just say 'guilty,' if you feel you are not guilty, just say 'not guilty.' Nothing else, understand?"

"Yes, Judge, I understand," replied Jimmie in her most charming manner.

"Do you understand the charges—disorderly conduct and driving without a license?"

"Yeah, I understand them, Your Honor."

"How do you plead? Guilty or not guilty?"

Jimmie didn't wait for him to finish before she burst out with an explanation. "I ain't done nothing wrong. I wasn't even driving that car. Whoever said I did is a liar and I want her to come here and say that to. . . ."

"HOLD IT! HOLD IT!" the judge raised his commanding voice, rapping his gavel. "Guilty, or not guilty. That's all you have to say. Nothing else. This is not a trial."

"Not guilty."

"Thank you," the judge said, annoyed. "A court date is set for the twenty-second at ten o'clock in this courtroom."

He focused on Homer and paused. "Homer, why are you here?"

"I come to bail out my wife, your Honor," he said, motioning to Jimmie.

"This is your wife?"

"Yes, sir, Judge."

"Well then, since she has no previous arrest record and you'll be responsible for her, then I release her in your custody without bail."

The prosecutor, a man with a baby face and dark straight hair stood up from his desk and objected. "But Your Honor . . . there is a man in the hospital in critical condition. If he should die, the charges will be changed to involuntary manslaughter, and under the circumstances, the State feels strongly that an amount equal to the degree of involvement be requested to insure the defendant's return to the court."

"Homer," said the judge, "are you going to make sure that your wife returns to this court as I have directed?"

"Yes, sir, Judge."

"Well, that's good enough for me. The defendant will be released in the custody of Homer Faison without bail."

"But your Honor," began the young lawyer, but the judge interrupted.

"I have known Homer for a long time," the judge interrupted firmly. "He's been shining my shoes at the Esquire for years. If he says he'll bring her here, then he will." He slammed the gavel down again. "Next case."

Jimmie Lee walked out with Homer in tow through the small wooden gates. The lawyer began putting his papers aside; the judge already looked bored again. When she saw Pat, Jimmie glared at Homer and asked, "What she doin' here?"

Pat sensed Jimmie's resentment at her presence in the courtroom. This was a world of rules, procedures, and the law dominated by white men. It was an arena that Pat, until that day, never knew existed. She noticed Jimmie's embarrassment. It was the first time Jimmie allowed the whites to have control over her in front of her daughter. Jimmie's disdain for the whites was beginning to spread like a rash. She was humiliated and angry with them and would do her utmost to outsmart them.

Pat felt guilty for being the cause of such contempt. But now that Pat was here, watching all of this, she wanted to know more.

"Momma," Pat asked, "why was you in jail?"

"You'd like to see me in jail, huh?" snapped Jimmie. It wasn't an answer, but from the tone, Pat knew not to pry further.

Back home, Jimmie, sullen and silent, downed a glass of gin. Homer went back to the Nugget. Pat went to bed, pulled the covers over her head, and attempted to escape into a fantasyland of pleasant dreams and the safety of Big Momma.

Pat awoke the next morning at about ten o'clock. Homer had already left for the shop and she stayed snuggled in bed. Suddenly, she overheard laughing voices in the other room.

"Tsk, tsk, that's awful!" It was Aunt Rosie. "How bad's the car?" Rosie asked.

"The car? Ha! It's all fucked up. He ain't never gonna be able to fix that sucker. You shoulda seen the midget fly off the front seat. Like a little rag doll, head first, right into the windshield!"

"Well you just better pray to God that he don't die, or your butt's gonna be in jail for a long time."

"Yeah, it would've been a lot better if he was a regular-size man—with a harder head," Jimmie said, laughing again. She couldn't contain herself. "Yeah," she went on, "but if he was a regular size then I woulda had a lot more trouble trying to pick him up and move him into the driver's seat."

A knock on the door interrupted their laughter. Two detectives from the Sparks Police Department wanted to know more details about the accident. They told Jimmie there was an eyewitness to the mishap—a woman who said Jimmie was driving the car when it hit the pole.

Jimmie Lee was adamant; she stuck to her story. She was polite and formal, acting as if it was all just a misunderstanding. The detectives suggested that she take a lie-detector test to prove that she was telling the truth. Jimmie pretended to be insulted by any insinuation of a discrepancy between her story and that of the witness. But then she reluctantly agreed to submit to the interrogation at the police station the following Monday.

Then the officers changed the subject to Pat. "This little white girl is supposed to be your daughter," said the older one. "Is this true?"

"Who told you that?" Jimmie asked.

The two men looked at each other. The younger one replied, "Homer Faison told the officer on duty last night."

Jimmie was silently fuming. As many times as the police came to the house in the past to quiet her down after a routine incident with one of the neighbors or one of her boyfriends, she never allowed anyone to see Pat. And now, Homer, of all people, volunteered the information that she herself so closely guarded.

"Yeah, she's my daughter," she said. "What about it?"

"Can you prove it? Do you have adoption papers, birth certificate—any legal documentation?"

Jimmie glanced up to the ceiling in thought for a second. "Yeah, I have all that stuff, but not here. My lawyer's got it and he's in San Francisco."

"Then I suggest you contact him and have it sent to you. I think you're gonna need them. This is not a police matter—not yet, anyway. We'll be turning over our report to welfare and they will contact you. In the meantime, the little girl can stay with you, at least for a day or two until the report is filed, but I think they'll probably take her into custody and place her in a foster home until this matter is settled."

Pat was very much aware of what was going on, even though she didn't understand all of the technicalities. When Pat heard the words "foster home" she became frightened. Her fear was over leaving Momma. Even if she was difficult, Jimmie Lee was all she had. The thought of being taken from her was terrifying—especially if it meant going to the white people Jimmie so hated.

While the adults chatted, Pat slipped out of the house, strolled down to the creek and sat at the side of the big boulder that jutted out a few feet beyond the bank. Even with the slight breeze that rustled the branches of the nearby willow tree, the water was still at that point in the small stream. In the distance, Pat heard the faint clacking of the train passing over the track. She stared down into the clear water, past her reflection. Her mind wandered to more pleasant thoughts as her fear dissipated. It wasn't long before visions of her real mother materialized. Pat's image of her real mother was a cross between Doris Day and an adult version of herself. As she sat, safely behind the boulder, she wondered if her mother, at this very moment, was sitting somewhere staring into her own reflection thinking the same thoughts. As her own image remained etched on the still surface, beneath it she caught glimpses of a woman in a pale green gown, similar to the one Doris Day wore in a movie. That was her mother, her real mother. The sounds of the stream became silent; her mind wandered. Dreams blended one into another, bringing her deeper and deeper into an imaginary world. A world of . . . peace and happiness . . . without guilt, or anger, or fighting . . . a world where she had everything she wanted. And everyone was the same color. *How could all this be happening to me? Now, after everything, they want to put me in a foster home! How could they be so mean to me? What have I done?* Suddenly, as if her dream had come alive, Pat was startled by a second image in her reflection. It was a black face with pigtails. It was Joyce, her girlfriend from the neighborhood who was just a year older than Pat.

"Where did ya come from?" Pat asked.

"God, I was standin' here fo' a long time and you ain't even heard a thing!" Joyce stood closer to the edge of the water and looked down into the spot where their reflections were. "Wut did you see, a fish?"

"No. I ain't see no fish. Jus' myself."

"Wut ya doing here so long?"

"Just thinking about her," Pat said pensively.

"Ya mean ya white momma?"

"Yeah. Someday I'm gonna find her."

"Miss Jimmie says you're white."

"No I ain't!" Pat yelled. "I'm mixed!"

"Then how come you ain't colored like everybody else is?"

"Cause my momma's white and her skin's white, but my Daddy's colored. And I'm colored on the inside, jus' like you is!"

Joyce didn't argue, she just picked up a stone and skimmed it across the water.

How come she doesn't understand? How many times do I have to tell her my story? I guess I'll be telling it forever. Finally, Pat smiled at Joyce and said nothing about it.

"If you say so, Patty, I believe what ya tellin' me."

"Hey, let's play the game." Pat said.

Joyce and Pat often played a special game they'd call the "her" game. The plan was to create ways for Pat to find her real mother, and act out reunion scenarios. But on this day, Joyce didn't want to play the "her" game with Pat. Then Joyce changed the subject, "Then how come the police was at your house?"

"Cause they want to take me away and put me . . . I mean they came to ask questions 'bout the car accident, that's all."

Joyce gave a perplexing glance. Pat knew Joyce didn't believe her, but rather then trying to explain, she said, "I hear Jimmie callin' me, I gotta go." Pat skipped off and left her friend wondering what was going on.

The police were gone by the time Pat reached the cottage, but she could still hear Jimmie cussing and ranting. This time it was Mrs. Atkinson, their landlady, upset at the frequent visits by the police. No one in the neighborhood wanted the cops snooping around. Since Jimmie, Homer, and Pat moved in, there were more cops stopping at their cottage in just a few months than at any time since the old campground days.

Jimmie had a kitchen knife in her hand and threatened Mrs. Atkinson. Aunt Rosie stepped in between them and hustled the elderly woman out the door. Jimmie was still screaming and cussing.

"Wut's going on?" Pat asked Aunt Rosie as she watched Mrs. Atkinson waddle toward the big house.

Aunt Rosie didn't answer. She watched cautiously, glancing back and forth between Jimmie in the cottage with the knife and Mrs. Atkinson, who kept looking back at them. When Rosie felt it was safe, she closed the door, leaving Jimmie Lee alone with her misery. Rosie placed her hand firmly on Pat's shoulder and motioned for her to walk around the side of the house toward the open field.

"Your momma's been drinkin' again, Patty. And you know how she gets when she's like that. She blames everything on you. But don't yo' worry, it ain't your fault, none of it. She says she wouldn't be with that midget if she didn't need the extra money to buy you things. And now the new trouble with the police. It's starting to get to her."

Pat looked down at the ground as they walked and began to cry. Rosie continued, "It's true. Your momma takes care of you, and makes sure you don't get into no trouble, and she sacrifices a lot for you. But she could be dangerous when she drinks.

"Down deep inside she really loves you, but when she's drinking, she thinks she actually hates you. She's told you that herself."

Pat loved Aunt Rosie and instinctively knew she was trustworthy. So why would she say such awful things about Jimmie—unless they were true?

"So I want you to promise me something," Rosie continued. "If at any time, you see your momma in one of her moods—that is, when she's drunk, and you feel danger brewin', then you come to me. I'll protect you. I ain't afraid of her. I got a lot of tricks and magical spells that'll keep the devil away. So taking care of a high-strung woman like Jimmie Lee is kid's stuff." She shrugged and acted sassy. "Why I got some special herbs and leaves that'll keep even the strongest evil from entering my front door. So don't you worry, child. When the time comes you just make sure you get your little behind to me. Promise?"

"I promise."

Pat knew Aunt Rosie believed in magic and incantations. Jimmie had often told Pat stories about her and how she learned about chanting, and spirits, and potions from her spiritual advisors in the South. Her psychic abilities, which Rosie said were a gift from God, were unusual. Pat never did understand how she knew so much about people, and events—particularly before they happened. Rosie taught Pat about ESP and paranormal mysteries that she had learned from books. That's all she ever read about—that, and the Bible. Her neighbors and sisters at the church believed she was a true witch. Aunt Rosie knew they talked behind her back, but never confronted them. Instead, she watched them step aside when she came near. She believed in the supernatural, and left everyone alone in his or her ignorance.

Homer and Pat stayed away from Jimmie and tried to ignore her antics. However, the following morning, she was a new person. She had a good night's sleep and was cool and relaxed. Pat was constantly amazed at her instant transformation. It was time for Jimmie to take a polygraph and make her statement to the police.

Pat trekked off to school that day, but her mind was far away. There was so much riding on the lie-detector test and Pat knew Jimmie couldn't fool the police. If she failed the test, then for sure she would go to jail, which would in turn force Pat into the care of an old, nasty white woman—a thought that made her stomach feel queasy. Even if Jimmie passed the test, there was still the matter of her uncompleted adoption. It looked as though there was no way out. As the thoughts rolled around in her head, Pat wrote down her feelings on small scraps of paper.

What am I guilty of?
Everyone blames me.
I have Negro blood.
I am not a Whitey.
I am not White.

It was all she knew how to do without letting anyone know her feelings; she felt ashamed.

As she folded the scraps of writing and placed them into her pocket, her face suddenly turned red. She realized that Aunt Rosie said her momma hated her and that was too distressing think about. As tears swelled in her eyes, she quickly visualized her Big Momma and all the love that woman had for her. She sensed her warm touch, her safe embrace, and sucked in her wonderful scent. As Pat wandered deep into her imagination, blocking out all that was around her, she could hear Big Momma's calm voice calling her.

"Don't worry, my child, my dear Pat. I'm with you. God has great plans for you. You'll make it through these trials. Everything will work out—you'll see."

She kept Big Momma's voice in her head, letting those soothing words fill her empty heart.

While deep into her daydreams, a voice rang out. "Patricia! Patricia! Are you with us today?" Her teacher snapped. Pat jumped in her seat but only for a moment.

When school let out, Pat remained aloof and sullen, avoiding her friends. Instead of heading home, she wandered by the stream and slowly headed back toward the open field behind the cottage, not wanting to face the reality of Jimmie failing the lie-detector test and trying to put the inevitable off for just a little longer. In her pocket, she felt the crumpled bits of paper and studied them one more time. Her words were private, her thoughts secret, and she dreaded letting anyone know her true feelings. She dropped to her knees and dug several holes. She placed the private reflections in an empty soda bottle and buried it, along with her embarrassment, in an unmarked grave. It was one of the rituals that Aunt Rosie taught her: the way to get anything she wanted was to bury her wishes in God's earth. It was the same custom that Big Momma mentioned. This powerful ritual of writing, then burying her thoughts gave her courage to defend herself against the endless rejection from the black neighborhood.

As Pat approached the front door, the merriment and laughter drowned out the music in the background. She stepped inside and scanned the familiar faces as each glanced back on cue, but no one nodded or acknowledged her presence, preferring to continue on with their prattle. She blended in easily without interrupting their impromptu celebration and allowed the jovial atmosphere to cheer her up. She recognized Jimmie's cronies—Barbara, her cousin, Blackie, Daddy-O from the hobo camp, and some other familiar faces. They each had a drink or cigarette while listening to Jimmie unfold her story with the flair and drama of a movie queen. She was at the center, on stage, performing her scene as if it was opening night. Pat caught only the tail end of the performance, but enough to know that Jimmie Lee beat the lie detector test. And that provided relief all around, even though she knew Jimmie would brag until the winter's snow. Although the truth might still come out if the dwarf recovered, for now that concern remained on the shelf while Pat savored the moment of her momma's triumph over the machine.

As the music echoed loudly off the sparse walls, Pat hummed along, tapping her feet to the syncopation. It wasn't long before Pat, bopping her head to the beat, became the focus of her momma.

Barbara pointed toward Pat, "Hey, that girl's got some rhythm!"

"Rhythm, shit!" said Jimmie. "This child's got more moves than a bedbug!"

The adults giggled. Pat felt embarrassed. She knew what Jimmie wanted her to do and warily dropped to her knees and slid under the table.

"Come on outta there. Show 'em how you can dance," she said as she dragged Pat by the arm until she was out on the open floor. Daddy-O turned the music up and the coaxing began. Pat hid her reddened face behind her arm trying to disappear, yet, still bouncing rhythmically to the beat.

"Come on Patty, show us your stuff. Yeah, they wanna see ya dance," Barbara said clapping her hands. The cheering only made Pat more embarrassed until she realized the only way out was to comply. Hesitantly, she started to shuffle her feet and prance about, allowing the music to take over, dancing until she became the main attraction.

"Look at 'er go, she's da only white Patty with soul!" Jimmie said. "Ain't no doubt 'bout where she gets them moves—not from da honky side, dats fo' sure!"

At that moment, Pat wished her skin were black like theirs.

CHAPTER 11

In the weeks that followed, the imminent crisis that Pat had anticipated slowly diminished. The attorney Homer pleaded with agreed to look into the adoption and that kept the Social Services at bay for the time being. The midget recovered from the coma. His family didn't want it known that their son was involved in an accident with Jimmie Lee and dropped the charges against her. Pat's anxiety dissipated as each calamity petered out. The only serious problem they had to face was Mrs. Atkinson. The landlord was adamant about getting Jimmie, Homer, and Pat out of her cottage.

Once a month, Reverend Mayfield, a Baptist minister, left off a pair of black leather shoes for Homer to shine and pick up the following day. Each time he encouraged the shoeshine man to attend his services, but Homer, not being much of a churchgoer, politely backed off.

Jimmie, on the other hand, was raised in the Pentecostal Church and had no time for the tight-assed Baptists. But local gossip inferred that Reverend Mayfield was okay as far as ministers go. His congregation had prospered and he was planning to build a new church. He also owned a couple of small houses nearby. Although Jimmie didn't have much use for his church or sermons, she did manage to persuade Mayfield to rent her one of the small houses on Wadsworth Street.

It was a finer home, slightly larger with two separate bedrooms not far from the old neighborhood near the railroad tracks and stream where Pat and her friends played their games. The prestige that came with living in a home owned by the minister boosted their confidence. Jimmie went to work making the new home comfortable by adding her own personal touch to a somewhat modest decor and sparse furnishings. She filled every empty spot with artificial flowers set in odd shaped bottles and vases. Reverend Mayfield was a more tolerant landlord.

Pat and Jimmie Lee spent a lot of time together at the new house, always with the TV turned on, but rarely watching it. Jimmie saw herself as having a special talent and longed to be on stage or in a movie. Pat watched with fascination as Jimmie performed, but cringed when she started singing, always out of tune and making up lyrics that made no sense to anyone but herself. When she wasn't singing, Jimmie hummed tunes that seemed to blend jazz or blues with theme songs from TV shows often sounding like Mae West with olives in her mouth.

When they weren't home together, they were at the Sparks Theater checking out the latest movie. Jimmie always critiqued the performances on the way home. "Tonight we're going to see *Imitation of Life,* and maybe even go for some ice cream later," she said to Pat. "That's the one with Sandra Dee and Lana Turner."

"And Mahalia Jackson and Juanita Moore," Pat added. "I heard that it was real good."

"I don't know what it's about, but we'll find out."

Jimmie was dressed in her white pedal pushers and a white embroidered sweater that accentuated her breasts. From the moment they neared the theater together, Pat felt the hostility. The white moviegoers standing in line peered at her with scorn. Pat tried to convince herself that it was her imagination stemming from the publicity that surrounded the controversial film. But as they walked hand-in-hand, she could feel the peoples' eyes pierce right through her, as if they were the street trash.

As they watched the movie, with the light-skinned actress Susan Kohner passing herself as white and disowning her black mother, Pat felt the odd connection to her own life. It was only at the end of the film, when the actress begs for forgiveness from her departed mother, when it was too late, that Pat and Jimmie Lee allowed the tears to flow shamelessly from their eyes.

Jimmie Lee turned and put her arm around Pat and said, "Are you gonna leave me like she did?"

Pat looked at her glassy-eyed and said, "Momma, I'm never gonna leave you."

As they walked together out of the theater, the eyes that had bore through her from the crowds were now soft and compassionate. She saw the transformation take place firsthand, and now understood that people could change if they were only shown the truth. It was then that she realized that someday she would let the whole world know her story and make her momma famous.

Mrs. Mayfield was a pleasant woman, polite and formal. She kept active both inside and outside of the church. She was particularly fond of Pat and decided to bring the little white girl along to a meeting with the black sisters from the church. Pat thrilled at their reaction.

"So whom do you take after . . ." asked Sister Ella, "with those big blue eyes and that golden hair? Is that from your mother's side of the family?"

"Yeah, my real momma is just like a movie star, like Doris Day," Pat said.

"And what about your daddy? What's he like?"

"My poppa is a Negro," she said. "It says so on my birth certificate." Pat felt them grip onto her words.

"Then how did you get here?"

"My real momma was forced to give me away when I was born cause she was too young to take care of me. So they gave me to my momma and Reverend Greenwade, when I was a baby. And then we got to be here." Pat knew the ladies were delighted at the straightforward history. She captured the spotlight, just as her momma wanted.

When Pat returned home, she told Jimmie about Betsy showing her off. Her reaction was indifferent. Although Jimmie didn't believe in the tenets of the Baptists, or the Pentecostals, or the Methodists, or the Catholics, or any organized religion, she knew that it would be good for

Pat to be exposed to the teachings of Jesus. Pat knew Jimmie believed in God, but she didn't believe in the hypocrisy that most of the sisters and brothers of the church practiced.

"Why don't you go to the services like Aunt Lucille does or like Big Momma and everybody else?" Pat asked Jimmie.

"I been to those churches, I grew up with those churches. I've seen the people, grown men and women, acting foolish when the Sprit gets on them in order to be saved. Huh!" Jimmie shook her head and continued. "They get saved one night and the very next night they out fornicating, fighting, cussing, stealing, and everything else just so they could go back the following day and have the Spirit jump their bones again.

"If I'm gonna sin, then there ain't no Sprit, or prayer, or two-faced minister gonna stop me." Jimmie was without illusion. Pat, however, didn't agree, but she kept her opinion private, not wanting to give Jimmie a reason to argue. She loved going to church. She loved the music, the dinners, and the comfort of knowing that she was closer to her angels.

"But that doesn't mean you're not going," Jimmie continued.

"I know, I want to go," Pat responded with enthusiasm.

The next day Pat was down by the stream with her friend Joyce Gaston and a few of the other kids from the area. They were skipping stones in the water, listening to a transistor radio and taking turns standing on the high rock singing the soulful sounds of their favorite songs, each performance worse than the previous.

Pat wanted to bring Joyce along to the Pentecostal Church. But Joyce and her family, along with all of the other people in the neighborhood, belonged to Rev. Mayfield's Baptist Congregation. Pat was the only one who was a "Holy Roller." For the Baptists, the policies of the Pentecostals were too strict. To be "saved" there were many rules to follow, most of which Pat didn't understand. And she never wanted the "Spirit" to jump on her. She prayed it wouldn't happen. Joyce and the other neighborhood kids teased her about being "saved," but Pat knew better. She had been to their Baptist church and the singing was okay. But the Holy Rollers— now that was music!

"This music's real good," Pat said to Joyce after they watched Stinger sing a Mathis song on the high rock, "but the music at my church's ten times better."

Joyce was caught up in the melody. Her eyes lit up like diamonds, then quickly faded. "Yeah, maybe, but my mother won't let me go to no Holy Roller Church. She says that the Spirit'll jump on me, and I don't want that! No Way! Uh-uh!"

"As long as you pray 'em away, the Spirits won't get on you. It always works for me."

After much prodding, Pat convinced Joyce to ask her parents one more time. They were conservative Baptists and didn't approve of Pat's church, but just this once, they let her go.

So, that Sunday, Joyce and Pat went together to the Pentecostal Church.

As they entered, Joyce surveyed the area and made a beeline for a seat in the last row. Pat walked past her, turned and said, "No, you don't want to sit there, you can't see nothing. Come with me."

"I can see jus' fine, I want to be right by the door in case I see that Spirit hoppin' around. Because if it comes near me, I'm gone."

"No, you don't understand, the Spirit don't go after kids. Kids don't sin, that's why my Aunt Lucille used to put me up in the front with the other kids. Cause the Spirit don't bother us over there," Pat whispered, "Now come on, follow me."

Joyce was frightened at first, not knowing anyone, nor what to do. They sat down in the front facing the congregation, where all the sinners usually sat. But from their vantage point, these were the best seats in the house. They could see everything.

Joyce sat quietly, trying not to be noticed as the services began. After the Rev. Webb made a few remarks about an upcoming social event and thanked everyone for being there, he asked for all the new members to stand up and say something about themselves. Joyce refused to participate, even with Pat's nudging.

The pastor then began reciting scriptures, each denouncing the devil and his work, and emphasizing its relevance to the congregation.

The organist began playing a slow hymn, which, as the Reverend Webb's sermon became more dramatic, puffed up into a funnel of passion. Pat motioned to Joyce, who was focused on the sisters of the church all dressed alike, to keep her eye on the organist.

Joyce glanced over to a middle-aged woman with thick, brown-framed glasses seated at the organ. She was twisting away from her sheet music to eye the sinners behind her while attempting to keep the tempo in sync with both the pastor's preaching and pounding of his fist and the congregation's rhythmic movements. The members swayed and sometimes bopped on the offbeat, each clapping at first to a distinctly different tune and then finally in unison. The harmonies were beginning to come alive. The organist picked up the tempo and the volume swelled. The pastor was right in line hopping to the music. As the pace quickened to a frenetic tempo, a woman jumped from her seat and shouted, "Hallelujah! Hallelujah! Let me be saved!" It startled Joyce and prompted another woman to scream aloud.

"Lord! Lord! May the spirit come to me!"

"Amen, brother!"

The organist felt her fingers ring out the music to the sound of the sinners. Suddenly, a man threw his arms in the air and yelled, "The Spirit's got me, I'm saved, I'm saved, Hallelujah!"

"Amen, brother!"

He shook all over in a spastic whirl. His eyes were white and his head forced all the way back on his neck. He leaped out of his seat. The others were now caught up in the fusion of the thumping and pounding, rhythm and clapping, savers and sinners. Other members started boogying to the music, and everyone on the beat.

Pat glanced over at Joyce whose grin was wide and bright. "This is the place! I mean the music," Joyce tried to explain as she clapped and stomped to the pulse of the beat, "it's it!"

"I know, I know!"

This was much more lively then anything the Baptists could dream up. Joyce was impressed. Everyone joined in unison to sing a few hymns. The pastor praised the Lord for saving all the sinners, allowing each to be congratulated by their brothers and sisters sitting next to them. And then it was time for Sunday lunch.

Pat could still feel the rhythm and kept humming between mouthfuls of peas, potatoes, collard greens, and chicken. That was the only thing that was awful about the Holy Rollers—the food was delicious, but it always made Pat sick.

Afterward, the service continued, but Joyce and Pat had had enough. They decided to take the afternoon off and not bother with the evening services. "That was great stuff!" As they snuck away from the adults who kept an eye on the young children, Joyce spoke.

"I'm sure glad the 'Spirit' didn't come on me! I saw all those people getting crazy and it didn't look like they'd ever recover."

"No, they get better," Pat said. "Most of them will be back in a couple of weeks to get saved all over again."

"There sure was a whole lot of 'em."

"Yeah, this was a great day for sinners!"

"Now what are we gonna do?" Joyce asked.

"I want some candy. Let's go the Laundromat near the bus stop. It's got that vending machine with the good candy."

Before they entered, they peeked in through the big glass window and saw that the store was empty. Two washing machines were going through their cycles toward the back. There was a shopping cart from the supermarket next to a dryer on the left. The two candy machines were opposite one another near the front entranceway. Pat walked up to the farthest one while Joyce looked at herself in the small mirror on the other. She called off the names of each of the candies: "5th Avenue, Butterfingers, Hershey's, Clark Bar, Licorice Sticks . . ."

Before Pat could complete all the names, a chunky white man with a red baseball cap and a dirty tee shirt that slovenly hung out over his gray trousers stood behind Pat and stared at Joyce. His unshaven jowls hung in layered rolls down his long face. He turned his head, looked at Pat, and said gruffly. "You can stay, but the nigger? She's gotta go." He pointed toward Joyce. Pat looked over at Joyce who was terrified by his appearance alone. Pat was stunned. No white man had ever called any of her friends "nigger" in front of her. They were together; they were the same.

"Well I'm a nigger, too! So we'll both gotta leave." Pat grabbed Joyce by the hand and ran out the door, leaving her dime in the machine. They raced back to the church, where some of the parishioners were gathered outside. Out of breath, they related what had happened with the white man in the Laundromat. Tempers flared and everyone within earshot was outraged. Some of the men wanted to burn his Laundromat down, but the elders squelched that idea.

Later, Pat discovered that someone had thrown a brick through the big plate-glass window of the Laundromat. Pat knew that the white man paid a hefty price for his racist slur.

Later, Joyce and Pat talked about that incident, trying to understand why some people were racist. After all, it was the whites that lied and cheated, and kept their people from getting ahead. That's what Jimmie Lee told Pat all the time, and there was no reason to doubt her, especially when she was sober. Pat was aware that the whites treated coloreds like the cockroaches of society.

The following Saturday, Jimmie forced Pat to go with her to clean houses. Jimmie hated the work more than Pat, but the jobs gave her extra money. Pat would rather be out playing or finding something to do over by the tracks.

"But Momma," she said, "you never let me help you so we can get done sooner."

"Never ya mind that. Take a book along and read somethin'. You gotta get an education so you won't have to kiss anybody's goddamn ass! Money rules this damn planet; the more you got, the better your chances of staying alive without too much ass kissing." Jimmie knew of no other way of earning money other then scrubbing for white folks. In the South, where she and her brothers and sisters were raised, no one in her entire family had an education, nor did they know of another way but to work as either a maid or janitor.

But working as a cleaning lady was often not enough. Although Pat never paid much attention to it at the time, there were periods when food was sparse. Jimmie hardly ever ate with Pat and Homer, preferring instead to drink. Many times Pat ate at Aunt Rosie's while Jimmie purposely spent suppertime away. Most nights after dinner, Jimmie wouldn't allow Pat to wash the dishes. She was a fanatic on cleanliness. On one of these nights when Jimmie sent Pat to bed early without cleaning up the dishes, Pat climbed out of her bed and peeked into the kitchen where Jimmie was leaning against the sink gnawing on the cold leftover chicken bones from Pat's plate. Pat watched, unnoticed. This was the same woman who ridiculed Pat for being the bastard child of mixed blood. There she was, doing without the very basic necessities of human survival in order to guarantee that Pat was well fed, fashionably clothed, comfortably sheltered, educated, and spiritually enriched. How could Pat hate this woman, or be embarrassed by her drunken outrageousness? She was truly an enigma.

Tears of understanding filled her eyes as Pat inspected her scrawny frame. She backed away silently, leaving whatever dignity Jimmie had left intact. With the cool, nocturnal breeze gently channeling its way through the narrow opening at her bedroom window, she climbed into bed, burying her head under the wool blanket and squeezing her eyes tightly as if to force her not to think of Jimmie. Instead, she tried to focus her vision on more pleasant matters and prayed to God to let her be able to one day change her life for the better.

As the months passed, Pat became more aware of the value of money. Neither Jimmie nor Homer allowed her to even consider working, no matter how menial or inconsequential the task. Her real job was taking care of Jimmie.

From the time she was seven, Jimmie would send her on errands because she knew she was capable. Everyone knew Pat, and those who didn't asked who the little white girl was, carrying the big bag of groceries. The response was always the same, "Oh, that's Jimmie Lee's kid. She says she's mixed." It seemed quite natural for Pat. She would have done anything not to make Jimmie upset. And the older she became, the more she worried about her momma.

Jimmie, as a housekeeper, was a scrubber and housecleaner and obsessed with disinfecting everything. Every six weeks or so, when least expected, Pat would come home from school and find their entire household scattered in the front yard. Nothing was left inside: tables, lamps, clothes, foodstuffs, her toys and old photographs, everything but the beds. Jimmie was inside, sprawled unconscious, and smelling of gin. It was usually hours before she awoke, but the entire house had been disinfected from top to bottom.

One day when Joyce approached the house with Pat, Joyce saw for the first time this spectacle, "What's this? You moving or somethin'?"

"No," said Pat. "It's bleach week!"

"What's that?"

"Momma's a cleaner, she has a thing about germs and dirt. So the whole house gets bleached. And when she don't use bleach, she scrubs it with something else."

"Do you just leave everything, outside?"

"Naw, we got to put it back, cause she'll be sleepin' for a while."

Together they carried all of the contents back inside the cottage. But before they were through, Jimmie was standing at the door.

"I heard that," Jimmie said, "I wasn't sleepin'. I left it there on purpose, waiting to see if any of those filthy Indians from next door were sneaking over here to steal something."

Joyce was perplexed and meekly asked Jimmie. "Why are the Indians gonna steal this stuff?"

"Cause those low-life redskins would steal anything; they'd steal the spots off ya dog if you wasn't watching them. Can't trust them. And my stuff here is better than anything they got."

"But Momma, I ain't never heard of them Indians stealing nothing."

"Never mind, you just stay away from them filthy animals. All they do is get drunk and steal. Everybody knows that. And they dirty, too. They never take a bath or even wash, so you just stay away from them. Why you think I bleach this place anyway? You think it's fun? Ha! It ain't no fun at all."

Jimmie Lee, as baffling as she was while intoxicated, was just as generous and righteous when it came to helping others who were less fortunate. Although she refused to let anyone clean the inside of her house, or so much as pick up a dirty cup or glass, the yard was something else. Often she would let the hoboes and vagrants rake and clean the area. For their efforts she would give them a sandwich, a beer, and always a silver dollar—legal tender that was abundant in Reno and Sparks.

Most of the hoboes who drifted from town to town were white men. During the latter part of the 1950s, however, their numbers were dwindling. Jimmie's favorite was a colored man named Daddy-O. She did more for him then the others. Homer was less enthusiastic about Jimmie's friends, particularly since he discovered his favorite shirt missing. When he questioned Jimmie about its mysterious disappearance, she was philosophical.

"If the white folks I works for can afford to give old clothes to us, then there's no reason why I can't give your shirts to someone that needs it." She stated emphatically.

"Shit, woman! That was my favorite shirt," Homer complained. "And then you give him a silver dollar to go with it!"

"Don't let it worry you. God will give us another."

As seasons changed, Homer lost more and more of his wardrobe, and Daddy-O was looking better. One day Jimmie thought it was time for him to complete his restoration and decided that she should cut his hair.

"Miss Jimmie, I don't need to have my hair cut," Daddy-O begged. "Ain't goin' nowhere."

"Hey guy, you got such a fine face under there. No need to cover it up with all this rag mop. It's just a place for the bugs to nest."

"But I don't wanna see me with no hair!"

"Have another beer, while I figure out what to do with this mess!"

While sipping her gin, she walked around Daddy-O, each time taking a closer look. For an hour, their irrational argument bounced back and forth, allowing each of them time to get high. Liquor made Jimmie determined, but less agile, especially with a pair of scissors in her hand. Her stamina won out and she butchered the poor defenseless hobo, leaving some portions of his scalp exposed while other sections went untouched. But Jimmie, bleary eyed and barely in control of her own body, was pleased with her handiwork.

When Daddy-O was finally allowed to see the results of this invasion, he was first unmoved, then stupefied, and then he cried. Jimmie couldn't understand why he was so upset. She never saw Daddy-O again.

Jimmie's sense of right and wrong varied depending upon the time of day, how much she had to drink, where she was, and who she was dealing with. It was wrong to chop off Daddy-O's hair when she was drunk and against his strong objections. If it had been Pat's hair, Jimmie would not have thought about doing it cause she felt responsible for Pat. It wasn't the same with the hobo.

Across the street from Pat's house lived Bertha Wilfong, a pleasant, elderly woman from the South who kept mostly to herself and rarely troubled anyone. Illiterate and unsophisticated, she scratched out a living by working as a maid, something she had done since the age of eight. She received letters from her sons and daughters who lived in another state, and often ask Pat to read them for her. Pat loved to read and readily agreed. They became friendly, and because Pat knew how to read, Bertha considered her very bright. At first, she asked Pat to write a letter for her to bring her family up to date on her health and welfare. Within a short time, she found other uses for Pat's talents such as paying bills, reading, or writing letters she sent to her friends. Pat received either a five or ten-dollar bill depending upon the amount of secretarial work required.

Each night, Pat told Jimmie what a wonderful person Mrs. Wilfong was, for which Jimmie had a sarcastic retort. Finally, Jimmie was fed up with superlatives about Mrs. Wilfong and decided to end Pat's career. She forbade Pat to perform any further clerical chores, even though she was being paid for her services. When Mrs. Wilfong objected and assured Jimmie that there was no reason to be upset, Jimmie went into a jealous rage, pulled a knife from the kitchen, and went after the old woman. "If you don't like me, then you don't like my goddamn daughter, either!"

Miss Bertha called the police. Pat defended Jimmie and persuaded the police not to interfere. "She had a bad day, that's all. Don't worry, I'll take care of her," Pat said.

The police left, and Pat continued to be a secretary for Miss Bertha—without Jimmie's knowledge.

CHAPTER 12

Reverend Mayfield was well respected in the community. He was sociable, forever promoting, and continually carrying his Bible. His preaching was emotional. He believed that everyone was a sinner, and the only way to be saved was to find redemption at his Baptist church, and a great many did. So many, in fact, that each service was filled to capacity with sinners, sometimes overflowing into the aisles. There was excitement and enthusiasm in his sermons, but more salesmanship than spiritual revelation. Reverend Mayfield had a reputation for being somewhat of a ladies' man. And this power was seductive. He took full advantage of it and knew how to get the most out of everyone. He was regularly coming up with new schemes for his fund drives, from bazaars and cake sales to raffles and Bingo. His chicken dinners were the core of his fund-raising program. Everything else supplemented them. He bought chickens wholesale, and then had them plucked, cleaned, and cooked by the sisters. The brothers did all of the manual labor. The children sold tickets—far more tickets than there were chickens to eat. Usually, only his loyal devotees showed up to partake in the festivities. Sister Betsy supervised the entire operation and Reverend Mayfield counted the money, and then reported the overwhelming success the following week. Each dinner brought him one step closer to his new church. Jimmie allowed Pat to participate.

Occasionally when Pat came home from school, Reverend Mayfield would be at the house visiting with Jimmic. Seldom did she find them discussing theology. More often than not, they would be quarrelling about the secular events of the day, whether it be people from the neighborhood, the noise from the trains, or who had the busiest casino. Being with Jimmie was a diversion for the minister. She cared little about his church or his fund-raising, but her sharp tongue, irreverence for institutions and a special knack for stripping away any pretense put on by the minister that may have fooled others, made Mayfield try even harder to gain her admiration.

Once, when Pat entered the house unexpectedly, Mayfield jumped up on his feet, quickly standing tall while tugging at his blue gabardine jacket. It was obvious that he did not want Pat to know what he and Jimmie were talking about. "How's my star pupil today?"

"OK," she answered, smiled, and then went to put her books away in her room. She returned momentarily noticing him push aside an empty glass from his place at the table.

Jimmie's wooden expression remained the same as she swallowed another sip of gin. She was in her quiet period, a preliminary stage of semi-sobriety in which she could still function normally. Reverend Mayfield broke the silence with a question directed at Pat. "I understand you have a birthday coming up soon?"

"Yeah, I'm gonna be ten, and Momma said we're gonna have a party . . . so she can invite all her friends."

"Great! Am I invited?"

"Sure, you can come . . . but only after the kids have the party," Pat answered while glancing up at Jimmie in the expectation that it was OK to invite her friends in the neighborhood.

Jimmie took another sip of her drink, "You're gonna be ten. And soon you'll be old enough to find your real momma, and then you'll leave me won't you?"

"Oh no, Momma, I ain't never gonna leave you, not ever!"

Homer wasn't a heavy gambler, but he did like the casino. It was a way to get a little extra money—money that he needed to give to Jimmie just to keep her from getting crazy. Sometimes he'd win 50, 60, sometimes

100 dollars or more. But more often than not he'd lose. Jimmie didn't mind where he was or what he was doing just as long as he came home with money.

Six months earlier, Homer had won big at the casino. He gave Jimmie most of the cash. That is, after he had bought a much-needed car—an old Packard with big heavy chrome bumpers, torn seats, and bald tires in the front. It was a dull green, bleached from its long life in the desert sun. Homer was very proud of his old car, the first one he had in a very long time. He kept it in good running condition and drove it all over town. The first time Homer dropped Pat off at school, three white kids questioned her.

"How could he be your daddy? He's colored and you're white," the eldest white girl said.

"Cause he's not my real daddy, he's my momma's husband," Pat answered.

"Your momma married a colored?" another white girl asked.

"Of course, why wouldn't she? But she's not my real momma. My real momma is white like you, even whiter, and beautiful, too! But my real daddy is a Negro. It says so on my birth certificate."

"You ain't colored. You're just saying that to be different." Said the second girl again.

"I am, too."

"You are not, you got white skin," said another white girl.

"I am, too! I'm just light-skinned, that's all? Why don't you believe me?" Pat pleaded.

"If you're colored then prove it."

Pat was frustrated. A few other white girls joined in, putting Pat in the center.

"Yeah, prove it!"

"I already told you what my birth certificate says. And birth certificates don't lie."

"We don't believe you, cause it ain't true. If you was colored, you'd look colored." The girl's voice got louder. "You got blue eyes and blond hair. No coloreds have blue eyes." She shoved Pat.

"I'm half-colored," Pat said calmly. "Half of my blood is white and half is colored."

Her poise infuriated the girls. One of them began to shout. "If you're blood is half and half, than what color is it when you bleed? Green?"

Pat gaped. They stared back with fury in their eyes. Suddenly she was pushed to the ground. Three girls piled on to hold her down while two others began scratching at her skin. "Let's see what color your blood is when you bleed. That'll prove it."

"Let's see if she's colored underneath. See if the white scratches off!" the shorter one yelled.

"No! Stop it," yelled Rhonda, a friend of Pat's. "Leave her alone!"

Pat began to scream as she struggled to free herself from their grip. Suddenly, all was quiet. The girls let her go and quickly ran off. Alone, her arm stung from the scratches, but there was no blood. She spotted one of the teachers heading her way. She quickly brushed herself off and followed the other girls into the building. Nothing more was said of the incident. She thought she knew these white girls, but when she saw the hate in their eyes, she knew they were harboring a prejudice that was rooted deeply within their spirit. Instinctively, she tried to prevent it from contaminating her own psyche. It was the second attack from girls who wanted impossible proof of her bloodline. Pat then knew she needed to be more diplomatic when confronted. She went about her business as if nothing happened without ever again mentioning it to anyone.

Pat did have her birthday party that year, but it turned out to be a disaster. At first, Jimmie Lee was quite pleasant, but then the alcohol took it's toll and she became feisty. She chased the children out first and eventually got into a scrap with anyone in view. The noise brought the police but no one pressed the issue. Pat was unnerved at the disaster and avoided her friends. Her embarrassment and humiliation only intensified. She prayed more than ever that Jimmie would stop drinking.

Dear God, it's me again. I know we have this talk every so often, and I know You read the notes that I leave. But please make everything right. Let me find my real white family, the ones with all the money so that I can get them to help make everything all right for momma. She tries hard, and she means well, but she just don't know how to stop drinking. I'll leave the details up to You. Thank You dear God.

Jimmie kept everything a secret. Whenever Pat asked her Momma about her real mother, she always reacted the same way, "Keep that vision of your white momma in your thoughts, right in front. Cause someday, you'll find a way to get in touch with her."

"I don't even know what she looks like, how am I gonna find her?" Pat asked.

"I don't know what she looks like either, but when the time comes, you'll know. It's just not the time." Underneath her comforting words, Jimmie remained apprehensive about the thought of Pat leaving her.

Life was usually more peaceful for Pat in Los Angeles whenever she visited her relatives. But, over the last few years, she had noticed a distinct change in the atmosphere, particularly among her cousins' friends. Race was becoming more of an issue with everyone, and the hostility toward Pat was more evident. She was proud of her black heritage. She did whatever she could to let everyone know that she was of the same race. She spent most of her time in the sun hoping to darken her skin.

"You better not be out in that hot sun again," Dolly stated critically, "you gonna fry your skin and look like a piece of bacon, all wrinkly and stuff."

"No I'm ok, I use the baby oil to make it darker," Pat said.

"And what's going on with your hair, it's looking like a cross between a raw beet and a sweet potato?"

"Nothin's going on with my hair, I'm just getting older and it's getting darker."

"Darker! You mean dark red," Dolly said as she shook her head.

Pat dyed her light-colored hair a deep reddish-auburn and began to wear trendy sunglasses to cover her blue eyes. Neither helped very much, which forced her to reveal her birth certificate with the line that read: *Father: Negro.* She prized that worn-out document, with its fingerprints, smudge marks and darkened creases along the folds. She was proud to be black and gratified to prove it.

As civil rights became more of an issue during the sixtiess, and "Black Power" its battle cry, her commitment was to that which she knew to be right: that everyone has a right to live his or her own life without interference. It was now Pat's turn to prove to herself and the rest of her world that she, as a black, was not going to be shackled to the oars of a galley like her ancestors.

Many people she knew in Los Angeles from early childhood became suspicious of her efforts to assimilate into a political movement that was becoming less amorphous and more defined along racial lines. Some of her cousins stood up for her and defended her status. However, Deedee wasn't one of them. While they were all playing near Dolly's house, a few of the older black kids from the neighborhood goaded Deedee into going after the white girl. At first reluctant, she then confronted Pat. "Who do you think you are, you white bitch?" she yelled, "Trying to make yourself black. I'm gonna cut your throat!"

"What?" Pat jumped back, "What's the matter with you? I ain't no white bitch, don't call me one. I'm half-black and you know it, too."

"I don't know no such thing. You been parading yourself off as some sister, talkin' the talk, and walkin' the walk, but you're like a piece of cheap glass, we all see right through you. Why are you in my family, anyway?"

Deedee's encounter was both dramatic and unexpected and Pat didn't know what had set her off. Things were never quite the same between them. Most others in the community who knew Pat supported her efforts to be black. She managed to reciprocate by causing as little commotion as possible. She was afraid others wouldn't understand or believe her.

In Sparks, the situations were always different, but the state of affairs was the same. Sometimes when her black girlfriends at school spotted her talking to two or three of her white classmates, they'd say, "Hey Patty, what's going' on?" or, "Patty, what's you up to?" Hearing the way they called her "Patty" irritated her the most. She knew what they were trying to say. While she was with her friends and they would see a "brother" with a white girl, she would smirk right along with them and say, "Look at that—what's he doing with a patty?" Yet she couldn't get the "high sign" from a black brother or sister when they met as strangers on the street.

It was just as bad with her white friends. Pat loathed how they scorned the black folks and treated them like the cockroaches of society. She knew she was despised for being with them. No one accepted her for who she was, or who she wanted to be.

The early teenage years were confusing for her. She buried herself in reading books and writing in her diary.

White, White!
I ain't White . . .
See THIS
Printed for all to know
The proof
Of my birth
It says—Father: Negro

Pat was never comfortable with the terms "Negro" or "colored"; it was unbefitting. She was relieved when "black" became popular. Among the whites, however, "nigger" was used almost exclusively, particularly within her crowd.

Rosalie, one of the four white girls from school that was part of Pat's white clique, nudged the dark-haired Clara as she pointed toward the pretty blond girl walking toward them. "You're the new girl," she asked as the girl was within hearing, "from Florida, right?"

"Yes, how did you know?" She asked in a friendly manner.

"Everybody knows. There's no secrets around here," said Rosalie. She then introduced herself along with the other girls in the group.

Pat was polite and friendly. She encountered a new friend without any pre-conceived notions about her history. "What's it like in Florida, I've never been there?" Pat asked.

"Oh it's great there. Always sunny weather, lots of bugs, those big kind like you've never seen around here," she said, "I hated those."

"I heard there were alligators in the streets," Clara added. "Is that true?"

"Sometimes, but I never saw one, other than in the swamps. The only thing that was in the streets were lots of niggers," she said with a chuckle.

Rosalie gave a quick glance at Pat then said, "Pat's a nigger. Ain't ya Pat?" She then leered at Pat waiting for her reaction. Pat was unfazed. She was used to the negative air. She peered at Rosalie.

The new girl gave Pat a disdainful once over. "Is that true? You don't look like a nigger. You got blue eyes. There are no blue-eyed niggers where I come from."

"Well, I guess I'm the first. And I'm not a nigger, either. I'm half-black and half-white. My father's Negro. It says so on my birth certificate."

The new girl looked around at the others suspiciously. "Anybody else here mulatto?"

Clara giggled. "Nope, Pat's the only one."

The conversation turned to the other cliques for just a moment before the bell rang for everyone to return to the classrooms

That night, Pat wrote in her diary.

I listen to the Beatles,
I love their FREEDOM,
but I can't tell anyone.
how I feel.
It's difficult living
in two worlds,
Trying to keep HARMONY

between the races,
without showing favorites
toward one, or the other.
I got PRESSURE
from both sides
it makes for a complex
set of RULES
designed Just for me.

CHAPTER 13

It was past midnight when Pat awoke to a commotion outside. She peeked out the window and discovered a parked limousine with a chauffeur opening the door for Jimmie Lee and a thin, young woman who sparkled in the dim streetlight. She wore skin-tight gold sequined slacks with a matching top that opened at the middle, accentuating her breasts which pointed straight out, and very high-heeled gold shoes that looked impossible to walk in. She was younger than Jimmie Lee and much younger than the white chauffeur. He was tall and thin, with a black cap pulled down just enough to shadow his eyes allowing just a glimpse of a thin mustache. "Let's go inside," Jimmie said, "you can meet her, if she's still awake."

Pat rushed back to bed, closed her door and pulled the covers up, feigning sleep. She could barely overhear their conversation.

"Why do you want to see her?" the new voice asked but to no response.

"Geo's got reasons. Don't you?" Jimmie said.

"Don't call me that, ever . . . ever. Do you understand?"

There was a long silence. Pat thought that perhaps they were whispering, but then she heard the door open and close, the car drive off, and then a still silence from inside the house. A minute later, she heard the woman again. "What happened?"

"He gets like that every once in a while."

"Scary."

"Well, Jamila, we'll just let you stay here on the couch tonight. He ain't coming back tonight."

The next morning Pat awoke to this beautiful woman sitting at the table having a cigarette with her coffee. She looked startled but then quickly smiled. "You're a whole lot more than what Jimmie described." Pat's body was changing, more mature.

Jimmie stepped out from her room and added, "Yeah, and she's got those new bumps in her shirt. Soon they'll be stickin' out bigger than yours."

The young woman broke into a wide smile and then asked, "How old are you, about fifteen?" Her voice was soft, refined, and somewhat seductive in its tone, and that impressed Pat. In all the different neighborhoods that Pat lived, she was never exposed to anyone who looked so flashy, yet so seductive.

Jimmie answered, "She ain't old enough, that's all you gotta know."

The woman gave a cautious glance up at Jimmie and turned to Pat. "Hi Pat, my name is Jamila."

"I'm gonna be thirteen. Who was the other guy?" Pat asked.

Jimmie and Jamila looked at each other, then Jimmie said, "How'd you know about the other guy?"

"I heard you all come making noise last night. Who was he?"

"Never you mind. He was just the chauffeur."

"Then why'd he want to meet me?"

"'Cause I told him how pretty you were and he wanted to see for himself, that's all." Jimmie said, and then went off into the bathroom.

Jamila waited for Jimmie to close the door and then turned to Pat, "Please come sit down here for a minute, Pat. I got something I need to talk to you about," she said.

Pat was intrigued and impressed that someone of Jamila's sophistication wanted to speak to her in such a serious manner. "What do you want to talk to about?"

Jamila placed her finger to her lips and whispered, "Well, I'm a bit worried about you being here with your 'so called' momma. You don't belong with her. You know that, don't you?"

"Whadda ya mean? Of course I belongs with her. My real momma's not old enough to take me in, she's jus' a child herself."

"She may not have been old enough when you was born, but she's sure old enough now, right? Besides, you're much older and mature than most girls and it's time you thought about what you gonna do with yourself."

"I go to school, that's what I'm suppose to do," Pat said.

"School!" she said, "I'm not talking about school. I'm worried about you being here with that crazy black woman you's livin' with. That's what I'm talking about. You need to be independent of her . . . you need to be out on your own, and doing the things you want to do. Let me tell you something," the woman paused and looked down for a moment. "When I was your age I couldn't wait to get myself out of the house, and my mother wasn't anywhere near as crazy as Jimmie Lee.

"Now what do you really want to do?"

"Well," said Pat without hesitating an instant, "someday I want to find my real momma. But that's gonna take some time."

"It's gonna take some money, too, isn't it?" Jamila stated.

"I suppose."

"How much money you got?" Jamila continued.

"I don't got any money," Pat said sadly.

"Well, you could make some good money to live on and be away from that crazy black woman at the same time."

"How?"

"Just do what I do. I can get you a place to stay in Oakland. You'd have to share it in the beginning, but it wouldn't take long for you to be out on you own. And you'd get enough cash to go do what you want—buy clothes, jewelry—anything."

"What do you do?" Pat asked naively.

"Most of the time I just hang out. But occasionally I party with some special friends. It's not bad at all. Everybody gets to have a good time." They heard the toilet flush and Jamila placed her forefinger up to her mouth. The conversation ended.

Over the next few days, the dialogue continued intermittently, always when Jimmie was out of listening range. The day before Jamila was ready to leave for Oakland, she tried to persuade Pat to go with her one last time. Pat's visions focused on all that she would do with a lot of money, and how it could help Jimmie. It was the first time that she had thoughts of independence, and that excited her. Jamila seemed kind enough and sincere enough to take care of the details. It was very tempting to be able to live on her own, have a real job, and not have to worry about Jimmie getting drunk and crazy.

What Pat didn't realize was that Jimmie's stealth at keeping a cautious eye was far more focused with Jamila in the house. Jimmie stormed into the house. "Patta, outside!" and pointed toward the door, "Now, out, I mean right now, go outside."

Pat rushed from the kitchen without so much as a breath.

Without warning, Jimmie grabbed Jamila by the arm, "I been watchin' you spending time with my Patta, and I know what you been tellin' her, too! You ain't takin' nobody with you to work no streets as a whore! I know who you are . . . I know how you got to be so chummy with me . . . and I know the chauffeur a whole lot better than you. You see, Miss Jamila, the chauffeur and I go back a long way—more than a dozen years to be exact. You see, we got us a history together," she paused and looked toward the door, "and a whole lot more. So, you can tell your boss that she's stayin' with me. Now get your skinny black ass out!"

A stunned and angered look overcame Jamila as she backed away from Jimmie Lee. "Hey woman, this here girl don't belong with you." Jamila said, "She's not your daughter. I can make her some good money."

"Neither you nor that sick fuck is gonna get your hands on her." Jimmie leered at Jamila, "You better get your whore ass outta my house now. I'll protect her from you and your pimp with my life." With one swift motion, Jimmie had the large knife from the kitchen counter pointed right in the woman's face. "Get the fuck outta my house."

Jamila's eyes lit up. She quickly snatched her belongings and rushed out the door, never to be heard from again.

CHAPTER 14

Pat was twelve years old and attending Sparks Junior High when her attention turned toward the opposite sex, particularly any good-looking black boys. The notice was reciprocated by more than a cursory glance, partly because of her now budding figure, which encouraged her to jot down her measurements each week, and partly for her complexion. She realized the lightness of her skin was an advantage rather than a liability.

A large commercial laundry hired her momma as a folder. Jimmie's fun-loving ways and outrageous antics attracted a like-minded group that she quickly assimilated into her clique. Pat rarely paid attention to momma's friends that frequently milled about the house, with the exception of Rudy, a man who was different from the others. Although slight in stature, the cut of his muscles wrapped tightly around his wiry frame made him quite conspicuous. He appeared much younger than his twenty-eight years with a light, olive complexion. His wavy black hair laid close-cut along the sides, a perfect frame for his smooth, soft face and bright sexy smile. He had a flat butt that, when viewed from behind, made him appear to be white. Most of the girls thought it was cute, but a few thought he looked Filipino rather than black. All of them, including Jimmie, had a crush on Rudy. At the gathering, he eyed Pat.

"I'm Jimmie Lee's daughter," she said.

Rudy feigned surprise "Get away! You're shittin' me!"

"No, it's true. She's my momma." Pat said smiling.

"You don't look alike."

Pat passed on her story and then asked why he was with such an older crowd. He didn't look more than nineteen.

"I just moved to Reno and I'm staying with my brother and sister-in-law. I took this job at the laundry until a better one opens up," he said.

"Yeah, but what are you doin' with them?" Pat asked.

"Oh, Jimmie Lee invited me over for something to eat and a beer. I didn't want to go home, so I came along."

Pat was fascinated with him, not only because he was handsome, or that his spirited, brown eyes were far more penetrating then anyone she had ever met, but also she found him to be very bright. When they chatted, she felt his undivided attention.

Over the next few weeks, Pat looked forward to his frequent visits. Each time, Rudy occupied the center of attention. The sixteen-year difference in their ages made the flirting subtle. She preferred to believe that her image was that of a sweet and innocent young lady living under rather unusual circumstances. In reality, she was much more mature for her age than any of her friends or relatives. She longed to be held and loved. Of course, she was aware of Jimmie's wrath and notorious temper and it kept her from showing even the slightest hint of romance.

Although Rudy never said more than a "Hello, good-bye," and "How ya doin', Pat," he managed to let her know, inconspicuously, that he wanted to be alone with her. The ploy was not to let Jimmie know what was going on.

Over the years, Pat learned many ways to get what she wanted without Jimmie knowing. Some of her methods were successful, others not. But when it came to Rudy, the stakes were higher. Pat fretted over what Jimmie would do to her if she became aware of even the slightest hint of her growing interest in Rudy.

Late one afternoon when Pat returned from school, Jimmie was home entertaining a few friends. She looked a bit ragged. Cigarette butts, coffee cups, and empty cans of beer were strewn about. People had been dropping in on her all day. Pat cleaned up a little in the kitchen, and then went about primping herself in an unusual experimental manner, striving to rearrange her hair or other part of her features to look more seductive. When it came to fashion, Pat was self-directed, never looking the same way twice, nor accepting any criticism from her friends.

After about twenty minutes of primping and trying to untangle another hair experiment that went awry, she heard laughter from the kitchen. She took notice of only one voice among all the others that made her skin quiver. It was Rudy. Quickly, she finished pampering her hair, took a deep breath, and burst out of the bathroom like a star athlete ready for a trophy. All eyes turned toward her, but she noticed only one. Casually, he glanced at her for just a second, but it was enough for her—he knew she was there.

They continued with their banter and laughter while Pat pretended to listen. Jimmie became bored and tired with drinking, and was in no mood to put up with a lot of people. As the chatter lagged, someone suggested that they all go to a movie. Jimmie declined, admitting that she was too tired. Rudy asked her if it would be all right if Pat came with them since they were all going together. To her surprise, Jimmie never hesitated and agreed without even a warning.

Seven of them piled into one of the cars and within a few minutes they were standing in line waiting to buy tickets to see *Sex and the Single Girl*. Pat was more than overjoyed. It wasn't as if they were on a date together, but they were almost alone out of Jimmie's reach. She had read enough True Romance books to know what to do next. She was prepared and hungry. Rudy and Pat sat next to each other, and before you knew it, she had him in a passionate embrace. There was no hesitation on her part. Pat was ready and willing to let him do anything he wanted. But quickly he pulled away.

"You're crazy, girl!" he whispered. "What's you tryin' to do—get me lynched?"

She sat up straight and realized that there were quite a few white people in the theater. Some of them, she was sure, wouldn't take the time to listen to her mixed-blood story.

Rudy looked at her. Pat returned the glance as lustfully as she could. She placed her hand on his leg and scratched gently, just like the woman in one of her novels. He folded his arms to mask the motion as he cautiously touched her. She wiggled slowly in her seat to get closer to him, trying not to look so obvious. "We need to be out of here," he whispered. "Let's go to the car."

Pat nodded and together they quietly exited the theater. Their first encounter in the car was uneasy. Her over-heated body kept her emotions in a state of chaos. But the first act of passion cooled it down and changed her forever.

"Are you OK?" Rudy asked afterward. When she didn't answer, he held his hand up to her face and kissed her tenderly. He smiled at her. "You're beautiful," he said.

She didn't feel beautiful. She felt ashamed, dirty, and dumb, but she wasn't going to let him know. He was the first person to show her the physical affection that she so desperately longed for, and she wasn't about to let him go.

"It was beautiful!" she said, then looked into his eyes and kissed him. "I love you, Rudy. I love you so much!"

He glanced down at his wristwatch and quickly started the car. "We'd better get going. The movie's gonna be out in just a few minutes. We don't want anyone to know where we've been. Oh, and don't forget. We can't let anyone know about this, OK?"

"I'll do anything you want—anything!"

"Good, then let's just keep this a secret."

When they returned to the theater, everyone was just walking out. She stayed in the car and acted as though nothing had happened. If she were ever going to see Rudy again, it would be impossible to say anything to anyone.

The following day she moped around the house, hoping that she would see Rudy again. In a naive attempt to heal, she was very careful not to be too active. Her emotions were mixed with remorse and elation, each jostling the other for position. When Rudy stopped in a few days later, the former lost out and she was again euphoric—in love for the first time.

For the next few months, not a moment went by without her thinking of Rudy and all the wonderful love he was giving her—something she felt she had been missing her entire life. They pretended not to notice each other while in the company of anyone even remotely connected to either one of them, sneaking away at every opportunity to be alone.

Rudy increased the frequency of his visits. Jimmie mistakenly believed that she, certainly not Pat, was the object of Rudy's attentions. But gradually, Jimmie Lee's suspicions surfaced. She noticed the subtle difference in Pat's attitude when Rudy was around. And more so each time she had another drink. For a short while, it became a game between Jimmie and Pat. Pat trying to hide any evidence that she was even remotely aware that Rudy existed, and Jimmie snooping about Pat's room trying to uncover any indication of the same—whether real or imaginary.

Pat never knew how Jimmie Lee finally found out about them. The only person who knew of their affair was Inez, Rosie's niece, who found out when she returned a jump suit that she borrowed from Pat weeks earlier. After a session of lovemaking with Rudy, some wet spots were visible on Pat's bed. Looking down at the mess, Inez asked surprisingly, "What's that?"

Pat took notice and her face turned red, "That's Rudy's," she said.

"Rudy's? Rudy's what?" Inez asked

"Rudy's stuff!"

"What were you doing with him?" Inez asked, even as she understood the answer. "How long has this been going on?" she began, but added, "Never mind. I don't want to know."

Inez shook her head and started pacing back and forth. "I can't believe this. I'm older than you and I'm still a virgin, and you—out screwing the finest wolf in the whole damn forest—my own cousin." Inez sat down in the chair opposite the bed.

"You are fast, girl. I mean F-A-S-T. I heard of some fast women in my time, but you are faster than any of them. I can't even get a boy to take a second look at me. I've got no shape, just straight—no hips, no breasts, just blue eyes! And everyone's afraid of them. Huh! Shit, girl. You got tits and everything! My Lord!"

Pat chuckled, but then she got serious. "You're not gonna tell Jimmie, are you?"

"Tell Jimmie! Are you crazy, girl? Why, if she even hint at a thing goin' on between you and Rudy, she'd cut my tongue out first, then choke you with it . . . and then she go after Rudy. Huh! I ain't no fool. I don't tell that woman nothin'—especially since she's got the hots for Rudy in the first place. That's all she has to do is find out you been cuttin' in on her stuff. I wouldn't want to be around when that happens! No shit sister! Not this child!"

Pat felt safe confiding in Inez. Inez knew Jimmie and feared her as much as anyone, but rather than allowing Jimmie to interfere with her life, Inez avoided any contact with her aunt for a while.

Pat and Rudy made love at every opportunity . . . sometimes at his brother's apartment, sometimes in the back of his car, and once in while, when they felt exceptionally daring, in her own bed while Jimmie was away. Pat loved Rudy. All she wanted to do was get married. Although they did their best to keep the tryst private, more people seemed to know what was going on between them. For a while, everyone she met either gave an evil eye because they were jealous, or the high sign and a wink. The latter made her feel wonderful. She gloated over the attention, secure in the knowledge that she was, indeed, very special for capturing the most prized stud in the whole world—at least the world as she knew it.

A few months after she met Rudy, Pat was sitting in her room reading a magazine when Jimmie burst through the front door, slamming it shut. There was silence for a minute and Pat didn't pay much attention, thinking that Jimmie probably had gone off to bed. Just as Pat started to reread a passage from a book, her concentration was broken. Jimmie appeared, her silhouette framed in the doorway to Pat's room, her breathing was rapid, forceful, like a locomotive building up steam. Pat felt sheer terror and instant guilt.

"Is this the way you pay me back for watchin' out for you your whole life? I protected you from all the whites trying to take you away, from the cops, from Big Momma, who was gonna give you away. And this is how you treat me!"

Pat cowered, wildly trying to guess the cause of this episode.

"You're only thirteen years old! And you're going to get pregnant!"

"What!" gasped Pat. "Pregnant?!"

"Did you think you could wrinkle the sheets with Rudy and not get knocked up? You wouldn't know what to do at all. You don't know nothing about nothing and here you go sleep with a man who's old enough to be your father! What the fuck is wrong with you? Are you crazy, you stupid white shit?"

Pat noticed her momma's eyes well up with hurt.

"You're nothing but goddamn white trash, sneakin' round, trying to get one over on me. Well, sister, you ain't smart enough, and you ain't pretty enough—and I ain't putting' up with no white patty tramp like you. You had your last goddamn ball in my house!"

Jimmie barked non-stop. Pat sprang to her feet on the far side of the twin-sized bed, trying to keep some distance between her and the impending violence. Jimmie lunged, swinging wildly, repeatedly missing her target with three out of four strikes. Pat relaxed when she realized that Jimmie's punches lacked power in her semi-impaired state.

Without waiting for panic to paralyze her, Pat spryly leaped to one side and scurried out of the room, leaving Jimmie sprawled on the bed. As she reached the far side of the kitchen table for protection, she detected Homer standing at the door.

"What all's going on here?" he asked.

Jimmie burst from the bedroom. "You mind your own damn business. This is my daughter and I'll do with her as I please!"

She turned to Pat and yelled, "Come here, you little whore, I'm gonna kick your ass all over this house!"

Homer tried to intercede but was swept aside. With Pat out of reach on the other side of the table, Jimmie groped for a weapon only to find a wooden spoon on the counter. Jimmie swung both ways and missed twice. Pat winced, protecting her face with her arms as Jimmie threw the spoon, stinging her on the arm.

"Stop it! Stop it!" pleaded Pat, tears coursing down her cheeks. "I love him. I want to marry him!"

"It'll be over my dead body if you do," screamed Jimmie as she began hurling anything loose: an empty tuna can, forks, paper napkins, an ashtray. "And my body ain't dead yet, so you can get your damn white ass outta here, cause I don't want you around anymore!

"And if you think that he loves you—ha! You just white trash. All he wants is to put it to you," she hissed, pointing toward the door. "So get your ass out. Go on, out!"

Still smarting from the objects thrown at her, Pat's wet cheeks were met by a cold blast of winter air as she opened the door, reached around for a sweater on the back of a chair and fled. Jimmie rushed after her, but Homer again interceded.

"Hey, Baby, you actin' like a fool. You're scaring the shit out of poor Pat. What's the matter wit you anyway?"

"I told you to mind your own business," growled Jimmie, "before I crack your head open! This is between that white hussy and me. I don't want her in this house no more. Let her do her trashy shit someplace else!"

CHAPTER 15

Pat stood in the cold night air with only a sweater to keep her warm. As she stepped away from the house, she felt the weight lifting from her shoulders. The light snowfall calmed her nerves. From the far side of Homer's old Packard, she heard the shouting and watched Jimmie's shadow bounce between the windows as she raged about the room. Suddenly, it all seemed as if it was something from another world—a lifetime away.

She turned and searched the dimly lit street for a friendly sign, but the houses that she had known most of her life suddenly seemed foreign and distant and smaller. She felt alone and lost. There were no angels about, only Homer's old car that provided shelter from the freezing elements. She climbed into the back seat where the broken window had been covered up by thin cardboard. The snow seeped in through the cracks and she still felt the cold breezes chilling her nose.

It was almost an hour before Homer opened the car door. "Hey, Pat, you must be frozen out here," he said as he covered her frigid body with a heavy blanket from her bed. It was the most comfort anyone had given her. Still, she spent the rest of the night with very little sleep, shivering to stay warm.

At daybreak, the snow stopped and the sun rose over the mountain. The house was silent. Down the street, she could hear someone warming up a car. The windows were covered with snow. The morning light brought with it some resolve. Without hesitation or thought, she walked over to the Gastons to wake up Joyce.

"What are you doing here so early in the morning?" Mrs. Gaston asked as she opened the door. "Is there someplace you and Joyce were planning on going?"

"Ah, no, Mrs. Gaston, Joyce don't know I'm here, but I can't go home," Pat said as she bowed her head. "Momma threw me out and I just wanted to get warm. Can I come in?"

Mrs. Gaston stared, and then glanced over Pat's shoulder to see if anyone else was around. "Yeah, of course, come in, come in. Let me get you some breakfast." She led her into the house and called for Joyce to get up. "Look at you, with those wrinkled clothes, reddened eyes, and hair plastered flat on one side, and tangled on the other. Where you been?"

"I slept in Homer's car last night." She told her what happened and soon Joyce was there listening intently to all of the details. They were naturally upset, but not surprised, knowing Jimmie Lee the way they did.

After they ate and Pat warmed up, she asked to use the phone.

"Who you gonna call, your momma?" asked Mrs. Gaston. "I'm sure she's worried sick over you."

"No," said Pat. "I got to call Rudy."

Joyce and her mother looked at each other, and then at Pat. Now they were stunned as they watched Pat dial the phone.

Rudy was sympathetic, but distant. "What are you going to do? Who you gonna stay with?"

"I want to stay with you. I love you and you love me. You said so. We have to get married," she said.

"Married?" Rudy said. The silence hung like a bead of water waiting to drop from the tip of an icicle. "Are you pregnant?"

"No, I'm not pregnant. Least I don't think so. But what's that got to do with it? You want us to be together, don't you?" Pat asked.

"Yeah, Sugar, you know I do," said Rudy. "But I got to tell you, the timing is real bad, I mean real, real bad."

"Why, what's wrong with now? What's going on?"

Born white, but adopted by an African American family, Fauna
believed she was biracial and her name was Pat for the first
twenty-two years of her life.

Fauna grew up in Sparks, Nevada in the 1950s. She is shown here (right) with her childhood friends from the predominantly African American neighborhood.

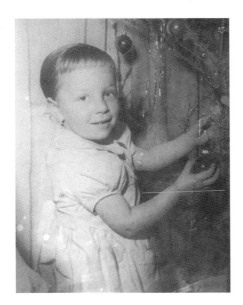

Fauna, Christmas, 1950s, Sparks, Nevada.

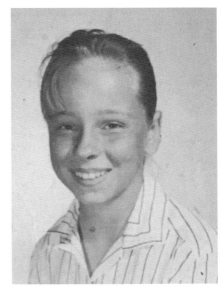

Fauna, age eleven, Sparks, Nevada.

Jimmie Lee (Momma) with Fauna, 1975,
Reno, Nevada.

Homer, the only father figure to Fauna,
who she loved and adored. Homer and
Jimmie Lee raised Fauna together from
the time she was a little girl.

Fauna, age fourteen,
Reno, Nevada.

Big Momma, Jimmie Lee's mother, was Fauna's guardian angel and grandmother.

Fauna, age fifteen, with Bobby, her first husband, who is father to Yvette.

Fauna and Billy (Fauna's second husband) in San Diego, California.

Fauna, age sixteen, working as a candy striper at the hospital where she discovered information about her biological family.

REGISTRATION DISTRICT NO. 3801	REGISTRAR NUMBER	CERTIFICATE OF LIVE BIRTH	STATE FILE NO.

THIS CHILD
1a. CHILD'S FIRST NAME: Fauna
1b. MIDDLE NAME:
1c. LAST NAME: Hodel
2. SEX: Female
3a. THIS BIRTH SINGLE TWIN OR TRIPLET?: Single
3b. IF TWIN OR TRIPLET THIS CHILD BORN 1ST 2ND 3RD?:
4a. DATE OF BIRTH — MONTH, DAY, YEAR: August 1, 1951
4b. HOUR: 10:15P

PLACE OF BIRTH
5a. PLACE OF BIRTH — CITY OR TOWN (IF OUTSIDE CORPORATE LIMITS WRITE RURAL AND NAME OF NEAREST TOWN): San Francisco
5b. COUNTY: San Francisco
5. FULL NAME AND ADDRESS OF HOSPITAL OR INSTITUTION — IF NOT IN HOSPITAL OR INSTITUTION, GIVE STREET ADDRESS OR LOCATION: St. Elizabeth's Infant Hospital, 100 Masonic Avenue, San Francisco

USUAL RESIDENCE OF MOTHER
6a. RESIDENCE OF MOTHER STREET ADDRESS (IF RURAL GIVE LOCATION): 1543 Vallejo Street
6b. COUNTY: San Francisco
6c. CITY OR TOWN (IF OUTSIDE CORPORATE LIMITS WRITE RURAL AND NAME OF NEAREST TOWN): San Francisco
6d. STATE: California

MOTHER OF CHILD
7a. MAIDEN NAME OF MOTHER—FIRST NAME: Tamar
7b. MIDDLE NAME: Nais
7c. LAST NAME: Hodel
8. COLOR OR RACE OF MOTHER: White
9. AGE OF MOTHER (AT TIME OF THIS BIRTH): 16 YEARS
10. BIRTHPLACE (STATE OR FOREIGN COUNTRY): San Francisco, Cal.
11. MAILING ADDRESS OF MOTHER (IF DIFFERENT FROM USUAL RESIDENCE): 100 Masonic Ave., S.F.

FATHER OF CHILD
12a. NAME OF FATHER — FIRST NAME: Information withheld
12b. MIDDLE NAME: concerning father
12c. LAST NAME:
13. COLOR OR RACE OF FATHER: Negro
14. AGE OF FATHER (AT TIME OF THIS BIRTH): YEARS
15. BIRTHPLACE (STATE OR FOREIGN COUNTRY):
16. USUAL OCCUPATION:
16b. KIND OF BUSINESS OR INDUSTRY:

INFORMANT'S CERTIFICATION
17a. SIGNATURE OF PARENT OR OTHER INFORMANT: *Tamar Nais Hodel*
17b. DATE SIGNED: 8-2-51

ATTENDANT'S CERTIFICATION
18a. SIGNATURE OF ATTENDANT: *Harold P. Gosselam M.D.*
18b. ADDRESS: 145 Guerrero

REGISTRAR'S CERTIFICATION
19. DATE RECEIVED BY LOCAL REGISTRAR: AUG 8 1951
20. SIGNATURE OF LOCAL REGISTRAR
21. DATE ON WHICH GIVEN NAME ADDED

13 COLOR OR RACE OF FATHER
Negro

Fauna's original birth certificate. Note the "Color or Race of Father" as "Negro."

George Hodel, Fauna's biological grandfather and the prime suspect in the Black Dahlia murder. (New York Daily News Archive / Contributor)

Tamar Hodel, Fauna's biological mother.

Fauna (right) with her sister, Deborah Elizabeth (AKA Fauna 2).

George Hodel's house in Hollywood, The Sowden House, which was designed by Frank Lloyd Wright's eldest son, Lloyd Wright.

Elizabeth Short, AKA The Black Dahlia, was found murdered in 1947. (FBI)

Fauna, age eighteen, holding baby Yvette on her second birthday, celebrating at Jimmie Lee's house in Reno, 1969.

Fauna, age twenty-eight, with her daughters, Yvette, age twelve, and Rasha, age one, 1979, Honolulu, Hawaii.

"Well, nothing's going on, that's the point. It's just that I don't got no place of my own and I ain't got the scratch to get one. So how we gonna live? Where we gonna live? Besides, you're thirteen years old."

"I'm gonna be fourteen."

"Right, fourteen, like that's gonna make a difference. We can't just get married. What do you think they'd do to me?" he said, then mumbled to himself soft enough for Pat to hear, "Gettin' married to a white looking momma who's not even a teenager." His voice lifted, "They'll put my ass in jail and send the key to Mars. They'd never let me out."

Suddenly, he sounded like a stranger to Pat. She felt a chill from inside her heart. There was silence on the phone, not even the sound of his breath. "I see," she said sorrowfully. "I understand. But what am I supposed to do?" She was devastated.

He responded immediately. "You should get a hold of one of your aunts in Los Angeles and tell them what's happened. They'll send you bus money quicker than shit. Besides, if your momma's on the warpath, then this ain't no place to be."

The suggestion was a good one, even though she was surprised by his cold response.

Mrs. Gaston called Aunt Lucille, who was outraged by her sister's handling of Pat's first love affair. She promised to send a bus ticket for Pat so that she could come stay with her in Los Angeles. Jimmie sent Homer over to the Gastons with her clothes neatly packed in a suitcase, along with all of her other belongings. When that happened, Pat knew for sure there was no way Jimmie was going to let her back in the house. Going to Los Angeles seemed the only choice.

A day or so later, the bus ticket arrived and she said her good-byes to Joyce and her other friends. It seemed she was going forever and her sadness was visible.

Pat boarded the bus, anxious to begin her life without fear and hopelessness. Yet, she knew she would be back, if for no other reason than to be with Rudy.

On the way to LA, Pat had plenty of time to think. She added some reflections to her diary.

In a drunken stupor
She ordered,
"Bitch, outta my house,
"Sleep in the car!"
I prayed in the car
. . . mostly I cried

But all she could think of was Rudy and how her life had changed since she met him.

Thirteen,
and the only "Love"
I knew Was the "Love"
I got When I "Gave"

Johnny's enthusiasm when he met her at the bus station was encouraging; she felt honored.

"We're gonna walk to the school to meet my sister, Barbara." he said, "That way, we can all go home together."

"It feels so different down here this time." Pat said.

"Well, you with me now, not your momma. You gonna feel the freedom."

As they neared the entrance to the school, a police car drew near them and slowed. "Keep walking,'" Johnny said tensely.

"Why?" she asked. "What's going on?"

"Never mind, just don't stop fo' nothing."

Suddenly, she heard a cop yell out, "Hey, boy. Where do you think you're going?"

"Who, me?" Johnny asked, and then whispered: "Get moving.'" So she did just that.

"Yeah, Boy. You. Come over here."

Johnny obeyed and slowly sauntered over to the car. Pat didn't hear what they were saying, and she was frightened enough not to look back. She wasn't more than a half-block away when the cop pulled up next to her in the car and stepped out. She stared at Johnny in the back seat, trying not to act ignorant.

"What's your name, Miss?"

"Fauna Hodel." She gave her real name.

"What are you doing here with him?"

The tone in his voice angered her and her defenses were alerted. "He's my cousin, and we're on our way to pick up my other cousin who goes to school here. And then we're goin' home."

"What's in the suitcase?"

"My clothes and stuff."

"Open it up. Let me take a look."

While standing in front of the school, Pat opened the suitcase. The officer began flinging the contents onto the pavement. She could hear the giggles when her bra hit the sidewalk in view of everyone and tried to maintain her composure as her face went flush. When he appeared to be satisfied with the humiliation, he told her to get in the back of the police car. They treated Pat very politely, but ridiculed Johnny as if he were a criminal. *These two overgrown cowboys, emissaries from the City of Angels, berating my innocent cousin, what bigots!* She kept her thoughts to herself, too frightened to be angry. They drove off to the police station and placed her into a holding area. For about two hours, she sat wondering what this was all about. Suddenly, Pat heard Aunt Lucille's voice echo through the hall.

"The boy's my son, and the girl's my niece. She came down here from Reno to stay with me, and you don't got no right to hold them. I want them released—right now! I'm a righteous God-fearing woman and an elder in my church. If I got to, I'll get the minister and the whole congregation down here telling you the same thing!"

After twenty minutes of haranguing, the police finally remanded them to her custody and freed them from the confines of the dirty cell. Aunt Lucille wasn't angry with Johnny or Pat, only with the police. They dismissed the incident and vowed to be careful to not provide any reason for suspicion in the future.

Even before the civil rights protests, the assassination of Malcolm X, and the riots in Watts, the blacks were always the first to be questioned for even the slightest infractions, whether real or imaginary. And now Pat was feeling the true effects of being black.

That night, Pat again wrote in her diary:

They say we: We say they:
niggers cheat . . . . . *cheated niggers*
niggers steal . . . . . . *sold niggers*
niggers con. . . . . . . *conned niggers*
niggers rape . . . . . . *raped niggers*
niggers kill. . . . . . . *killed niggers*

Not even knowing
Who or what
I was . . .
No wonder!
I wasn't accepted
I couldn't even
Accept myself

For the first few days, everything was peaceful in Los Angeles. Aunt Lucille went about her business as usual, Barbara continued to go to school each day, and Johnny and Pat spent most of the time together. Pat couldn't enroll in school for at least another two weeks. Each afternoon, she would go out and see what was going on in the neighborhood. Some of the kids she knew, but because of her light skin, most were very distrustful of her.

On the third day, while she was washing the dishes, she heard Johnny talking to someone at the front door. "No, she ain't here," she heard him say. "I don't know when she's coming back. Maybe never!" Seconds later, he rushed into the kitchen, his eyes widened like an owl's.

"We got two dicks at the door asking questions about you," he said, "I told 'em that you weren't here."

"Why they looking for me? I ain't done nothing wrong."

"Don't know, but I ain't gonna let 'em know where you're at. I know how these cops are. Once they get a hold of you, they never let go!"

"Yeah, but I ain't done nothin." Just as she said that, she saw the two men looking through the kitchen window at her. Before she knew it, they were at the front door again and there was no place for her to hide. They took her into custody for being a runaway.

Jimmie had filed a complaint against Pat in Reno in order to get her back, telling the police where she would be in Los Angeles. The police would not return Pat to Reno unless Jimmie sent a bus ticket. Jimmie decided that letting Pat spend a night or two in Juvenile Hall would be her way of punishing her for stealing Rudy away. It was easier doing it that way than calling Pat or Lucille on the telephone and going through a heated argument. Jimmie was vengeful, and still very angry at Pat for going out with Rudy. She was angrier still at her sister for taking her in.

Juvenile Hall, however, was no place for the fainthearted. Pat felt fear the moment she entered—a loneliness unprotected by Homer and the safety of her neighborhood. Not even the wrath of her momma frightened her as much. This was a new world and Pat's initiation into the California Penal System was humiliating. She was stripped, searched, scrubbed, disinfected, and inspected painstakingly by two middle-age women who'd had more than their share of practice.

She was then located in a female holding cell with ten other juveniles. All were either Hispanic or black and appeared to be veterans of the system. For ten days and nights, as the only white-skinned girl, she was deemed an outcast and left alone, a situation she welcomed. She overheard their stories, watched them in anger, or in a moment of joy, or having sex, or in pain. It was both an education and a revulsion. LA was far removed from the spirit of Sparks.

Each day was filled with boredom, anxiety, and frustration. She didn't know how long she would be there, nor was she aware of anyone helping her to get out. No one from her family came to visit. The fear from not knowing what would become of her life continually weighed heavy on her. She cried herself to sleep each night.

On the tenth day, she was informed that a bus ticket, sent by her mother in Reno, was waiting for her. An escort from Juvenile Hall drove her to the depot and gave her ten cents out of his own pocket. She left before lunch, glad just to get out of Los Angeles.

CHAPTER 16

Jimmie and Pat didn't say much to each other that evening—no pleasantries, no questions, no story telling. The tension was there, but they were both too emotionally drained to begin to sort out all that had happened over the past two weeks, let alone the animosity Pat had harbored for the past twelve years. There was so much they needed to say, but Pat knew it would be a waste of energy to confront Jimmie now. All of it was becoming tiresome. All she wanted, was to be left alone to experience a normal, uneventful life like other people.

Jimmie was humming an unfamiliar tune while her eyes were half-closed. Pat stared at her, a woman she now considered pathetic. Pat's mind wandered toward her real mother. *Would knowing who she was perhaps energize Pat's life?* Pat began to feel closer to this faceless stranger than ever before. At the same time, she felt guilty for wanting to be with her. Pat still felt loyal to Jimmie.

In the days that followed, Jimmie and Pat acted quite civil toward each other, almost as though they were old friends. There were no apologies. Each of them allowed the other the time to heal their wounded egos. Finally Jimmie confessed that she didn't want her baby Pat to grow up too fast.

Pat's longing for Rudy continued. It was difficult at first to make contact with him. Jimmie had let it be known that Pat was off limits to boys, not to mention men, particularly Rudy. At first, he refused Pat's phone calls, but about a month later, when Pat finally did get to talk with him, it was as though they had never been apart. The romance still burned. They snuck off together as often as possible, making love whenever they were alone. Rudy was very cautious about their being seen together. He maintained a healthy fear of Jimmie's temper. But Pat's thoughts of Rudy occupied all of her time. Her obsession to marry him intensified and Pat became careless. Jimmie again found out that Pat was seeing Rudy.

It was a Sunday afternoon and Reverend Mayfield was visiting with Jimmie at the house, enjoying a beer or two. Pat was doodling on a piece of paper at the kitchen table while pretending to do her homework. "Looks like you got somethin' else on your mind besides your school work," Jimmie said to her. Pat didn't answer.

Then Reverend Mayfield said, "Yeah, I think I know what it is."

Pat noticed Jimmie steal a glance toward him. "Never mind, 'you know what it is.' If you kept your mind off the sisters and your hands off the bottle, you wouldn't have no problems."

Mayfield just raised his eyebrows and took another sip from his drink, then said, "The only problems I got is to keep the church filled."

Jimmie put her hands on her hips, looked straight at Mayfield, then said, "Well, Rev. 'give-me-more-for-the-building-fund' Mayfield, you spent so much time raffling this and baking that, borrowing from everywhere, then hounding everybody for more, and more, and more, that they just fed up with you begging."

"Well sure, that's true enough, but how else was I supposed to build the church? Now, I got to support it out of my own pocket," he said with his nose in the air.

"You didn't have to build the biggest, chicken fried, pie baking and most expensive church in the whole State of Nevada. You could've done with a lot less. Those diehard churchgoers you got would've listened to you anywhere. Shit, you could preach to them from the back of a pickup, they don't care," she said.

His reputation as a womanizer and drinker cost him his congregation. Few regular parishioners attended his services and those that did, continued to gossip about his carousing. He maintained control of the Sunday school, but he had to force the children to go to his services.

Every Sunday he chauffeured all the children from their homes, and bribed them with money just to add bodies to his otherwise empty church. He would buy lunch and chauffeur everyone home after he was through preaching. They went just for the money and food and to have a good time. He spent every dime trying to keep his church open.

The dreamy-eyed teenager kept doodlin', half-listening to them chat about nothing important. But Jimmie interrupted her again. "What's the matter," she said. "Ain't you talkin' today?" Jimmie looked casually at Mayfield.

"You were right the first time," he said. "That child is far away from here. She must be in love!"

When Pat heard the word "love," her heart jumped. She looked up at Mayfield and wondered what he was talking about. As she turned toward her momma, their eyes locked. Pat saw her guilt reflected in Jimmie's hardened gaze. Pat tried to cover up the scribbles, but it was too late.

"Rudy!" Jimmie rasped as she leaned over the scrapbook. "Is that all you been thinkin' about?"

"No! Of course not!" Pat answered.

"Then why you writin' his name, doin' all those scratches over that pad? You think if you draw his picture he'll pop right out of that damn paper—just like a cartoon? Huh . . . that ain't never gonna happen, cause you ain't never gonna see that man again!"

"Sounds like little Pat has herself a boyfriend," Mayfield chimed in grinning.

Pat saw Jimmie's head turn toward him, her finger in his face, "You mind you own damn business! She ain't got no damn boyfriend!" Jimmie said.

Mayfield held up a hand. "Hold on there, Miss Jimmie. You shouldn't talk to me like that. And besides, Pat should be going out with young boys her own age—to parties and all. It's natural. Why, when I was her age. . . ."

"I don't care what you was doin' at her age," said Jimmie. "You ain't my damn daughter. And you ain't in heat over some twenty-eight-year-old Casanova!"

"Ahhh, I see," said Mayfield. "it's just a phase she's going through. She'll get over it in no time at all."

Pat sat in awe, watching the two of them discuss her life and her heart as if they knew what she was feeling. She covered her ears, trying to block out the embarrassment and moved her mind into her dream world.

"It ain't no phase," said Jimmie. "She's already tasted his sweet cakes and that's only gonna make her want more."

"You can't blame her for that, living in a promiscuous environment like this. It's your fault. You're the biggest influence. The Bible says. . . ."

"The Bible says shit!" exploded Jimmie "You don't know what you're talking about!"

"Jimmie Lee," said Mayfield, "it's because you haven't been going to my church and listening to my sermons, that's why you let things like this happen. Why, I know this Bible inside and out, and it's your responsibility to take care of her moral upbringing."

"Don't you talk to me about 'moral upbringing,'," Jimmie snarled. "Not when you out screwing all the sisters like there's no tomorrow. And another thing, if you stayed off the bottle, your church'd grow like scum on a pond."

Mayfield's eyes widened. Pat saw the defensive look of a man with exposed secrets. "What do you mean?" he said. "Why, I live by what I preach. I live by the Bible. I've read it through and through—seven times. And I know everything in it."

Jimmie Lee sprang to her feet and scowled at the flustered preacher. "You may have read it through and through, but until "it" goes through you—you don't tell me a shittin' thing!"

She turned toward Pat and continued, "And as for you, Miss, if I ever hear any more shit 'bout you sneakin' round wit' Rudy, I'll kick your queeny white ass into Thursday!"

"I didn't do nothing. And I ain't white! I may look white, but I. . . ." Before Pat could catch her breath and finish her statement, the preacher, now indignant, stood up, stuffed his hat onto his head and said, "You had better mend your ways, Sister, or the Lord's gonna come down on you like a truckload a wet tobacco!"

"And you had better mind your own business," Jimmie interjected, "or I'm gonna come down on you with the fat end of that bottle! Now get your lumpy ass outta here."

"You ain't heard the end of this, Jimmie Lee Faison!" Mayfield stormed out of the house, mumbling something about the wrath of God evicting Jimmie. She ignored his remark and focused her attention on Pat, simultaneously pouring herself another drink.

"But Momma, I really love Rudy!" Pat blurted out. "And I want to marry him."

Jimmie stood with the glass up to her lips. She said nothing, then slowly placed the glass down on the table and folded her arms, sitting in silence. Finally she said, "OK, Miss Know-It-All, if you want to marry Rudy—then that's what you'll do."

The following day, Jimmie went to the courthouse to find out the legal requirements to marry at thirteen. Pat was anxious and overjoyed at the idea. She immediately called Rudy to let him in on the wonderful news. But to her surprise, he wasn't as enthusiastic. He was aloof and guarded, trying to dismiss the exciting news as just another plan that would go awry. At the time, Pat was unaware that he was being pressured by his brother and sister-in-law to stop seeing Pat altogether. Not because she wasn't a nice person, but because she was only thirteen years old, which was young enough to keep Rudy in jail for a long time.

When Jimmie returned with the details from the court, Pat realized that she wasn't as mature as she thought. The law was clear. Pat had to wait until her sixteenth birthday. The love she longed for was right at her fingertips, yet too far away to touch.

Pat continued to scheme on new ways to be alone with Rudy, always trying to fool her momma and disregarding the consequences. With each tryst, she noticed Rudy's enthusiasm diminish. He became more distant. She preferred to believe it was fear.

As one season rolled into another, Pat continued to attract boys her own age. Each Friday or Saturday night, Pat's clique from school got together for house parties. Jimmie encouraged anything that took Pat's mind off of Rudy. But Pat was still detached. Her limited experience with a man made it difficult for boys her own age to compete. One of her friends was a fifteen-year-old boy, who they all called Pickles. He was big for his age, over six feet, with the body of a grown man, wide shoulders, and broad hips. In spite of his imposing size, his nature was gentle and friendly.

Jimmie emerged from her room half-lit while Pickles was standing in the kitchen, talking with Pat during one of his rare visits. "Where's my drink?" she asked, holding a straw broom in one hand.

Pat looked around, pretending not to know what she was talking about. "I dunno," said Pat, continuing to wash dishes. "Must of finished it."

"No, You threw it out!" shouted Jimmie. "Didn't you?"

"No, I didn't," said Pat. "I dunno where you left it."

"Yes, you did. There's the goddamn glass—empty, sittin' on the drain board. You always throwin' away my drinks; every time I get one, you throw it out!" Jimmie said. "I'm sick and tired of you sneakin' about touchin' my stuff."

"I didn't do it!"

"I'll make sure you never do it again!" Her movement was quick and deliberate. She grabbed her daughter by the back of the hair and pulled her down on to the floor. In a flash, Jimmie had the broom handle across Pat's neck, her foot holding it down, forcing Pat to squeal in agony as she tried to hold it back from crushing her windpipe.

"I'll kill you!" shrieked Jimmie. "I'll kill you, you no-good bitch!"

Pat's eyes flooded with tears and suddenly the weight was lifted. Pickles picked Jimmie up off her feet and placed her to one side. She began beating on him and screaming louder than before.

"Mind your own business, stay away from me, stay away!" He barely felt her punches. Pat looked up and saw his big, black frame standing over her, shielding her from the violent attacker while Jimmie pounded on his back. "Get out my goddamn house! You don't belong here stickin' your nose in with my family. Get out!"

Pat stood upright, while Pickles remained motionless, allowing her time to catch her breath. Pat rushed to her room and locked the door with a small wooden chair propped against the doorknob. Pickles ambled out without a word.

During the night, Pat awoke to a sudden coolness. Silently, in the darkness, she began to shiver. She tried to move her arms to warm the chill, but her limbs did not respond. She tried to move just her fingers, but again, nothing moved. Her body felt paralyzed. She heard nothing, not even her own breath. Suddenly, a brilliant white light appeared from the closet. Her heart fluttered and her bed began to shake vigorously.

Beads of sweat crept from her forehead onto her brow. As the white light grew brighter, Pat fought desperately to close her eyes, but she couldn't move. It was hopeless. Fear overwhelmed her.

And just as her heart pounded loudly enough to hammer the silence, an apparition of Big Momma appeared, surrounded by a brilliant glow that emanated from the closet. To Pat, Big Momma seemed to have come through from the "other side." The soft, reassuring voice whispered in her ear. "Pat . . . Pat," she called, "get out of this house. If you don't, someone's gonna die—and it will probably be you!"

Big Momma had always loved her. Pat knew she was telling the truth.

The light faded, the shaking stopped and the chill vanished just as quickly as it appeared. Pat relaxed. Her arms and legs moved freely. She sat up in bed; a sheet pulled up close to her neck. Her fears subsided. Exhausted and confused, she fell asleep in spite of her strongest efforts to keep watch.

In the morning, she waited until Jimmie and Homer left the house before calling Aunt Rosie to let her know what had happened. Pat was afraid and wanted some type of protection. But instead of Rosie, Roxy answered the phone. "My mother's not here," Roxy said. "She already left the house."

"But I gotta talk to her. Where'd she go? To work already?" Pat asked.

"What's the matter with you? You in some kind of trouble?" Roxy asked.

After Pat relayed the events of the night before, Roxy took matters into her own hands. "Well, you get over here, right now. Soon as I hang up I'm gonna call the Welfare Department."

"Wait, don't be rushing into stuff like that," Pat said. "I mean we just can't go down there and say what happened. Who's gonna believe me?"

"Well if I believe you, why wouldn't they? They ain't no different than me. I talked to those people before lots of times. Like when they was interviewing my momma about the woman who used to live next door. She was trying to be a foster parent and they came to the house. They ain't so tough. Ain't no tougher than you."

"But I don't have to do nothing, right?" Pat asked. "I mean, we could jus' go talk to them and see what they got to say."

"It couldn't hurt. They might be able to help," Roxy said, "Who knows?"

The social worker assigned to her case was Mrs. Morrissey, a woman in her late forties. She spoke softly and didn't seem to be surprised at the fact that Jimmie had tried to kill Pat. "I hear this every week," the woman said, "so don't feel afraid. You're not the only one out there who is in trouble. Just know that it's our job to protect you from danger, no matter who causes the problem." Mrs. Morrisey put down her pen and folded her arms, sitting back on her small office chair. Her eyes flickered back and forth from Pat to Roxy, finally settling on Pat.

"I'm still confused. Tell me again how you got to live with your momma." She said.

"I already went through that twice," Pat said. "I was adopted, period."

"But my concern is that you're so white. You don't look like you fit in with your family," Mrs. Morrisey said.

"Well, I do belong; I'm mixed, half-white, half-black. Some mixed people are real dark brown, others are light brown. Their skin is mixed and stirred. Mine ain't. I'm black inside and white outside," Pat said. "And I can't never change any of that. It just is."

"Okay, I'm still confused, but I get the picture. Let's take care of one problem at a time. The way I see it, the first thing to do is to relieve the tension at home. I'll call your momma, Jimmie Lee and. . . ."

"No, no, you can't even think 'bout doin' that," said Pat. "If she finds out I talked with the Welfare Office, she'll go crazy!"

"Very well," said Mrs. Morrisey, "then we'll just have to place you in the hands of a foster parent—someone recognized by the State to be responsible for you, at least temporarily."

Roxy interjected. "Why can't she stay with us? My mother always said that if Pat can't handle Jimmie, then she should come stay with her."

"Is she a foster parent?" Mrs. Morrisey asked.

"I dunno; she knows how to take care of us kids."

"Yes," Mrs. Morrisey said, "but she must be qualified by the State and registered through our office. Now in the meantime, they will remove you from the house where you live—tomorrow. Since you believe that it's too dangerous to confront your so-called mother, I'll just leave her an official notice telling her that the State has decided to remove you from her care for your own safety. She will then have to contact them, and they know how to deal with her."

Roxy and Pat exchanged skeptical looks. They knew this woman had no idea who she was dealing with, but under the circumstances there was no choice but to continue with her plan.

"For the time being Pat, we will assign you to the care of Mrs. Boykins, a registered foster parent."

"Mrs. Boykins!" Pat exclaimed. "I know her. She used to babysit for me a long time ago."

"Besides," said the woman, "she is not far from where you now live, so it'll make the transition simple."

They talked for over an hour. They filled out forms, with Pat giving details of her life, and answering questions from as far back as she could remember. Mrs. Morrissey seemed very confident in her ability to deal with Jimmie. As Pat sat in the chair watching her type as they talked, she became very nervous, thinking about Jimmie's reaction to her leaving.

The following morning, after everyone had left the house, Pat called Mrs. Morrisey and told her that the coast was clear. Within a half-hour, the woman knocked on the door. Cautiously, Mrs. Morrisey surveyed the entire house and followed Pat into her room to help pack her clothes. When Pat opened her closet, the woman was dumbfounded at the amount of clothes that hung neatly on the crossbar. When Pat saw the look on Mrs. Morrisey face, she knew that she must have painted a much more dramatic picture then was actually the case. Pat had never mentioned Jimmie's good qualities, like making sure that Pat was well dressed. After packing, Mrs. Morrisey left a typewritten letter on the kitchen table. They tiptoed out like two thieves in the night.

Although Mrs. Boykins was expecting them, it was obvious that she wasn't very excited at the thought of risking the wrath of the notorious Miss Jimmie. "How long is she gonna need to stay here?" Mrs. Boykins asked.

"Why do you ask?"

"Don't get me wrong," said Mrs. Boykins. "I love Pat. Why, I been takin' care of her, feedin', changing diapers, babysittin' and the like since she was brand spankin' new. And I don't mind doin' it again, just like I do with lots of little ones. But I'm getting too old to wrestle with her momma. I've seen enough of that woman's temper to last me a lifetime."

"She won't be that bad, especially since you have the protection of the Welfare Department. It's out of her hands," Mrs. Morrisey said.

Mrs. Boykins eyed her skeptically. "You ain't listening to a word I'm saying! The woman is crazy!" said Mrs. Boykins. "She don't care about no Welfare Department—or anyone else for that matter."

"Well, I'll do what I can to make other arrangements, perhaps with Mrs. Bilbrew, if they can get her registered as a foster parent. In the meantime, Pat will have to stay with you. Just try to keep her out of the way of Mrs. Faison."

The woman left and Pat moved in with Mrs. Boykins for a few days. It wasn't long before Jimmie discovered Pat's hideout. The following evening, Jimmie knocked on Mrs. Boykins door asking for Pat. Mrs. Boykins hid her in a living room closet, close enough for Pat to hear them arguing. Mrs. Boykins lied. She told Jimmie that she had no idea where Pat was—certainly not at her house. Jimmie made a few harmless threats then left, but even minor threats made Mrs. Boykins very nervous.

While Aunt Rosie cheerfully agreed to become a foster parent, it still took some time for her to fill out the necessary paperwork and go through the normal investigation. The Welfare Office cooperated and expedited the paperwork.

Jimmie, however, was not about to sit back and let the State interfere with her family. Jimmie uncovered the name of the caseworker, Mrs. Beth Morrisey, and began a campaign of terror. Each day, Jimmie made dozens of anonymous phone calls to Mrs. Morrisey at the Welfare office threatening to cut out her heart. She discovered Mrs. Morrisey's home phone number and warned her to be careful starting her car in the morning because of a bomb, while other times she'd say she was going to set her house on fire, or kidnap her children. Jimmie's threats succeeded. The Welfare Department transferred the woman to another district and assigned a man to Pat's case—at least temporarily. Pat learned the seemingly confident Welfare Lady had a nervous breakdown.

Aunt Rosie quickly qualified as a foster parent and welcomed Pat with open arms, a comforting smile and an old coffee can.

"What's in there?" Pat asked when she saw her near the front door.

Rosie opened the top and let Pat take a peek. "It looks like egg shells. And what's that? Seeds, dried leaves, and what else? Bird feathers?" Pat asked in wonderment.

"And some other special things that most people never heard of," said Rosie. "Now you just head on up to your room and put away your belongings. You know where they all go."

Pat turned to go to her room, but she was still curious and turned to watch her aunt. Rosie stepped outside the front door and spread some of the contents at the entranceway. Pat overheard her murmuring something about evil spirits.

"What are you doing?" Pat asked.

"I'm just making sure your wicked mother don't bother you no more. I got spells that'll keep the likes of her away—and a whole lot more. This stuff is more powerful than she'll ever be. That crazy woman will never cross this threshold. Don't you worry about that.

"Now that that's taken care of," she brushed her hands together and then turned to Pat. "Well, what are you doing? Don't worry, between this, and God, and His angels, no one will bother us. So don't just stand there—go do something. You can't just stand there and do nothing. Always keep busy. Always keep busy. Idleness is the devil's workshop. Get goin', get goin'."

Rosie's energy level was always high, she was constantly chattering about something. She seldom let anyone finish a sentence without interjecting her point. There was rarely a lull when she was around. She believed in all psychic phenomena: reincarnation, telepathy, and anything else in the realm of the unexplained. Many times she sat Pat down and passed on stories about mysterious events or odd people that she knew.

Rosie was confident in relaying her opinion, and Pat believed her without question, whether it was history, religion, politics, or medicine—particularly medicine. Aunt Rosie's herbs cured almost anything. She had a sixth sense that gave her an inside track on anyone who was ill, sometimes before they knew it. She was quick to the rescue with a special cure. Without asking, she took charge of their care. More often than not, whether through the body's natural healing process, or due to Aunt Rosie's herbs, minerals, and home remedies, the patient was better within a few days, a week at the most. No one understood her methods, and certainly no one dared to argue, she preferred it that way.

One exception, of course, was Inez, Rosie's niece. She got the brunt of Aunt Rosie's natural cures. A few years ago, when she first complained of a sore throat and slight swelling in her neck, Aunt Rosie became concerned. Without outside consultation, she diagnosed her with complete confidence. She proceeded to confine her to bed, keeping her bundled with blankets and having her drink plenty of liquids. But the illness worsened and Inez's lump got bigger. Rosie looked one more time at her swollen neck and quickly made another diagnosis: mumps!

"How did I get the mumps?" Inez asked.

"You just get them, that's all. You get them from somebody else who's got them. That's how you get them. Who have you been near that has the mumps? Probably one of the children at school; that's how you must have got it."

Inez looked puzzled. "I don't know of anyone who has the mumps. No one has said anything about it."

"Well, it don't matter much now, does it? You got it and we need to take care of it." Rosie said emphatically.

"What are you gonna do?"

"I got a sure cure for the mumps that's been around the family a long time." Rosie looked up and thought a minute. "It may have been a cousin of mine, twice removed on my father's side that had it. I think. No, no she wasn't a cousin; more like an in-law or something. Anyway, they didn't know what to do about it, so they went to their minister and he sent them to this old man from the congregation who once worked on a fishin' boat in the Gulf. And he really knew his stuff when it came to cures. Well, this old man passed on the remedies for lots of ailments. Mumps was one of them. And the remedies have been with me for a long time. But it doesn't matter. We'll fix it anyway. But I want you to know something—it's really serious."

"I know it's serious; I'm the one who's got it," Inez moaned. She looked up at her aunt as Rosie shook the thermometer briskly in her hand, trying to bring down the reading. "What is the mumps, anyway?"

"It's what kids get when they ask too many questions. Now open your mouth." Inez complied and Rosie placed the instrument under her tongue. "I'll be right back."

Aunt Rosie returned with a can of sardines and she proceeded to cover Inez's chest with the fish.

"Oooooo! What are you doing? What is this? Are they alive?"

"An old Cajun remedy," Rosie said. "It'll draw out the infection."

In spite of Inez's strong objections to the odor of dead fish resting peacefully under her nose, Aunt Rosie insisted that was the only way to cure her body. The fish stayed. By the next morning, the smell had penetrated the entire house. Inez complained louder then ever. After five days, it was unbearable and even Aunt Rosie couldn't take it any more. She removed the hardened herrings while the mumps remained. Only after another week of bed rest did the infection finally subside. It was another year before Inez even looked at another fish.

For almost a year, Pat stayed with Rosie. She transferred to Traner Junior High. Without Jimmie Lee's presence during that time, Pat's constant fear and guilt dissipated. Everything seemed to have changed for the better. She made the Honor Roll. She became more outgoing, more independent.

At Traner, Pat only socialized with her black friends. She wanted to be black like them; that was the fabric with which she was most comfortable. Rosie never objected to Pat going to most of the house parties and dances with the kids from school. Her bright blue eyes, light hair, and agreeable personality, however, made her stand out among the girls, most of whom resented the attention she got from the boys. Pat overheard some of the black girls say that it was only because of her skin color, or lack thereof, that attracted the black boys. She viewed the bigotry from both sides, and knew it would never go away.

What she missed, however, was the affection that she no longer received from Rudy. The pressure that Rudy's brother and sister-in-law put on him about getting involved with an under aged white girl, young enough to be his daughter, was too intense. Out of self-preservation, he moved to California.

When Bobby Ward, seven years her senior, moved into Reno from Selma, Alabama, he was the new guy in town and very popular. He showed interest in her, she reciprocated without a second thought. Although his glory days at high school were long over, Bobby maintained his status among the teenagers by keeping in touch with the younger set. By the time Pat learned of him, he was already a minor celebrity.

He was very different from Rudy in both stature and personality. Bobby was tall and thin, with a darker complexion and angular face. He was a good deal more considerate than Rudy, genuinely interested in her as a person, not just her young body. The parties and dates continued, and she indulged her freedom more than ever. Any details of their liaison were kept from Rosie.

Pat did not see Jimmie while she stayed with Rosie, nor did Jimmie ever set foot into Rosie's house. Pat thought Jimmie was either too stubborn or Rosie's powerful concoction did its job. Reverend Mayfield had evicted Jimmie for her belligerent behavior. She and Homer moved into a new housing project in Reno. Pat thought for sure that Jimmie would be out of her life once and for all.

It was an especially warm Saturday night during the summer. After stepping out of the shower, Pat slipped into a thin oriental print robe that immediately clung to her moist skin. The air was heavy and close. Pat set up the ironing board in the living room and pulled out a paisley blouse to press for a night out with some friends. She kept the windows open in a futile attempt to capture even the slightest breeze, but only the light from the street came through. Without a warning, the screen door flew open, replaced by a menacing silhouette. It was Jimmie Lee looming in the doorway. Pat first reaction was to remember to remind Aunt Rosie that her eggshells finally wore out. She was stunned, but acted calm, as her momma got right in her face. She felt the danger.

"I'll teach you to leave me and run away to some social workers!" Jimmie screamed as she jerked Pat by the collar of the robe and tossed her around like a toy doll. "You're coming home with me—and this time you stayin' put. Your days of spreading lies about me are over!"

Pat struggled to free herself. "No! Leave me alone—you're hurting me!" Pat yelled. "I didn't spread no lies. Everything's the truth."

"The truth! Ha! You ain't got the slightest idea about the damn truth!"

They struggled and knocked over the ironing board along with her dress. "The iron! The iron!" warned Pat, but Jimmie didn't care about anything except dragging her out the door half-naked.

A car was waiting at the curb with the motor running. With one swift movement, Jimmie opened the door and forced Pat into the back seat by her hair. Pat screamed and fought, but Jimmie refused to let go.

Pat yelled to the black man who was driving the car. "Stop the car!" pleaded Pat. "Don't you see what she's doin' to me?"

Jimmie slapped over and over. Pat fought back, trying to hold off the blows. "Stop the car! Help me!" The driver remained silent as he continued to drive. "Someday," Pat declared, "you're gonna pay dearly for this."

"You're not going nowhere, Bitch," snarled Jimmie. "You staying with me—where you belong."

For the first time, Pat lost all control. "I hate you," she screamed. "You rotten nigger!"

Jimmie continued to slap and punch until they reached the curb in front of her apartment. The struggle spilled out onto the sidewalk, causing the several people who were trying to cool off outside to gather nearby and watch the commotion. As if on cue, two white policemen arrived on the scene and separated the two of them. The smaller officer put his arms up and faced Jimmie, "All right what's this all about . . . the neighbors complained that someone was being assaulted?" he asked Jimmie.

Jimmie didn't waste a second. "No one's being assaulted, I was trying to save my girl from a life of misery and shame. I caught her makin' it with some black man and it's my responsibility to drag her ass back home. She's blaming me for interfering! Well I got a right to interfere. After all," Jimmie continued with enthusiasm, "she's only fourteen and still underage! What would you do if it was your own daughter? I'm her mother, I raised her. I am gonna make her understand right from wrong. I want her in my house and she's not going out for a month."

Pat's mouth dropped and her eyes bulged out. "What a liar!" she shrieked. The larger officer held her at bay. "She came bursting into my aunt's house and dragged me out and started beating me for no reason! I left the iron on!" Pat was getting panicky. "I have to unplug the iron. The house can catch on fire."

Then the two police officers exchanged combatants, and the smaller officer tried to calm Pat. He wanted to confirm her age and relationship to Jimmie. Pat confirmed that part of the story, but waved the rest off as pure nonsense and again explained as quickly as possible what really had happened. Pat begged the officer to take her back to Rosie's house.

Within moments, they were on their way back to Rosie's where the iron and dress were on the floor. Luckily, the iron was unplugged. The policeman was satisfied that Pat was telling the truth. Pat had won this small battle. After filling out his form, they drove Pat to Mrs. Boykins' house, where she stayed until Aunt Rosie came home.

Later that night when Pat was in her room at Rosie's, she stood in front of her mirror and looked deep into herself. The events of the evening wore heavy in her mind and heart. She was really alone, not knowing where she belonged. Rosie's was great but temporary. Momma's the strongest pull, but that was impossible under the circumstances. The sadness was in her glassy eyes, her lids heavy. She was uncomfortable with a frown; it was unnatural for her. She realized that Jimmie Lee would never change. Pat had relished the short time of freedom living with Aunt Rosie, who taught her to stand tall and not bow to fear. She was proud of the way she had stood up against Jimmie Lee. She yearned for her real mother and decided that she was old enough to start searching for the woman of her dreams. She indulged herself in the fantasy; it made her feel confident. The sadness went away.

But this feeling of enthusiasm, optimism, and empowerment soon came to an abrupt halt when Pat discovered a few months later, to her utter amazement, that she was now pregnant with Bobby's baby. She was fifteen.

CHAPTER 17

Pat knew something had to be done quickly. She did not want to let Bobby know now that her period was late, the obvious consequences of their lovemaking. Pat confided in Donna, one of her friends at school. She wasn't one of her close friends, but it was rumored that she had experience at these sorts of things.

"Take aspirin," Donna said. "Lots of aspirin. That'll make your period come quicker." Pat did this for three days, two at a time every two hours.

"Nothing happened," Pat said when she met Donna the next day.

"All I know is it worked for me," Donna shrugged and walked away.

Pat ignored any further advice from her girlfriend and went right to the source.

"I missed my period." She blurted out to Bobby while they were driving home from school. He shook his head then sneered, but he was silent, his eyes on the road. "It's been three weeks, I took a bottle of aspirin, but it still hasn't come, so I think I'm pregnant."

Bobby looked at her apprehensively, "A bottle of aspirin, what for?" he asked.

"That's what someone told me to do," she answered, her eyes downcast.

"A aspirin ain't gonna do shit." He said, and then added, "how'd you get yourself pregnant anyway? I thought you were safe." Pat didn't answer.

"I guess I'm the father, right?" Bobby asked half-jokingly. Pat's eyes bore through him. "Just kiddin', that's all. I know I'm the one."

"You're the only one," she said, as her eyes began to swell. "What are we gonna do? Momma's gonna kill me."

"Momma, huh. Don't you worry about you're momma. We'll just get married and have the baby."

"Where we gonna live? My Aunt Rosie ain't gonna let me stay when she finds out," said Pat.

"Well, for now, we don't tell your Aunt Rosie, till we get everything figured out." Bobby said to her confidently.

"What about money? I guess I'll quit school and get a job. Or maybe stay in school and get a part-time job." She said, thinking out loud.

"I'll get a second job," Bobby said, "but we got to get married, real quick. Cause, I could get drafted anytime, and sent to that Viet Nam. People are getting killed over there, and then you'd have to do this all yourself."

"I got to do this by myself, anyway." She paused, and then added, "They don't draft you when you're married?" Pat asked.

"No, you get exempted, especially when you got a kid," he said with confidence.

The idea of living together enlivened Pat's interest, but she knew that a quick marriage was not possible, having explored that path with Rudy. But each day she waited the more anxious she became.

A week went by, and Pat noticed that Bobby seemed to act much older than his twenty-one years, and more concerned about her than before.

"When are you gonna tell your aunt about this?" Bobby asked. "You can't just surprise her and one day just go out and bring home a baby!"

"Why not?" she said, "Momma did it with me."

Bobby gave her a cynical look. "You know that ain't the same thing. Your momma wasn't pregnant for nine months. You will be, and there's no way of hiding that. Besides, you need to be with someone who knows about babies, and your aunt is gonna be a whole lot easier to deal with than your momma."

But Pat instinctively knew that Aunt Rosie would not be the one to have the last say in this matter. Jimmie was her main concern. "I just want this whole thing to disappear. I pray everyday, ten times a day, just to make it go away." She said fearfully. "I'm fifteen years old, I'm too young for this. This isn't want I wanted now. My whole life is changing and I don't know where it's going."

Bobby put his arm around her and held her close. "Divine intervention is not gonna happen. Nobody's gonna make this go away. We got to deal with it."

She looked up at him with glassy eyes and said mournfully, "I don't know how to be responsible for another human being. I'm unmarried, I'm in the tenth grade for God's sake."

"Think of it this way," Bobby said, "if you're a mother, and you're responsible for a baby, then you don't have to listen to what Jimmie says at all. You'll be your own boss. We'll have a place of our own, with our baby and we can do what we want, whenever we want to do it."

Pat sniffled and gently dabbed the tears from her cheek. She thought for a moment then said, "Perhaps you're right. We would be independent, like a separate country almost. Ok, then, let's go tell my Aunt Rosie."

"Aaaah, now wait a minute." Bobby paused and looked down his nose at her. "You need to tell Aunt Rosie. It's women's stuff and all. I don't want to interfere with that, so I don't need to go."

"You're afraid of Aunt Rosie, aren't you?" she asked.

"Afraid! Shit no, I ain't afraid of nothing. I'm a stranger to her," he said. "How's it gonna look if I walk in and say. 'Aunt Rosie, I'm your new nephew.'"

"Fine, I'll do it myself. I know she's gonna be angry, and I know she'll be disappointed in me. But at least she will be able to help me. She'll know what to do."

That night, Pat asked Rosie to sit down with her; she had something important to talk to about.

"What do you mean, you think you're pregnant? That's impossible! We can't have that. No, no, no—not in my house. "Who's the one you been messin' around with, huh? It was that Ward boy, wasn't it?"

"Yeah, but I don't understand how it happened." Pat realized—and Aunt Rosie's expression confirmed—that it was a foolish thing to say, but it was too late to act intelligent at this point.

"Who knows about it?" demanded Rosie. "Does your boyfriend know?"

"Yeah," Pat murmured.

"Well we can't let anyone else know. No one. You hear?"

"How am I gonna hide it?"

"That's your problem, not mine. You got yourself into this damn mess, and you're gonna get yourself out. I can't have anyone know that you got knocked up while living here—under my roof! What will everyone think of me? I'll tell you what they'll think. They'll say I'm running a shittin' cathouse! That's what they'll say." She looked away from Pat, paused for a moment, placed her finger up to her mouth, turned back and said coldly. "Well, there's only one thing for you to do. You can't stay here no more."

"Where am I gonna go?"

"That's not my problem. You better get your old man to take care of you now that you got one. He's part of this, too, you know. I want your butt outta here as soon as possible."

Pat didn't expect this from her aunt. Rosie had always urged Pat to come to her with her troubles. And now that she was in a spot, she was throwing her out. It took a couple of days to get over the initial shock before she cleared her head and told Bobby that she was homeless.

"I wasn't expecting this so soon," Bobby said to her. "I figured we got five or six months before we get to move in together. My part-time work at the laundry ain't gonna get us nowhere. And there's no room at my house, that's for sure."

"I know that, I just don't know what to do. Rosie just told me to go to my old man and . . ." she paused and thought for a moment while Bobby just ignored her.

She decided to give Homer a call at the Esquire that afternoon. Pat heard the joy resonating in Homer's voice as he recognized her. It was more than six months since they last talked. "Pat, it's so good to hear from you! How you gettin' along these days with Rosie?"

"Oh, fine, Homer," she lied. "Just fine." She didn't have the courage to tell him what was happening. She was his little girl. His heart would have broken. "How's things with you?"

"Pretty good," he said in his slow drawl. "Business could be better at the shop, but I manage." There was a long pause. Finally Homer said, "Jimmie's been on the wagon, you know."

"How is she?"

"She misses you, Pat, very much. She talks about you all the time as if you were in school or something, waitin' for you to come home—like you used to do when you was little. Remember that?"

"You say she ain't been drinking?"

"Nah. She's dry as a pretzel. It's been over two months since she's had a drop. Looks better, too." There was another long pause; Pat wondered whether or not to tell Homer about her condition. Finally Homer said, "Why don't you give her a call. She'll be real glad to hear from you."

"Maybe I will, Homer. Maybe I will. You take care of yourself. I'll be seeing you."

The next day, Pat took Homer's advice, but instead of calling Jimmie on the phone, Pat decided a personal visit would be better. She arrived at the new housing project late in the afternoon. She found the apartment where Jimmie and Homer were living, and stood at the entrance, trying to find the courage to ring the buzzer.

Without her knocking, the door opened. Pat was startled; Homer was standing there. "Hello, Pat. Come in, come in." he said.

"Homer." She said nervously. "Got the day off?"

"Nah. I ain't been feelin' too good. Let me look at you." Homer held her by the shoulders and looked straight at her with gentle brown eyes. "You look fine, just fine," he said softly; her fears subsided.

"Your Momma's in the kitchen." With a conspiratorial smile, he motioned for her to go into the other room. Pat took a few steps and then turned back toward him. He crinkled his nose and gestured toward the kitchen with his hand. It was just the encouragement she needed. She filled her lungs then exhaled slowly.

Jimmie was sitting on a chair at a small table near the window. She stared at Pat for a moment.

"Hello, Momma. How are you?"

Jimmie didn't get up or respond, just looked her over, eying her daughter bundled up in a heavy winter coat. She turned away and said, "You're pregnant, ain't you?

"Surprised?" Jimmie said.

Pat felt her knees weaken. She thought to herself. But how could she possibly know? Aunt Rosie was much too embarrassed to let out the secret, and I said nothing to Homer to alert him.

"I know your whole life—from when y'all first came home from the hospital. I watched you put off things you didn't want to do. I know your every mood. I know when you're lying and I know when you tellin' the truth. You can't put nothin' passed me—'specially no baby!

"Now take that silly coat off and set yourself down. There's lots we got to talk about."

Pat was paralyzed for a moment. Her skin tingled. Finally, she had the courage to ask, "You're not angry?"

"Angry, no. I tried to keep you straight. Did everything I knew how to, but you was just too strong-headed to listen to anybody. You was always different, not jus' because you was half-white, either. Nah, it was the things that you'd always do when you was by yourself. Like when you was always gathering stuff, pieces of paper, and lists of things, and you was always writing down things and saving them. I could almost read your mind. I thought you'd be something special, somebody who is somebody, not someone like me, not a cleaning woman."

Pat watched the expression in Jimmie's face change from disappointment to compassion. She knew she did the right thing by coming over.

"I wanted to be somebody, too," Jimmie continued. "I knew what I was gonna be from the time I was a baby back in Mississippi. Then you come along. At first, I was really pissed. But you started to grow on me and I decided that you had a better chance at being somebody more than me, cause you looked so white. And then when I saw you was smarter than the rest, I just knew I had to keep you safe. I tried to keep you away from that Bobby Ward and anyone like him. So, I ain't angry with you Patta, not today anyway."

Homer was right. Jimmie was sweet as can be when she was sober for any length of time. Pat found it difficult to hold back tears as Jimmie lectured her on being a mother, while treating her as an adult without chastising. For three hours Pat quizzed Jimmie about pregnancy and babies, occasionally questioning Jimmie's reliability and depth of knowledge. Pat listened patiently; grateful she was no longer alone.

The next day, Pat moved in with Momma and Homer. Pat knew that Jimmie was back in charge. The convenience of allowing Jimmie to make some decisions early on was worth any abuse, at least until Pat learned what to do. Pat was relieved when Jimmie's first order of business was to remove her from Traner Junior High. The peer pressure and humiliation Pat was starting to feel was nerveracking at best, and Jimmie insisted on enrolling her in a maternity school in Reno.

The class was small, only eight girls—all white. Pat learned some of the basics about having a baby, quickly realizing that most of the stories Jimmie told her were slightly off the mark, a mixture of the facts of life with the fiction of Jimmie's imagination. Pat realized then that if she were going to raise a child, it would be far different from the way Jimmie had raised her.

The small group of expectant teens became close to one another, each sharing their experiences. Pat never let on that her boyfriend was black. She somehow felt there was no need for them to know, at least not yet.

Pat was not upset that Bobby never came to the school to pick her up. She knew he was working hard to save as much money as possible for them to get married. When they were together, he'd ask Pat, and beg Jimmie Lee, to let them get married. The answer was always the same. Each time Pat saw Bobby in Jimmie's presence she would see the contempt spewing from her momma's eyes. Jimmie told her at every opportunity that Bobby was completely unworthy, and couldn't understand what she saw in him in the first place.

Pat usually took the bus home, but when one of the girls offered her a ride home from school, she accepted without reservation.

"It's really nice of you to give me a lift home," Pat said to her young driver.

"I know." The girl answered. "It feels great to be old enough to drive. I mean really, I'm gonna have a baby, the very least they can do is let me drive a car."

"Oh, you're so right," Pat giggled in agreement.

"It will be so much more convenient to not have to depend on everyone for a ride here and a ride there; taking the baby to the doctors." The girl continued, "I bet you can't wait to get yours?"

"Yeah," Pat answered, "but it'll be awhile before I can get a license. There's just too many other things I got to do before then.

"Turn left on the next street," Pat said as she motioned with her hand.

Pat noticed the startled expression on the girl's face as she directed her toward the projects.

When they were close to Pat's house, the girl asked, "you live in the nigger section?"

Pat was infuriated by the ignorant remark. "Yeah, and that's my mother!" Pat pointed to Jimmie, who sat alone on the front stoop.

"Oh my God. I'm sorry. I didn't know. You look so white."

Pat got out of the car and slammed the door. The following day she met the girl at school.

"I'm so sorry I said that yesterday," she said to Pat, "I really didn't know you were black, you look so white."

"That's OK, don't worry about it. I'm used to it." Pat smiled graciously.

Each day, as the life inside her grew, Pat became more aware of herself—not only the physical changes in her body, but the emotional changes as well. Each morning she wondered what the day would bring, how her baby would turn out—if it indeed would be black, or perhaps lighter skinned like her. With every breath, she was closer to being a mother and her obsession to find her real mother grew even stronger. She again studied her birth certificate, searching for clues that may have been overlooked, but still she knew nothing.

The Welfare Department became involved again when they discovered that Pat had moved back to Jimmie's and changed schools. Their meddling was just another interference that irked Jimmie more than Pat. Jimmie was determined to finish them off once and for all.

By the spring of that year, Bobby got another part-time job. Along with his job at the laundry, he managed to save enough money to afford a small apartment of his own. He was outside Pat's house whenever he wasn't working. It was a weekday and Jimmie was sitting at her favorite spot on the stoop. Pat and Bobby moped about. Jimmie kept one eye out for the Welfare people and one eye on her daughter. She noticed Pat was nervous.

Bobby leaned over to Jimmie and said, "I know I can take care of her and the baby when it comes. I know I'd be a good father, too. I know it." He paused a moment then continued, "We can't do nothing without your permission. They'd put her back in a foster home if we tried to get married without you. I just want to get married. Hey, everybody does it. Why can't we?"

Jimmie never looked at him. She pretended to be uninterested by yawning then exhaling with gusto, and finally brushing her hair away as if she was too bored to even gesture.

But Bobby was persistent. Over and over again he pestered Jimmie to allow Pat to marry him. He was determined to take care of his soon-to-be-born child. Jimmie finally acknowledged his presence.

"How you gonna take care of my daughter?" Jimmie asked. "You think it's easy? You have any idea what you need to take care of Pat? She's a handful, you can bet your ass on that one, Bobby Boy!"

Jimmie's eyes darted to Pat who was about to interject, "What? You think you're not a handful?" Jimmie said confronting Pat. "I got news for you, Miss Patta. Did you think that keeping you fed and healthy and out of trouble was easy? Well, see for yourself what happened as soon as you're out of my care—you get yourself pregnant! Just walking around town, or taking your white ass to the store was a chore. If you was black like the rest of us, no one would mind, but you're not. It was dangerous just to keep you in the house in the first place. Now you wanna be out in the public with a black husband and black baby—who you two think you're kidding? Ain't nobody gonna make it easy for you."

"It's too late for that now," Bobby said, "the baby is gonna be here no matter what. We can't send it back."

"And I'll never give it up like my real momma did to me," Pat added defiantly.

"So, that's it, ha!" Jimmie stated with full contempt. "You think she could've done a better job than me. Your high and mighty princess gave you away. And she gave you away to me. And after all I done for you, the first chance you get, you'd leave me flat. This is how you show appreciation?"

"No, you misunderstood," Pat pleaded. "I would never leave you, no matter what. But I want to raise my own baby."

"Is that right?" Jimmie asked Bobby sarcastically.

"Oh, yeah," Bobby was taken by surprise. "More than anything else. And I'll take good care of her, too! I got my own apartment, and I'm working two jobs. I got enough money for us to live on. Don't worry about that."

Jimmie turned to her daughter next. "Do you want to get married?"

Pat really didn't care what happened to her anymore, just as long as all the bickering and tension stopped. Pat answered unemotionally. "Of course, why not?"

"OK. Then it's settled. You," pointing to Bobby, "be back here at six o'clock with the best man. And wear a suit! I'll take care of the rest."

"Momma, what are you gonna do?"

"You both want to get married, don't you? Then that's what you gonna do—today. I'll show the Welfare people what I think of them and their rules."

Bobby didn't understand what Jimmie was up to; he really didn't seem to care, either. Without another word he made a dash for the car.

Jimmie phoned Reverend Webb and told him to be ready for a wedding at around six. They then proceeded to make plans as to what Pat was to wear and whom she was to invite.

The day was hectic. First, they went to the clerk's office to secure a license. Once there, Jimmie told Pat to lie to the clerk about her age. But she didn't have to, no one asked for proof. When they returned home Jimmie was frazzled at the thought of Pat leaving permanently and drank until she was completely tight. A couple of months on the wagon didn't change her attitude. She still managed to keep control of everybody.

Bobby returned at about 6:30 with his brother. Even Jimmie thought he was handsome in a new suit. He handed Pat a neatly wrapped flower box that contained a beautiful corsage, which Jimmie promptly placed in the refrigerator. Neither Pat nor Jimmie were anywhere near ready for this special occasion. Jimmie had the three of them waiting on her hand and foot, almost as if she were getting married. In her condition, it took forever. Finally, at about 11:45 that evening, the four of them were ready to walk out the door on their way to Reverend Webb's.

Jimmie knocked on the door of the unlit house where the minister lived, then knocked again and yelled out, "Hey, Mr. Reverend Webb, open up, it's me!" She knocked twice more before a light came on and the door opened. Reverend Webb looked as though he had been sleeping for hours.

"What you doing here?" he mumbled, "Is something wrong?"

"I told you we were coming over to get Pat married, didn't I?"

"Yeah, but that was this afternoon. What are you waking me up in the middle of the night for?"

"Don't sweat the details," Jimmie yelled, "let's just get this show on the road."

Jimmie didn't understand Webb's look of disbelief when he shook his head in obvious consternation. Jimmie just followed his motion to come inside. Within a few minutes, the minister, clad in his pajamas, filled out paperwork, which both Bobby and Pat signed. He arranged them in a proper setting and read the marriage vows. Within fifteen minutes, it was all over. Pat was now Mrs. Bobby Ward, pregnant, in the tenth grade, with still a few months to go before her sixteenthth birthday. Jimmie didn't shed a tear.

Bobby and Pat moved to his small apartment on the south side of town. As an expectant mother and housewife, Pat's confidence soared. She sensed empowerment, and a knack for taking on responsibility, including her new husband. Her days were filled with school studies; her evenings remained free for Bobby. At night, her dreams came alive, alternating between the faceless woman who gave her away and an infant that bore skin both black and white. When she awoke, the images were gone, but the longing remained.

Yvette was born on August seventh, only six days after Pat's sixteenth birthday. Her skin was a light caramel, her head bursting with straight black hair.

"She's the color I'm suppose to be," Pat said to Bobby as she saw him enter her hospital room.

It was the first time he laid eyes on his daughter. "At least she'll know who her father is; and she'll know she's black like me," Bobby added with a smile.

"Well, at least my baby won't grow up with the same bigotry that I dealt with," Pat said, "she'll be proud of who she is."

"What are you talking about?" Bobby asked, "It'll be just the same, she'll be treated just like me."

"Yes, but at least the blacks won't be prejudiced because she's white," Pat added.

"Well, she's half-white, ain't she?" Bobby asked slyly.

"A quarter," Pat said, "she's just a quarter white."

"Yeah, that and a dime will still buy you nothing."

It wasn't long after the baby arrived home that Bobby and Pat realized the apartment was much too small.

"I found a new apartment on Spokane," Pat said, "it's perfect. Two bedrooms, a full bath—there's room for everything."

"How much is it gonna cost?" Bobby asked. "I don't have anything extra as it is, and this baby's a whole lot more expensive than we thought."

"I know; I've got a job," Pat said nonchalantly.

"A job! What kind of job? What about school? Who's gonna watch the baby?" Bobby was relieved, but perplexed.

"I can't go back to school with the baby. She needs too much care.

"I was over Momma's talking to her and she. . . ." said Pat before Bobby interrupted her.

"Your momma's involved with this? Then that could only mean trouble. What's she want you to do be a maid like her? Cleaning people's houses?" Bobby said.

She knew he was annoyed, but continued anyway, "As a matter of fact, that's exactly what I had in mind. But Momma threw a fit when I mentioned it and told me that if I needed money than I should go talk to one of her neighbors, Mrs. Williams who just happens to be the personnel director of St. Mary's Hospital. So I did."

"Well, what she say?"

"Mrs. Williams said that I was way too smart to be working as a maid."

"Damn straight, you're too smart. That's why you married me," Bobby said.

"No seriously," Pat continued, "she told me I shouldn't throw my life away by being a maid. Of course I told her that it wasn't a career choice; I just needed money for the new apartment.

"Anyway, she told me to apply for a file clerk's job and she'd make sure I got hired."

"Well, who's gonna take care of Yvette?" Bobby asked. "I can't, I'm working two jobs now."

"I'll get Momma—she's the only one," Pat added.

"But I thought you dreaded her watching the baby?" Bobby said.

"I do," Pat paused for a moment then added, "but I'm praying all the time that everything will be alright."

CHAPTER 18

Catholic nuns administered St. Mary's Hospital and they were efficient, methodical, and ever-present. They managed the lay staff quite easily. Pat began using her legal name, Fauna, and was assigned to filing in the accounting department. She worked alongside a young girl named Luanne, just two years older than herself. Luanne worked there for almost a year before Fauna arrived and was asked by the supervisor to instruct Fauna on her duties. The filing position amounted to nothing more than moving patient records, insurance forms, letters, and folders from one filing cabinet to another, simple tasks that required no thought. Luanne's real expertise, however, was social. She loved to talk and made friends easily. She was so adept at piloting Fauna through the machinations of the hospital, that by the end of the first week, Fauna already knew the histories of everyone she met—the nurses aides, the maintenance people, the office manager, and even one of the doctors.

"So what about you," Luanne asked as she placed a stack of files on Fauna's desk, "aren't you in school?"

"I had to quit school, I'm married," Fauna said, "and I have a baby daughter, too. Here, I got a picture." Fauna watched Luanne's eyes lock-up as she showed the girl Yvette's smiling brown face.

"She's your daughter?" Luanne asked, "So—her father's black?"

"Well, yeah, but I'm half-black myself," Fauna added.

Luanne's mouth was moist and steadily dropping, but she managed a reflexive gulp, "Your black? How can that be, you look white as me?"

"My father was black, and my mother, she was very young, and was forced to give me away when I was born cause they were society people. So, my momma who raised me was black and I just grew up that way. Cause I am black. It says so on my birth certificate." Fauna said.

Luanne was silent for a moment than asked, "Did you ever meet your real mother?"

"No, never," Fauna said, "but I will—one day I'll find her. When I look through these files I try to put faces on them, but none of them look like my mother would look."

"Oh yeah, I used to do that when I first started, too." Luanne said, "but I don't bother with it no more. Luanne stepped around to the other side of the desk, closer to Fauna, "Where did you come from? I mean were you born?"

"St. Elizabeth's in San Francisco," Fauna answered.

"I've heard of that hospital," Luanne said.

"You did?" Fauna said. "You're the first person I ever met who knew about where I was born."

"Wait," Luanne said, "I don't know the place, I just heard the name mentioned once or twice because it's run by nuns like this one."

"But still, it's amazing. I mean the connection, don't you think?" Fauna asked.

Luanne shrugged her shoulders, "I guess." She sauntered back to her desk, "So how did you get here?"

"My momma worked as a maid in a restroom at the Riverside when she was asked to adopt me."

"The society people asked a single maid in a restroom to adopt their baby?"

"Oh Momma wasn't alone. Her husband was a shoeshine man," Fauna said, "but he took off when I was real young."

Luanne's mouth hung low as Fauna slowly walked away.

The next day, Fauna's story was known throughout the hospital. A nun with creamy white skin in her mid-forties wandered in and out of the accounting area. She frequently glanced at Fauna in a way that made her feel uncomfortable. Fauna feigned busyness to gain her approval. "Who is that nun?" Fauna whispered to Luanne.

"Which one?" Luanne asked.

Fauna turned and noticed there were now three nuns chatting near the office. "The one with the big wire-rimmed glasses. She never says nothing, just keeps looking at me."

"Oh, that's Sister Hillary," Luanne said. "No one knows what she does, but it seems like she's always in the middle of something."

"What do you mean?" Fauna asked.

"Well, I don't really mean in the middle of something specific, but the other nuns are always looking for her. I don't know if she hides or what, but they always seem frustrated whenever they ask about her," Luanne whispered, then added, "but it's a good frustrated, you know what I mean? They always seem to smile, like she's doing practical jokes or something."

One of the nuns left the area and the shorter one came over, handed Luanne a box filled with forms and said, "Luanne, I need you to take this over to admissions, please."

"Ok," replied Luanne.

The nun thanked her and followed her out of the room.

Fauna found herself alone with Sister Hillary who appeared to be hovering about with her arms folded inside the sleeves of her habit. To Fauna she looked like a floating spirit with sparkling blue eyes.

Sister Hillary peered down at Fauna with a Tony the Tiger grin and said, "So, you're the young lady who has a daughter, and a husband, two mothers and a mysterious past."

Fauna said, "Yes, Sister, but I only know one mother."

"I'm Sister Hillary," the nun said, "and you're Fauna."

"Yes, you know a lot about me." Fauna said.

"Oh no, I know very little. Just the rumors about you were given away to a colored maid in a restroom?" Sister Hillary said. "Is that true?"

"Uh, huh." Fauna nodded.

"And what other rumors do you have to tell? You must tell me more.

I love a good story," Sister Hillary said as she pulled up a chair and sat next to Fauna.

"Where do I begin?" Fauna said, and then proceeded to relay her saga to the inquisitive nun. She ended with a plea for help in searching for her real mother.

"I understand your frustration," said Sister Hillary sympathetically, "but there isn't much I can help you with." Fauna's shoulders drooped. "At least not officially."

"Oh, what can you do?"

"Well, I'm not sure, other than offer encouragement right now. But we must keep this very quiet." The nun said as she lifted two fingers and then twisted them at her lips, pretending it was a key, which she tossed in the air. She smiled, "The other sisters will not approve of my meddling, so we'll need to communicate surreptitiously."

"What does that mean?" Fauna asked.

"Stealthily, on the QT." Fauna's eyes glazed over. "Under cover," said Sister Hillary.

"Oh, I get it, like James Bond." Fauna said.

"Yes, like James Bond. When I find something out, I'll use the code name 'Lucy', but don't expect too much."

"Who's Lucy?"

Sister Hillary stood up and shuffled toward the door. She turned and whispered to Fauna *Peanuts*. Then disappeared into the hallway.

The nun's enthusiasm and keen interest were all the encouragement Fauna needed to keep her focused over the next year and a half to do something, anything, to find her real mother. One evening, with Yvette put to bed and Bobby working late, Fauna again found herself studying carefully the only link to her past—her birth certificate. *There has to be something here—something that would get me a step closer—but what? St. Elizabeth's Hospital, Tamar Hodel, my mother, Dr. Torkelson, the physician, father 'Negro', date.* Her eyes widened. *Oh, how stupid, stupid, stupid. How dumb not to have seen it all these years. Of course! The attending physician, the doctor, would know where my real family was. He'd have records, just like at St. Mary's!* Immediately she wrote a letter to Dr.

Torkelson in care of St. Elizabeth's Hospital in San Francisco asking him for any information regarding her mother, Tamar Hodel.

The following day, Fauna told Jimmie what she had done.

"Patta, I know you been looking for her your whole life. What do you thinks gonna happen when you find her?" Jimmie said.

"I don't know, I just need to know stuff," Fauna said.

"What stuff you need to know? Why'd she do it? Who's your real daddy? And when you get the answers, what you gonna do? Go move in with her? I'm sure your 'white' momma'll be real happy to know she got a black granddaughter and a black son-in-law, useless as he is. "

"Momma, that ain't true," Fauna said.

"She gave you away cause you was suppose to be mixed, now you really are mixed. Yeah, she'll be ready to take you in now."

"Momma, I'm not gonna leave you, no matter what you say," Fauna said. Neither was entirely convinced.

Yet, in spite of Jimmie's abusive and manipulative manner, Fauna was devoted to her. It was a new maturity that appeared with having a child that kept Fauna loyal. On one hand, she accepted Jimmie's contempt of the whites, knowing how much Jimmie hated being a minority. She knew Jimmie blamed all whites for keeping her from reaching her potential, putting her life on hold while manipulated into caring for a mixed-race girl who looked white and was trying to be black. And on the other hand, Fauna felt Jimmie's loving and protective instinct as a mother when she was sober, but she lacked the biological attachment that only Fauna's real mother could provide. Fauna knew that she was the center of Jimmie's woe. She knew it was the reason Jimmie continued to drink. Jimmie drank heavily, stopping occasionally for a month or two, vowing never again to touch the bottle. Inevitably, at the first sign of tension, or sometimes for no discernible reason, she resumed her unattractive role as the neighborhood drunk, keeping everyone in abeyance with her outrageous displays and violent temper. Everyone, that is, except Homer, who by now had become immune to Jimmie's antics, and Reverend Mayfield, who had his own reasons to stay lit.

Mayfield's congregation had withered away to an occasional tourist visiting the area for the first time. Abandoned by his flock, he discovered Jimmie's warm heart and a soft shoulder to cry on—and a bottle of gin. They became a team, sharing their sorrows and officiously advising anyone who listened. They talked about everything, occasionally causing a ruckus for lack of something more productive to do. They sat and drank together and Jimmie usually outlasted the minister.

———————

Bobby dreaded the thought of going over to Jimmie's house, and avoided her as much as possible, stopping just long enough to pick up Yvette whenever Jimmie optioned to baby-sit.

In early November, as Bobby was ready to leave with the baby, Jimmie stopped him. "Oh, a letter came here addressed to Miss Fauna Ward. Is that some relation of yours?"

"You know who Fauna is," said Bobby.

"Oh really," Jimmie said, "When she was living here, her name was Patta. Now that she's married to you, you not only changed her last name but her first name, too! What's next? You gonna try to change my name? Stop trying to be something you ain't!"

"I didn't change nobody's name, she did that herself, besides, it's her real name," Bobby grabbed the letter and left without another word.

Minutes later he was with his wife. "What did I ever do to your momma? That woman makes me crazy. Except I know I ain't crazy. So that means it must be her." He handed Fauna the letter. Quickly, she went off by herself and read it in silence.

October 31, 1969

Dear Fauna,

Dr. Torkelson has referred your letter to me requesting information regarding your mother. Fauna, I would not say your mother gave you away. Your mother was a very unsophisticated girl who would not have been able to care for you because she was immature and was dependent on her mother financially. Her mother did not believe she was capable of rearing a child.

Your grandmother did make all the arrangements for the adoption, of course, with your mother agreeing. It was a private adoption; therefore they were not consulted and had no part whatever in the placement. We do not know the whereabouts of your mother; in fact, her parents have heard nothing from her since she left them after you were placed with your adoptive parents.

God love you and keep you.

Sincerely,

Sister Ann, ACSW
Director of Social Services

It was the letter Fauna had hoped for, but it told her nothing whatsoever about the whereabouts of her real mother. She was dejected, but still there was a ray of hope. At least someone actually knew her mother, even if for only a brief time seventeen years ago.

The following morning Fauna showed the letter to Sister Hillary, "Don't look so depressed, dear; you've learned quite a bit from this letter. For instance, they know that your mother did not give you away, but was obviously forced to do so by her mother and grandmother. Also, your grandmother was not very wealthy, and your adoptive mother must have known your grandmother or more probably your great-grandmother, but she is not telling all. It also appears that your real mother was not nearly as mature as you were at the same age.

"So you see, things aren't always as bad as they appear on the surface," Sister Hillary paused, gazing at the ceiling. "In about two months, I have to go to San Francisco on hospital business. Perhaps, if I get a chance, I'll snoop around and see what I come up with. In the meantime you can write another letter."

"To who?"

"The Missing Persons Bureau, of course." She left holding her finger up to her lips, reminding Fauna to keep everything a secret.

With the exception of Jimmie, Fauna kept the secret. Jimmie seemed delighted by the letter, even though it wasn't helpful.

Fauna wrote to the Missing Persons Bureau in San Francisco, but after weeks with no response, Fauna's thoughts turned to more pressing matters such as trying to keep Jimmie out of jail. From what the police told Fauna, Jimmie had came home by taxi and stabbed a cab driver in a dispute over the fare. Jimmie was in bad trouble this time. Although the driver was not seriously injured, the police had their fill of Jimmie Lee Faison episodes. They thought it best to keep her locked away for a while.

While her mind was occupied with Jimmie's plight, her body was caring for two households while working full-time at the hospital.

Finally Fauna received a letter from the Missing Persons Bureau; the investigation had turned up nothing. There were no records of Tamar Hodel whatsoever. Fauna wasn't discouraged, just very disappointed. Except for telling Momma during her frequent visits, Fauna kept the details to herself.

To make matters more complicated, Luanne, Fauna's co-worker at the hospital, had decided to run away from home. She moved in with Fauna and Bobby, making their small apartment that much more crowded.

A few weeks after Luanne moved in with them, Fauna found a note on her desk at work.

"I found some interesting things in you-know-where. Meet me at 3:00 near O.R.
— Lucy."

Fauna was so busy with everything else going on in her life that she forgot about Sister Hillary's trip to San Francisco. Fauna met her as planned. The nun motioned Fauna toward an empty room.

"I got your note . . ." Fauna said.

"Shhhh," Sister Hillary peeked through the opening before she closed the door. "We mustn't be too careful, spies everywhere you know."

"Did you find out anything about my mother?" Fauna said. "Where is she? Did you see her?"

"I told you not to expect too much, and no, I didn't find your mother, Fauna. I'm sorry. But I did go to St. Elizabeth's and managed to talk my way into seeing the records of your mother's case that were tucked away in some old files."

"You got the records! How did you manage that?"

"Never mind," Sister Hillary said. "Let's just call it professional courtesy."

Sister Hillary sat down and opened her notebook, "Now let see, I found out that your grandfather was a Russian Jew who was considered a genius. Your family was very wealthy. They left San Francisco and moved to the Los Angeles area, but it didn't say where. The only thing that was useful was an old address on Fillmore Street where your grandmother was living at the time. I checked out the old house, but she no longer lives there. The neighbors aren't very talkative, if you know what I mean.

"Nearby, there was a small church which I had been to many years ago, so I decided to stop by." Fauna gave her a quizzical glance. "I don't know why, either; I guess I came down with a bout of nostalgia or something. Anyway, I met this woman, an old woman who seemed to belong there for some reason. We chatted a bit. During the conversation she asked why I came to San Francisco and specifically this church. I told her why I was in the neighborhood, and the next thing you know, I let out the whole story of your life!"

She paused for a moment, and checked out in the hallway. "I am sorry, I really had no right to tell anyone what you told me in confidence, but this woman seemed so interested, I just found myself talking and talking."

"That's OK, Sister," said Fauna. "It doesn't matter, everybody knows already. So what did she say, anyway?"

"Well, that's the interesting part. This woman said it was Providence that brought me to that church and brought us together. Although she didn't know these people personally, she had heard of them. She said that it sounded as if your mother was a real troublemaker, and that she caused her family a lot of pain by becoming pregnant. If she was any kind of mother, this woman told me, she would have tried to find you a long ago, and that it would probably be best for you to let go and get on with your life, and leave your real mother alone."

"That's it?" Fauna asked.

"Sorry, yes. That's all."

Fauna was disappointed at not learning more, but later she began to think that there was something that didn't sit right. Sister Hillary wasn't telling her something, Fauna felt, but she was too confused to identify it. It would have to wait.

A few months later Jimmie was released from jail. She looked older and not very well. Her sobriety didn't last. She began to drink again. Fauna put the thoughts of finding her mother on the shelf. Her job, Yvette, and Bobby, were keeping her quite busy.

Fauna spoke to Luanne about the letter from the Missing Persons Bureau and about Sister Hillary's discovery that the family had moved to the Los Angeles area.

"Maybe you could hire a private eye, you know, like on TV." Luanne said.

"No, I can't afford that. There's gotta be a cheaper way."

"I know, how about a newspaper ad. I see that all the time, people put ads in for missing cats, rings, everything," Luanne said.

"Yeah, but which paper?" Fauna said. "There are dozens of papers. I don't even know where to look."

Fauna folded her hands, "There must be something Sister Hillary wasn't telling me. That old woman at the church must somehow be connected."

"I know, I'll check the phone book in Southern California," Luanne said.

Fauna straightened up, "That won't cost anything, either," she said.

The following day, Luanne spent her lunch hour at the public library and searched most of the cities on the West Coast. She found three Hodels listed in the white pages of the Los Angeles directory. She was surprised and delighted to see her friend's name in print. She returned and gave Fauna the information. That evening, Fauna called all three numbers and began asking questions about Tamar. The first two had no idea what she was talking about, but the third call Fauna made was to a Marion Hodel in Manhattan Beach.

"Hello, Mr. Hodel?" She didn't wait for him to reply, since this was her last hope and she was anxious for a confirmation. "I am trying to locate Tamar Hodel. Do you know her? She's an old friend of mine. I haven't seen her in a few years."

"Tamar Hodel?" he said, "Why yes, I do."

Instantly, Fauna's whole body tingled. She felt flushed. "I'm her daughter!" she said.

There was silence; he said nothing. Then Fauna's voice began to quiver. "It was from a long time ago. She gave me away when I was born—to a Negro family in Reno. Do you remember anything about that?"

Again there was silence. Then he spoke, but this time his voice was more guarded, deliberate. "Now there was something about someone in the family, a distant relative whose name was Tamar."

Again, Fauna couldn't wait for him to answer. She was sure he knew who she was. "You do remember? Do you know where she is? What does she look like? Where can I get in touch with her?"

"No, I'm sorry, I can't remember anything. You'll have to find someone else who may know. Good bye." The line went dead. She knew by the tone in his voice that he indeed did know something. But what, she didn't know. Fauna thought about calling him again, but decided it would be less threatening to write him a letter explaining her circumstances in detail. Maybe that would refresh his memory, maybe he would help.

Fauna told Momma of the phone conversation. "I'm not surprised he hung up on you. Those whites don't want to get involved with no black people, especially ones that's gonna bring them a whole heap a trouble," Jimmie said.

Fauna moved toward the window and folded her arms, looking out at the street.

Jimmie continued, "What do you think they're gonna do when they find her, huh? I'll tell you what. They gonna keep it to themselves. Besides, how do you know if she even wants to see you in the first place? Don't you think she would of tried to get in touch with you after all these years?"

A week later Fauna received a letter from California.

May 29, 1970

Fauna

I am so very happy and glad that you followed up your phone call with a letter, because as it happens you did contact the right "Hodel."

Your grandfather is my cousin and is now living in the Orient. However I don't have his address, but will secure same from his son who is living in Los Angeles.

Steve Hodel, your grandfather's son, contacted me about 4 months ago trying to trace some family history. I hadn't seen him since he was about 5 or 6 years old and your grandfather had him at that time. This is over 30 years ago.

As soon as I can get in touch with Steve and get your Grandfather's address I will send it on to you, and he might also have information on your Grandmother.

This is a short note but wanted to get it mailed at once as I know this will be of interest to you.

Sincerely

M.E. Hodel

P.S—Your mother would be a half sister to Steve.

MEH

Her knees weakened as she sat down at the kitchen table. Her heart pounded as she read the letter over again, concentrating on each word, one at a time. Her hands quivered and a chill tightened her skin, yet she felt warmth inside of her heart. It was a dream; this couldn't be real! All the dreadful times she spent alone, wondering if her mother was real, or whether this life she was living was just a bizarre cosmic joke played by a restless God. It was now close to affirmation. They were real; her mother was real!

Fauna immediately wrote another letter with a long list of questions and sent it off to Marion. She told anyone who would listen what had happened and what was going to happen, as if she already knew the results of Marion Hodel's search. Fauna envisioned a gala awakening by a host of relatives gathered around an enormous fireplace all awaiting her arrival. A party! No, a formal reception with speeches and gifts and flowers with everyone making a fuss over Tamar's long-lost daughter! It would be wonderful.

Within a week Fauna received a second letter in response to her enthusiastic query.

> *Dear Fauna 6 – 5 – 70*
> *Again, a very, brief note to let you know that I received your second letter and am still trying to get your grandfather's address in the Orient. I haven't been able to contact Steve for the last week or so.*
> *As soon as I do will forward the information on to you, and at that time I hope that I will be able to have found out more information from Steve. As I said before I know how anxious you are and that is why I am writing these short notes so you will realize that I am working on this for you and not just forgetting the whole thing.*
> *Sincerely,*
> *Marion Hodel*

Fauna was impatient and did not want to wait a minute longer to hear from him, but she knew it was best to let matters take their own course. She prayed for strength so as not to fall apart and make a fool of herself. The following day, another letter arrived from Marion with the complete address of her grandfather in Tokyo. This was it! Fauna knew if she persevered and prayed hard enough, she would have what she wanted. Without a moment's hesitation, she sat down and wrote a letter to her grandfather.

Bobby was just as excited and gave her all the encouragement she needed. He knew how anxious she was to find her grandfather or possibly her real mother, and did his best to keep her occupied with chores so that she wouldn't burst with excitement. Jimmie softened somewhat, too. She realized that inevitably Fauna would renew contact with her imaginary rival. Jimmie calmed down her behavior so as not to be alienated from her Patta. She became encouraging, maternal, and considerate, often giving opinion as to the eventual outcome. But it fell on deaf ears, since Fauna's mind was already set and nothing was going to change it.

A month before her ninteenth birthday they received another sad message from Los Angeles. Jimmie was informed that Aunt Lucille died during the night. Fauna was heartbroken. It meant that they would all go down to Southern California for the funeral, an event that she did not look forward to.

On that same day, Fauna received another phone call. The operator said it was overseas. She was too grieved to think of who it could be, and at the time she really didn't care.

"Fauna Hodel?"

"Yeah, that's me."

"This is Dr. George Hodel. I am your grandfather."

The blood rushed to her head. Her emotions were awash in a sea of confusion. She didn't know what to say. Her mind was blank. He was her grandfather, and her feeble attempts at an appropriate salutation surely distorted his perception of her.

He got right to the point. "In your letter there were many questions, all directed toward one purpose." He paused. "Why do you want to get in touch with Tamar, your mother?"

Fauna was stunned by his frankness and mystified by his question. Yet somehow she felt she would not get another chance. "Dr. Hodel, if my trying to find Tamar puts her in any danger, or interrupts her lifestyle in any way, please don't tell her. Just send me a picture so that I can lay down to rest this obsession that I have."

He chuckled then said, "I can assure you that it will not endanger her lifestyle. She's in Hawaii. You mentioned in your letter that you were married and had a daughter."

"Yeah, her name is Yvette," she said.

"Let me ask you something. Is your husband Negro?"

"Is he Negro? Sure he is. I'm part Negro myself. A black family raised me in a black community. Why wouldn't I marry Negro?"

"Yes, of course. I will let Tamar know that I spoke with you and she'll be in touch. I would love to meet you. The next time I'm on the West Coast, I'll make sure that I make time to meet with you."

"Oh good. In fact, we're on our way to Los Angeles in just a little while. My Aunt Lucille just passed away and I'll be there for at least a week."

"I may be able to get there at the same time. Why don't you give me the address and phone number where you will be staying and I'll get in touch."

Fauna gave him the information and was delighted that he warmed up somewhat.

Then he said, "Fauna, this is very important: Under no circumstances are you ever to call or get hold of Marion Hodel—ever! I'll explain it to you when I see you in LA."

She agreed and they said good-bye. She didn't understand. What was going on? Immediately Fauna called Marion Hodel, but there was no answer.

CHAPTER 19

Jimmie was unusually solemn. On the trip to Los Angeles for the wake and funeral, she reminisced about her sister and their early days in Canton. Fauna drove while Yvette slept in the back seat.

"Lucille was always going to church, more than all of us put together. She took right after Big Momma," Jimmie said. "I remember once when Big Momma was too sick to get out a bed. It was a holiday, like Easter or something. Lucille thought it'd be shameful not to go to services that everybody was planning on. As much as Big Momma complained, and she was sick, too—I mean really sick, Lucille wouldn't take no for an answer." Jimmie paused then looked over at Fauna. "She made Big Momma go to church. She was stubborn like that, forcing everybody to do what was right."

"I know Momma, I heard that story before, about a dozen times," Fauna said. Jimmie turned away toward the window and the endless farmland outside. Fauna bit her bottom lip and said, "I talked to my grandfather yesterday. He called me." Jimmie did not respond, just sat looking out the car window. Fauna relayed the conversation she had with George Hodel. Jimmie said nothing, just reached into her bag and gulped from her flask of gin and 7-Up.

Fauna ignored Jimmie and focused on something that was much more personal to her: Tamar. *I wonder what she's like? Maybe, my grandpa will have a photograph. Of course he will, it's his daughter. I wonder what he's like? As soon as she returns from her vacation in Hawaii, I know my grandpa will tell me that he spoke with her. Soon I'll meet my real grandfather. He'll adore me because I am his long-lost grandchild, and he'll tell me everything.*

As her mind drifted back, she heard Jimmie going on about Aunt Lucille and their childhood. Fauna was no longer comfortable with the small minds, petty arguments, and lack of ambition of those around her. Something new was about to open up for her and she refused to permit past prejudices to interfere.

By the time they reached Los Angeles, they were worn out from the journey and the emotional drain. Jimmie had consumed too much gin. She was becoming irritable.

Aunt Lucille's home was busy. People from the church, relatives, friends, and acquaintances milled about renewing old friendships as if the solemn occasion were a class reunion. Jimmie entered first and then Fauna brought in Yvette, closing the door behind. A few heads turned, but most people didn't know Jimmie and merely acknowledged her presence. Dolly came up to Jimmie, put her arms around her and said, "Our sister's gone."

"I know, and I'll miss her," Jimmie slurred.

Dolly stepped back to look at her sister, quickly noticing the glassy red eyes and the slight stagger. Before she could say anything, her brother Willie advanced toward Fauna with a big smile and a warm, enthusiastic greeting. "I can't believe how much you growed up, and into such a beauty. My, my, you is something else to look at. A pleasure!"

Jimmie got in his face, "I knew you'd say hello to the white bitch before your own kind," Jimmie's anger silenced the room. "That's the way you are—always trying to act high sadity in front of an audience."

"What?!" said Uncle Willie. "Don't be givin' me a hard time; I ain't seen either of you in years. Can't I say hello to my niece without you acting jealous of your own daughter?"

"Jealous?" Jimmie shot back. "Of who? Her? Ha! That's a laugh. I'm still the prettiest one in the whole family and you know it, too!"

"Pretty, shit!" said Willie. "You nothin' but an old drunk . . ."

Aunt Dolly forced her way between her siblings. "Hold on!" she said. "Stop trying to disgrace the whole family in front of all these people. Ain't you got no shame? Your sister ain't even cold and you both fightin' like you was a couple of six-year-olds!"

It didn't end there, but Fauna made her way out of the room, not wanting to be associated with either one of them. She was in no mood to listen to a scene that had repeated itself hundreds of times in the past. That no longer upset her; Fauna learned to bury her embarrassment. In spite of the strong emotional grip of the affair at hand, Fauna kept reviewing her conversation with her grandfather.

She was forced back into reality when a familiar voice interrupted her privacy. "Hey, Pat, it's good you could be here."

Without hesitation, Fauna put her arms around him. "Johnny, I'm so sorry about your momma, she was like a second mother to me. And you, you're like a brother. I feel so sad and I know how bad you must feel. I'm sorry." Tears filled her eyes.

"Thank you, sister," he responded coarsely by pulling her too close so that her breast was crushed against him. Fauna pushed away and noticed his eyes, half-closed, reddened, and glassy. His gaze was blank, a look with which she was familiar.

She felt uncomfortable as his eyes peered lustfully at her breast.

"Pat," Aunt Dolly interrupted without warning, "please do me a favor. We need for someone to go run an errand. Would you please go to the corner store for me?"

Fauna was relieved, "Oh, sure."

The evening air, crisp and cool, was a refreshing change from the smoke-filled house. After taking a few deep breaths while standing on the top step, Fauna noticed a car parked across the street with someone hunched down in the driver's seat. She stepped down to the sidewalk and saw that he was a white man, highly unusual in this neighborhood. Fauna wondered if perhaps it was her grandfather, wanting to get a glimpse of her before he decided to introduce himself. But on second glance, the man was too young to be anyone's grandfather and certainly not distinguished enough to be what she imagined.

Going to the store in the black neighborhood was an event for her. She was always self-conscious among the residents. At times like this, she wished she could pin her birth certificate to her forehead. Although she was nervous, she acted indifferent, as if she belonged there. Fauna reflected on her real family, and wondered when George would call, or perhaps he had already. Through all the confusion, perhaps Dolly or Johnny had forgotten to mention it. She made a mental note to ask them as soon as she got back. And poor Johnny, why was he acting so strangely? But these questions would take a back seat to more important matters, particularly George. Meeting him would be the highlight of her young life, and the anticipation was exhilarating. He would be the one to provide all the information about her real mother and answer those questions that plagued her from the beginning.

Fauna wondered what he looked like. She wondered if she bore much resemblance to him, or, more to the point, did she look like the faceless woman of her dreams? But still, there should be something physical that bound them together?! It must be the eyes!

From hearing his refined voice over the phone, Fauna expected him to be at least six feet tall and slightly balding with glasses. Anyone as smart as her grandfather must do a lot of reading. His image remained with her when she returned to the house. At the top of the steps, Fauna turned and noticed that the car with the white man was gone. She brought in the bag of ice and milk for Dolly. "I meant to ask you before," she asked, "did anyone call for me or leave a message?"

"No, I don't think so," said her aunt. "Were you expecting Bobby to call?"

"Oh no, not him. Well yes, him, too. But I was really expecting my grandfather, George, to call me."

'Your what?" Dolly asked.

"Oh, I didn't tell you? I've been in contact with my grandfather, George Hodel. He's a doctor. In fact, he's coming to meet me here, in LA."

Fauna told her the entire story about how she had contacted her grandfather. Dolly stared, holding the bag of ice.

"I didn't know you knew anything about him," said Dolly. "Jimmie Lee always kept it hush-hush."

"Momma didn't tell me much either. I did everything on my own. She's been telling me that someday she's gonna give me the whole story, but every time I ask . . ." she paused and shrugged her shoulders.

The next few days Fauna shuttled between the funeral parlor, the house, and the church. Twice she spotted the same car with the white driver sitting in a slouched position and thought it merely curious.

Two days passed without a call from George. On the third day, Fauna ignored his warning and called Marion in a final effort before going home to Reno. He answered the telephone on the fourth ring.

"No, no, I don't know anything," his slurred speech was slow.

"What's wrong Marion? You sound frightened," she asked.

"Leave me alone. I can't talk to you. Don't call here anymore." And then Fauna heard the dial tone.

She sat down at the end of the couch and put her hands over her ears and gently squeezed her head as if she could force an explanation for his peculiar behavior. But all she came up with was more questions.

She slouched back into the couch, discouraged that as close as she was to finding out who her family was and where she came from, the answers were still beyond her reach. *How could anyone do this? How could George be so callous and unfeeling as to let me sit and wonder without even attempting contact? He must understand how important this is and how long I've waited. How can they abandon me for the second time in my life? Maybe Jimmie was right; maybe these whiteys didn't care much for me even though one of them was my grandfather.* Her heart was broken, filled with anger.

Bobby began working full-time as an apprentice painting cars at the auto body shop. There was no room for advancement, but he liked what he was doing and the money was adequate. After work, he'd come home to eat, then spend most of his evenings with his friends, gambling at one of the casinos. For a time his luck held steady and he managed to save a bit of money. He was free to do as he pleased. But they were not as close as they once were.

Their life together lacked the excitement she expected. Slowly, she began to drift away. Her aspirations were not compatible with his and she was restless to move on. Her heart was buried in disappointment and gloom over not having heard from George.

The hospital, however, was a far different world. Fauna immersed herself in work, becoming more proficient and undertaking responsibility. She received training as a keypunch operator and later was promoted to work in the mainframe computer department. The pay increase was small, but the training by a bona fide tech person gave her more prestige than anything else up to that point in her life. With the promotion came responsibility and confidence.

As much as she wanted to be free of Jimmie and her meddling style, Fauna's own complacent nature was easy fodder for Jimmie's guileful manipulation. Fauna wanted to create an environment that would ease Jimmie's pain—a comfortable home, a new car, enough money to eliminate the pressures of poverty. And a complete medical examination to free her momma from alcohol addition, a disease which was taking its toll on her frail and aging body. But as the months passed, Fauna knew that Jimmie was getting worse. She coughed up blood and had violent tremors, which were first misdiagnosed as her unruly temper.

"Momma, you've got to let Homer take you to the doctors," Fauna said, "Cause whatever this is, it ain't right."

"Never mind that. These doctors only tell me the same thing—it's a cough I got for years," Jimmie said. "What do you know about it anyway?" Jimmie turned in the kitchen chair and raised her hand to shoo her daughter away. "Jus' cause you work in that hospital don't mean you know nothing. You know even less since you're with that knucklehead you call a husband." Jimmie began coughing, "He ain't getting you nowhere, just feeding off you."

Fauna reached into the kitchen cabinet and grabbed a glass for water.

"Don't use those glasses, they for my company." Jimmie said.

"What company?" Fauna asked.

"Never you mind what company. If you were a right child, you'd know what company."

"I'm sorry Momma. I can't help it if I look white, but I know I'm half-black. You think I like having this white skin?" Fauna's head dropped as she leaned on the sink. She whispered, "I know part of this is my fault for. . . ."

Jimmie interrupted, "I tell what's a right child, one who respects they momma, that's a right child, and one who stays with they momma when she needs them the most." Jimmie started coughing again.

After weeks of urging, Fauna finally forced her momma to the hospital for a checkup to determine the extent and cause of her bleeding. Jimmie protested as they entered Washoe Medical Center.

"There ain't nothin' wrong with me," said Jimmie. "All I got is the flu. A little rest in bed and some aspirin'll clear that."

"Aspirin won't do anything. And you don't got no flu," Fauna replied.

"This blood thing," said Jimmie, "is because I'm worried 'bout you—livin' with that good-fo'-nothin' lazy nigger."

"He ain't lazy! You always say that. Bobby works very hard."

Jimmie got louder, "What's gonna become of you? I wanted the best for you. You should of married that doctor at the hospital who's been after you for all this time. He'd be the right one! No! Not you. You pick some fool who ain't goin' nowhere."

"Momma, lower your voice. Everyone's staring at us."

"Let 'em stare," rasped Jimmie, her voice rising up to a shout. "They probably never saw no white nigger-lover like you before."

"Momma, please," urged Fauna, "You're embarrassing me . . . again."

"And you're making me sick! You're the cause of this whole thing. It ain't the drinking. I know what's wrong with me! I don't need no doctor to poke and pry and pinch and stick stuff down my throat! It's you living with that dumb bastard!"

"Momma! Please!" They finally reached the examination room, where the nurse made Fauna wait outside. Jimmie shouted and cursed at Fauna for dragging her to the hospital, insisting that she had the flu.

Fauna sat in a nearby waiting room for more than two hours, watching the nurse and doctor go in and out of the examining room, at first without expression, then with exasperated looks. Fauna suspected Jimmie of giving them a hard time. Finally, a young, pudgy doctor came out and approached her.

"Mrs. Ward?" His voice was high-pitched. "I'm Doctor Edwards. Your mother—she is your mother, right?" He looked at her with a mystified expression.

"Yeah, she adopted me when I was a baby."

"Well, she's very ill. We need to do some tests to determine exactly how far the disease has spread and if there is a chance to slow down the progression. She'll need to be hospitalized."

"Hospitalized! For how long?"

"A week. Perhaps two. Does she have medical insurance?"

"Insurance? No! Of course not, Momma don't believe in insurance. Besides, she can't afford it even if she did. How much is it gonna cost?"

"I'm afraid quite a bit. But if there is no coverage, then I'm afraid there's not much they can do as far as the testing is concerned. We'll have to treat her as an outpatient. I'm afraid her chances aren't very good."

"Oh, no," Fauna began to cry, "You can't let nothing happen to her. She's my mother. You gotta do something."

"I'm going to keep her here for a day or two. By the time the hospital finds out about her not having coverage, maybe you'll be able to raise some money to take care of her bill. I'll do what I can."

He walked away leaving her emotions racing in a circle. Fauna didn't know what to do, but she couldn't let Jimmie die. She went to the lady's room to wash her face and dry her swelling eyes. She couldn't let her Momma see her crying. That would tip her off that it was serious, and who knows what she would do then.

"The doctor said you gotta stay here for a few days," Fauna told Jimmie. "They need to do some tests."

"Yeah, I know all about it. That nice young doctor told me—said I gotta stop drinkin' or it's gonna kill me."

"They all told you that for years. Now maybe that you heard it from someone who knows, you'll stop. Now, you don't have a choice in the matter."

"I know it," said Jimmie, "They ain't gonna keep me here very long, once they find out I ain't got no money for these tests."

"It ain't right," said Fauna, "You gotta have those tests. I don't understand why they just don't do 'em. Why does it always have to be money? Don't they care?" Fauna felt her eyes fill up again and turned away from Jimmie, making an excuse why she had to leave so abruptly. "I'll be back later. And don't worry, everything will work out."

Fauna drove to her momma's home and stayed just long enough to pick up some of her momma's personal items, praying all the way. She returned to the hospital to find that her momma had been moved into a ward with ten other impoverished patients. She looked tired and frail. She told Fauna they had given her a pill and said no more. Within moments, her momma's expressionless eyes closed slowly and she went off into a gentle sleep.

Fauna stayed with her for what seemed like hours, contemplating how limited her options were, and praying to God for His guidance and intervention, offering her own soul if it would do any good.

The medicinal odors emanating throughout the ward irritated Fauna. She made her way into the chapel, knelt at a pew in prayer, and stayed there for hours, until her knees became raw. She was forced to put pads over the bruises. Fauna believed that God wanted something in return for the miracle she was asking; aching knees were all she had to offer.

She left the chapel and wandered about the hospital halls, slightly disoriented. She stumbled upon the hospital offices and noticed a door ajar with the title "Administrator" painted on it. Without a second thought, as though the hand of God had guided her there, Fauna walked in and sat down at one of the two leather chairs opposite the desk. She had no plan in mind, nor did she know what she was going to say, but somehow this is where she had to be.

Before Fauna had a chance to make any cohesive plan, a middle-aged man in a western-style shirt and cowboy boots walked in and said rather coarsely, "Who are you?"

Introducing herself, she explained that she was employed at St. Mary's Hospital in the accounting department.

"So?"

The conversation went downhill from there. Fauna explained her mother's case and their financial situation and asked for help.

"There is nothing I can do," the man told her as he picked up a phone call and turned away from her in dismissal. "The hospital has a very strict policy concerning indigent patients."

Her next call was to the Welfare Office. They politely informed her that what the hospital said was correct. Fauna was desperate and alone. She needed someone to help her—someone like her real mother, who she knew would understand and perhaps find a way. . . . perhaps through George. George! That was it! Suddenly, Fauna was full of enthusiasm. He would help. How could he refuse his long lost granddaughter!

Fauna checked on Jimmie to see if everything was all right. She was still asleep in the same position. Fauna hurried home to find the address that Marion had given her in Tokyo. Fauna thought about writing him to plead her case as strongly as possible, but realized that mail would take too long. And there was little time, according to the doctor. To expedite matters, she sent a telegram. It was more of a complaint about the manner in which her momma was being treated than a plea for help. Fauna didn't know if he would even get the telegram, much less respond. But it was worth a try. Perhaps he had a way of providing an insurance policy or exercising some loophole in the state laws that would provide for momma. After all, he was a doctor and should know more about it.

The next few days were hectic. Fauna was trying to take care of her household while also spending as much time as possible at the hospital with Jimmie, who was anything but an ideal patient. Even in her weakened condition she abused the nurses, offering advice where it wasn't needed or even wanted, and in general, causing a ruckus in the ward. The doctor then kept her sedated.

On the fourth morning, Fauna walked to the ward where her momma had been staying, and found her bed empty. She rushed to the nurse's station just as the administrator stepped off the elevator.

"Oh, Mrs. Ward, I'm so glad I found you," he said, "I tried to call you this morning, but there was no answer."

"Where's my mother?" Fauna said.

"I want to let you know that arrangements have been made . . ."

"Arrangements? What arrangements, did she die?"

"No, no, arrangements to have the best possible care for your mother. In fact, she is now having tests to determine the best course of treatment. We moved her out of this ward. She'll have a private room so that they can extend the care that she deserves. Now, why don't you go down and have some coffee and relax. Everything that is humanly possible is being done. I will have one of the staff inform you when she is comfortably back in her room."

Fauna was stunned, "How did all this happen?" Fauna asked, "Who's paying for it? Was it the Welfare? Did they change the rules?"

He hesitated, "Let's just say that it's all taken care of. I'm not permitted to go into any of the details, but arrangements have been made. Ummmm—we'll just leave it at that."

Fauna was curious, but not enough to understand that he didn't want her to know how these "arrangements" had been made. Fauna decided it best not to make waves and let the matter rest as he suggested, and happily walked to the coffee shop to wait.

Fauna spent at least two hours lingering in the snack shop, but no one called. She went to the front reception desk and asked what room Jimmie Lee Faison was assigned, and then quickly made her way to the new room.

"How y'all feelin'?" Fauna asked Jimmie.

"They poked and needled me," said Jimmie. "I feel like a pin cushion. How'd ya get them to do all this stuff? And a private room, too!"

"Well, you always said you wanted to be famous," smiled Fauna. "They must have realized who you were and decided to give you the very best."

"Bullshit! I ain't famous yet, but I could've been an actress, I'm a good actress. I could've been a singer, too, but I guess I'll got to leave it to you to become famous," Jimmie paused, "Except you ain't headed in that direction at all."

"Well," said Fauna, "I was just fooling anyway. I got no idea how this all came about. The guy in the office just told me that everything was taken care of. So, let's just leave well enough alone."

"About time I got something from whitey. They been taking from me long enough," Jimmie said.

Fauna remained at her side most of the time until her momma was released the following week, still wondering how the hospital bill was paid. She concluded that her prayers were answered, or her mysterious grandfather had acknowledged her telegram in a most confidential way. She thanked God.

For the next few months while Jimmie recovered and remained sober, Fauna visited a few times a week to do some of the household chores. Jimmie sat in her favorite chair by the window, while Fauna struggled with the coffee pot. She felt her momma stare at her and abruptly stopped. "What?" Fauna said.

"I ain't said nothing," Jimmie turned back toward the window, "nothing I ain't said before."

Fauna sighed, and then pushed her hair back from her eyes. "Well, then why you looking at me like that?"

"Cause you look frazzled," Jimmie said, "I already warned you about what would happen if you married that so-called husband of yours."

"That's not why I'm frazzled. I got a lot to do, that's all."

"If you'd of put your mind to it you could of married a doctor or a lawyer," Jimmie said, "and now, you'd have nothing to worry about, could've had the easy life. But instead you slide deeper down the drain with that car washer."

"He ain't no car washer, Momma," Fauna said, "and you know that."

"He's lucky he's got that."

"I got other things that are more important right now, I can't be arguing about Bobby," Fauna said.

"He's gambling, ain't he?" Jimmie said.

"How'd you know?"

Jimmie smirked without saying a word.

"I know my life ain't perfect yet. But it will be someday, it will."

"It won't till you get rid of that husband. You the one who's taking care of everything anyway. You work, you take care of your baby, you take care of him. The only one you don't have time for is the one who raised you."

"Momma, that's not true. I'm here all the time. What more can I do?"

"If you don't know what to do by now, Patta, then I can't tell you."

Fauna felt the coolness glide over her skin only to be quickly replaced by a hot flash. She sensed guilt replacing fear, guilt for being born, guilt for unsettling her real family, guilt for Jimmie's drinking, and that responsibility was deeply ingrained. Fauna couldn't abandon her now, not when Jimmie needed her the most. Appeasement was again the only course of action. The breakup of her marriage seemed to be the path of least resistance.

Fauna buried herself in extra work at the hospital to delay making a decision. The computer functions became mechanical. Her mind traveled in ten directions at once. She was weary of feeling ashamed at not being darker skinned each time someone questioned her mixed race, yet she continued to tell her story to anyone who listened. She loved Yvette, she liked her job, and she was deep into her search, but still she found herself daydreaming more and more of her real mother and her family. More than a year had gone by since George had called her. Her wounds of disappointment were healing, and again she felt a strong urge to connect with Tamar. Many nights she sat up in her bed, in the darkness, visualizing what her mother looked like, forcing her dreams to become reality. Each morning she tried to make them go away, but she couldn't control the visions that lurked about her mind. But her most basic needs never altered. She had to know why she was so white for someone who was half-black. She had to know why she was given away, something that Jimmie had always known but refused to tell her.

The obsession finally got the better of her one morning while she was sitting in bed. She began calling the directory assistance throughout California. First, San Francisco, then Oakland, San Jose, Sacramento, Los Angeles, San Diego; but they all led to dead ends. At each rejection, immediately she thought of another city until all of the larger population centers were covered. Suddenly, as if the sun burst through the clouds, Hawaii snapped into her head. George had told her she was in Hawaii, but Fauna hadn't given it a second thought. Everyone knew that nobody lived in Hawaii, they just went there on vacation and she assumed the same for Tamar.

Information for Honolulu responded with a phone number that Fauna jotted down. She broke out in a cold sweat, fidgeting nervously. She sprung out of bed and raced into the bathroom flapping her arms. She glanced in the mirror at flushness in her face. She heard the pounding of her heart as blood raced through her body. *What to do? What to do?* Her emotions were in chaos. She felt stupid for going through such a complicated process, only to find so simple a solution. Tamar did exist, and all Fauna had to do was dial her number. The dream was now a reality. She fell to her knees to thank God and her angels.

Fauna composed herself. She needed to finish the final leg of her odyssey. She took a deep breath and walked back to the phone, terrified and euphoric at the same time. She closed her eyes tightly and thanked God and her angels, again and again. Almost unconsciously, Fauna dialed the eleven digits. Before she realized what she was doing, she heard a single ring on the other end of the connection. A clear melodic voice that sounded like an echo answered.

"Hello."

"Hello, Tamar?"

"Hold on," she heard the voice say and then a muffled "It's for you."

"Yes, this is Tamar. Who's calling?"

"Hello, Tamar?" Fauna recognized her sweet, wonderful voice—a voice that she had heard thousands of times in her dreams—a voice that would make her life complete. "This is Fauna. Your daughter." There was silence on the phone and then Fauna spoke again.

"What? Fauna?" Tamar sounded confused. "Fauna is right here. Hold on a minute."

Fauna didn't understand. She jotted down the name Fauna with a question mark on her note pad. Then she heard Tamar call to someone else. "Fauna, it's for you."

In a moment, another voice answered, "Hi. It's me."

"Hello, is this Tamar?" Fauna asked again.

"No, this is Fauna. Who do you want?"

"What? I wanna speak with Tamar."

"Well, OK. Who is this?" she asked.

"This is Fauna, her daughter she gave away as a baby twenty years ago." Again there was long silence. Then Fauna heard the second voice call to someone else.

"It's for you. She says she's Fauna, your daughter."

Suddenly Fauna heard laughter on the other end of the phone, almost as if they were having a party.

"Hello, this is Tamar. Who is this?"

"Tamar," Fauna said, "This is your daughter. You named me Fauna when you gave her away in 1951. Do you remember?"

There was a long pause. "Fauna? Fauna. . . ." Fauna heard a sniffling. "Is this really you? I can't believe it! How did you find me?"

"I got your number through information. You sound just like me."

"This can't be happening! This isn't real! Oh my God! I didn't understand who you were. Fauna, I thought you wanted Fauna, my daughter, my other daughter. Her name is Fauna, too. This is unbelievable, she began to giggle. "Since you were born, I had been sending my love to you, wherever you were, every day, and finally that love came through."

Then Fauna heard her say to someone else, "It's Fauna, the real Fauna."

"Oh Fauna," Tamar said as she came back on the line, "It's so good to hear you." She was crying and laughing at the same time. "You can't know how much I've wanted to hear from you. Oh, I didn't give you away as a baby. I was forced to give you up for adoption. I didn't have any choice in the matter."

Fauna listened carefully, but through the emotions, almost unconsciously, Fauna asked, "Tamar? Can I call you Tamar? I don't know what else to call you."

"Of course."

She stared into the dresser mirror trying to put a face on the real voice of her dreams, but she only saw a reflection.

"Is my real father a Negro?" Fauna asked.

"Is your father a Negro? Oh no, of course not. He was some Italian playboy from the neighborhood where I grew up. I don't even remember his name."

Fauna felt the shockwave tighten her skin from the top of her head to the tips of her toes. She was flushed with rage and iced to the core at the same time. Her fingers turned white as she tightened the grip on the receiver and pressed hard against her ear trying to make the words disappear back from where they came. Her knees began to buckle and she slowly melted to the floor with her back leaning against the bed. She swiped her mouth with the other hand removing the sweat that covered her. She took a deep breath to stiffen her resolve, trying to stay conscious. Her exhale released what felt like thousands of pins jabbing at her from inside her head. She was dazed, trying to meld the sound she was hearing with the vision of her dreams. It made no sense.

All of her life Fauna had defended her blackness, forced to prove it over and over with a worn out birth certificate. The sun never set without the thought of "race" at the forefront. Her earliest recollections were the contrasts in skin color; the blackness of Jimmie Lee, Chris Greenwade, Homer, Rosie, Bobby, Yvette. The blackness of her friends, and virtually everyone Fauna knew. There was never doubt in her mind that she was of mixed race, and only through some quirk of genetics and the complexity of DNA was her skin white. By her culture, she was black. By dying her hair, and tanning her skin, Fauna wanted desperately to be black. She defended it at every opportunity, proving her mix with her love for the family that raised her.

Now, through five simple words, the only person in the world who knew beyond a doubt shattered her soul. *"Oh no, of course not."* That was all she heard, not another word.

CHAPTER 20

One lie,
One little white lie . . .
Caused me to fight
For
The rest of my life

She wrote in her diary. Her life was a sham, and the deception was too profound to discuss with anyone. With each passing moment, she knew less and less what to do. Her life was set on a new course into waters never before explored, and she was too disheartened to come on deck. The dilemmas that she envisioned, resulting from a young girl's action more than twenty years earlier, overwhelmed her. Humiliated and ashamed were the words she used to herself over and over again—and questions, questions, always more questions. *What kind of sick minds would interfere so boldly with another person's life?* She didn't know if anything was real anymore. She had desperately wanted to be black all of her life, now that she knew that her proudest attribute was a lie, she was a calamity. She could never tell her momma.

That evening while she was tucking her precious child into bed, Yvette looked up at her and said, "Mommy, I'm not sleepy yet. Can I stay up?"

"Sure, but you'll have to stay up by yourself, because I'm drained and I'm going to bed, too."

"But can you stay with me for a little?" Yvette asked, her beautiful brown eyes irresistible.

"Well, maybe just a little," she said and looked down at her little girl. She smiled and couldn't help but share her wonder out loud. "You're a vision, Yvette, a perfect vision of what I should be. All my life I wanted to know my real momma, to know for sure if I was of two races. I look at you, my baby, who I love more than anything, and I know that you're what I wanted to be. You're my living treasure."

Yvette smiled and cuddled close to her mother.

"Now get some sleep," said Fauna.

"OK, Momma," Yvette said, "I love you."

It was a most inopportune time in her marriage with Bobby to discover the truth about her lineage. They were already having difficulties communicating. He gambled more and more, and she was tired of paying the bills. Now that a challenging new world was opening up to her, she became bored with the routine of married life. But instead of becoming entangled in hateful accusations, Fauna brooded quietly, waiting for events to unfold. She prayed to her angels for a change in direction. She wanted to make something of herself. She wanted to fulfill what she believed was a Divine Plan.

A few weeks after her fateful call to Tamar, a rainbow-colored letter arrived from Hawaii. She set it down on the kitchen counter near the sugar jar, reluctant to know its contents. She poured herself a glass of cold water and sat down at the table just long enough to take a sip. She stared at the envelope, and then realized that nothing could be more painful than the phone call. She reached over and promptly tore it open. Before she unfolded the scalloped-edged stationery, a photograph tucked inside dropped to her lap.

For the first time, the woman of her dreams was no longer faceless. The image centered around a woman with dirty blond hair seated on a couch. She wore a blue housedress with one side pulled down far enough to expose her left breast, allowing a suckling infant that lay across her lap to nourish itself. To the woman's left was a young, dark-skinned teenage girl with another baby on her lap. Above the girl's head, in the white margin "Fauna II" was written in purple ink. At the feet of the woman two little boys, both in their underwear were seated on small stools: one busily eating out of a bowl and the other staring directly into the camera lens. Below each child was written what appeared to be their names: "Joy," "Love," "Peace," and "Starr."

Fauna flipped over the photo, and on the back was a hastily written message:

For you, Fauna, taken by your grandfather when he was visiting. Fauna II's father is a Negro folk-ballad singer named Stan Wilson. I will write soon—children keep me pretty busy.

Then there was the main letter. Fauna read it slowly.

Dearest Fauna, I love you.

Hello. I am so happy that you answered, that we answer the call of our hearts. I am sitting at the edge of the sea watching your little brothers, Peace and Joy, run into the water and I will join them when I am through writing, light candles and wait for your answer, so sorry that I lost you—Has been a long sad time for me in my mind and heart.

Please tell me of your life, of your heart, of how you have lived. I said that your father was a Negro because I love black people so much and thought that you were mine to raise with love. Before I knew that I could not keep you with me, it was too late, and I did not know what to do. Your actual real flesh and blood father was a local playboy, Italian, in our neighborhood, maybe about 22 years to my 16 and I don't remember his name because I pushed him from my memory because our understanding levels were so different.

I live now in a house in Kailua with the children: Peace (4) and a Leo too; a boy, Joy, an Aries 2 in July and his mother, your sister Deborah, or Fauna II, who will be 17 in October (Scorpio). She waits for her baby's father Michael to join them in Hawaii, from LA; and my latest baby, whose name is Love, is a smiling boy and a Gemini.

I am not married but am fortunate enough to share my life with a beautiful friend named Wendy. She is visiting with us after a time apart from us—he will be returning to Dixon, California by the end of September for a few months before he returns to live with us here and open a health food restaurant and other happy things. So, I believe Dixon, California is close to Reno. It would be beautiful if you could meet and talk. I will send the address to you. Write please send me a picture of you and your loved ones. I love you,

Thanking God, all power, love that I am able to speak these sweet words.

Tamar

Also enclosed was a hastily written note on plain white paper. It was in Tamar's handwriting:

P.S. Here is the phone number of my dear friends, Michelle Phillips and Warren Beatty. . . . I would like for you to call them. Also, the number for Kenny Ortega is. . . . You can ask them questions about me, if you want.

Fauna studied the photo carefully; she was captivated by the image of her mother, Tamar. She read the letter again and again trying to understand what wasn't there—something between the lines. But after several hours of mind-squeezing agony, going over each scenario, Fauna was drained. She felt empty; her whole life had been a lie. She stood up from the table and wandered aimlessly about the house in a state of perpetual numbness. She hid the letter in a safe place with her other secrets and decided to accept it for what it was, at least temporarily: a brief, informative note introducing her to her half-brothers and half-sister—Peace, Joy, Love, and Fauna II.

She could never let anyone read it. It was evidence, proof that she was not black! For the next few days, she avoided everyone. She prayed for a glimpse of the bright side of all of this. She wrote another reflection in her diary:

When yet a seed
I loved you so
Now full bloomed
It's doomed. . . .

Fauna's self-confidence was at a low point. She needed to restore her poise. Living on a meager income from day to day only added to her angst. That had to change. Her life had to change. She made up her mind to be in control again. Help came in the way of Bobby's sister, Jean. While visiting Fauna early in the evening, the conversation moved away from the baby's latest discovery.

"I can't believe Bobby's missing all this with his own daughter," Jean said.

"I know, when he ain't working, he's with his friends at the casino," Fauna replied, "he thinks he's got a system of some kind, but all he keeps doing is using money we don't got."

Jean was sympathetic. "He's always been that way, thinking he could strike it rich, but he don't realize that he's got to take care of his own first." Jean walked over to the stove to heat some tea. As Fauna watched her shapely figure shuffle back and forth, she suddenly turned toward Fauna with the same twinkle in her eye that made her so likeable. Her skin was very dark, and her hair short and wavy, but with a style that made her perfectly even features only accentuate her smile. "You need to make more money girl," Jean said.

"Don't I know it." Fauna said, "I need a new job. The hospital don't pay me enough for what I know how to do. It was okay in the beginning, but now I've been there for a long time."

"And they ain't giving you any more money, right?" Jean asked.

Fauna nodded and picked up Yvette who was starting to cry. "She's getting tired, time for her bed." She carried the baby to her bedroom and came right back.

"No, they say that the budget's too tight for any pay raises," Fauna said.

Jean set the two cups of hot tea on the table and sat down opposite Fauna. "I'm gonna look for a job at the EOC where I work."

"Ain't that a civil service job or something?" Fauna asked.

"No, I don't mean at the same place I work, but through the companies that work with us. We promote minority works projects, minority jobs, any time there is something to do with money and minorities, we got our fingers in it. That's why they call us the Economic Opportunity Council."

"It's like a employment agency, right?"

"Right, except it's only for minorities." Jean said.

"Well, I'm a minority. My birth certificate says my father is 'Negro'."

Jean grinned, and then said, "You sure don't look like no minority, but since you got the paper to prove it, then that's all they should need."

"I'll come down tomorrow, after work," Fauna said.

"Bring the baby, too, just in case. At least *she* looks like a minority."

Jean found an opening for a CRT Operator at Western Union and Fauna applied. However, convincing the EOC that she was half-black required her to tell her tale in the same persuasive manner that she had done so many times before. It was a unique appeal for understanding, each rendition fresh and interesting, as if the latest listener were the first to uncover her remarkable account. Fauna concealed the truth about her real father. In a sense, she was in denial. Instead, she used all the skills she learned growing up with her momma, easily manipulating the system to convince the EOC that she was a minority and did indeed have a high school diploma. She started work with better pay within a week. She also recognized that she would always need to explain herself.

It was obvious to everyone that Bobby and Fauna were having a difficult time with their marriage. They had fallen into a pattern of deliberate taunting. The more time he spent with his friends at the casinos, the more Fauna resented his lack of attention. She kept busy with Yvette, Jimmie, her new job, and her ambition to understand who she was and why she was on this planet. She felt driven to not only get ahead, but to also uncover the secrets of her real family.

Whenever they discussed the problems that kept them at odds, Bobby tried to placate her in some way, which usually lasted about two weeks. During one such respite, she took inventory of her possessions. Among the clothes, dolls, old photos, school projects with silver stars pasted across the top, parts of toys, magazine cut-outs of her favorite movie stars, odd slips of paper with phone numbers long ago disconnected, and her fragmentary diaries, there stood out the notes from her first conversation with Tamar. The pain of that debilitating call held open her wounded heart, blinded her rationale, and blocked any cognitive associations whether real or imaginary. But the name *Dorothy Barbe* was scribbled and heavily underlined. Below it, an address and phone number in San Francisco. The name resonated in her head as she said it aloud. It was Tamar's mother, her own maternal grandmother. It was just the mechanism Fauna needed to rekindle her quest.

She dialed the number and was more prepared than before. "Hello, Dorothy?"

"Yes, this is she."

"Hi, this is Fauna, Tamar's daughter. The first one."

"Oh!" she said, clearly surprised.

"I know this is unexpected, and I'm real sorry to bother you. I've talked to Tamar on the phone in Hawaii and she sounded so nice. She even sent me a picture."

"Yes, I'm sure she did. What is it that you want from me?"

"I've been thinking about you for a long time and I'd really like to meet you sometime."

"Meet me? Whatever for? I'm not important. No, you don't need to meet me. Besides, I'm not feeling very well and I don't need to have company."

"Yes, but you're important to me and it'd mean a lot just to finally meet someone in my real family. All my life I wondered what my family's like. I really need to meet you and you're the closest to me from here in Reno. Can I come next week?"

"Next week? Oh, no, not next week. That's much too soon." Dorothy was fumbling for an excuse. "Perhaps, sometime later."

"But we'll be in San Francisco next week. I promise I won't take up no time at all, and I just want to meet you and talk with you about my family."

"We? Who is we?"

"Oh, you didn't know? My husband, Bobby and I have a daughter, too."

"No, you must not bring anyone with you. I cannot meet with a stranger to discuss anything with you. You'll have to come alone. There's too much to talk about with you. And with a stranger, even a husband, it would be too much interference."

Fauna was delighted, "Fine, we'll be there on Friday."

"I will only meet with you alone. Your husband will have to wait in the car. And you must ring the bell four times so I'll know who it is. Otherwise I never answer the door."

With Bobby in tow, Fauna arrived in San Francisco. She was surprised to learn that Dorothy's apartment was quite old and run-down, not at all what she expected. They rang the bell four times as instructed, and waited only a few seconds before an elderly, dour looking woman answered the door. She was petite, with graying, short hair. Underneath her sagging jowls, her face was stern with a chiseled look about it. Her glasses, too, were dated, as were the slacks she wore. A "Victorian matron," Bobby later described her, and he was right. She had the air of someone who had been lost in another era, trying to retain the dignity of what might once have been her glory days.

Dorothy looked at them coldly. Fauna smiled and said, "Dorothy? I'm Fauna." Bobby looked at Fauna strangely. He had never called her Fauna; it was always Pat.

Dorothy was stone-faced, eyes darting back and forth between the two of them, and then fixing on Fauna. They widened, almost as if she was in shock. She caught herself staring, and then hesitated only momentarily to look them over. "I thought I made myself clear when I told you that we must meet alone," she said.

Bobby understood. He had lived with prejudice his entire life. "I know you both got lots to talk about, so I'll just leave. Be back later." He was gone.

Dorothy motioned her inside. Fauna's need to know, after coming this far, doused her spark of resentment at what appeared to be this woman's narrow-mindedness regarding Bobby.

Entering the small parlor was like walking into a museum. Fauna was overwhelmed by the amount of unusual pieces: oriental objets d'art, nudes, oils of Hawaii, and the finest she ever observed up close. Fauna's enthusiasm was obvious; she was fascinated. Dorothy watched closely as Fauna's eyes roamed from one sculpture to another. She saw Fauna marvel at a copper piece of a mother and child. "Do you like that one?"

"Oh, it's like something I've never seen before. It's beautiful."

"It's by my sister, Beryl. She and her husband Ray Boynton are both well-respected artists. Many of these pieces are from their studio—the sculptures, and the drawings, and some of the paintings. The other pieces we've collected over the years."

"What about the nudes? Are they also by him?"

"No, of course not, those are by Matisse. Not originals of course, just copies, but they look fine, don't you think?"

Fauna gave a nod and smiled.

"I'm sorry for staring," Dorothy said, "You look so . . . so white."

"Yeah, I guess I take after my mother's side," Fauna said, surprised at how quickly this woman seemed to be warming to her despite the frosty reception. Perhaps, Dorothy rarely had company and hungered for the chance to gossip, especially with someone who was completely in the dark. Fauna felt trusting, realizing that Dorothy was relieved to find someone to confide in about the family secret that she had carried around all these years.

"I'm sorry," said Dorothy, "about wanting to speak to you alone. I don't have anything against your husband. But it is the neighbors. They would be very concerned about his blackness," she said.

That surprised Fauna. This was San Francisco; the Fillmore area was mostly black. What difference did it make? Could it be all in her head? Or has nothing changed, was everyone racist?

"There is a slight resemblance to the family," Dorothy continued, "I just hope you haven't inherited your mother's temperament."

"Why," asked Fauna, half amused, "What do you mean?"

"Oh, please!" said Dorothy, suddenly alarmed, "You don't want to know!"

Fauna hesitated, trying to collect her thoughts. "Dorothy," she began, "I came here to find out about my life. I've been in the dark about my real family for twenty-one years. I don't think you understand how important this is to me. My life has been one question mark after another. I need to know where I came from."

"I'm sorry, you're right," said Dorothy, "Please sit down. Would you care for some tea or something?"

"Sure, that'd be good, thanks." Dorothy shuffled into the kitchen while Fauna sat on the edge of her chair, looking around the room searching for something that would help her connect to this family, but the furniture and wall coverings and artwork and lamps were never in her dreams. It was a different world, foreign and musty, a place where history is kept, but a history of which she knew nothing. Fauna closed her eyes and breathed deeply, trying to feel her real past, but only Jimmie came to view and a world far different from this. Moments later, Dorothy returned with a silver tray. The cups and saucers carefully placed with what Fauna assumed was an accurate arrangement. Dorothy poured a cup of tea from a dainty silver teapot and asked Fauna if she wanted cream and sugar. Fauna said "Yes", and allowed Dorothy to fix her cup. Dorothy sat back on the solitary, wing-backed chair opposite the coffee table.

She looked up at Fauna warmly and said, "You have a right to know. You want to know about your family. Wait here, I'll show you."

She rose from the old chair and walked into another room, immediately returning with a cardboard box stuffed with yellowed papers, envelopes, folders, pictures. She handed Fauna a file folder with a neatly buttoned manuscript titled:

Fillmore Family Record
Descendants of John William Fillmore
Of New Brunswick and Illinois

And some of his Ancestors
I.A. DeFrance
November 1971

"What's this?" asked Fauna.

"This is a history of my family, that is, our family. Actually, it's a fairly detailed account of the Fillmore family, of which both Tamar and myself are included. It traces the roots back to their beginnings in the seventeenth century when Captain John Fillmore first arrived in Massachusetts from England. It's fascinating."

"Really! That's amazing! I'd never imagined," said Fauna, perusing the material.

"Yes, it gets quite interesting just before my great-great-uncle, I think it is, Millard Fillmore, the former president, is introduced; but don't bother with that now, take it with you, or make a copy and return it to me, perhaps on your next visit."

"Yeah, of course, it does seem involved." She put the folder down and asked again. "What about Tamar? What's she like?"

Dorothy looked uncomfortable, looked away, took a deep breath, and placed her hands up to her chin. "Well, you might as well know the truth rather then hear rumors, or lies from Tamar."

"Lies? What do you mean?"

"Tamar has always been a problem. She makes up stories. Not your average childhood fantasies that most children do when they have an imaginary friend or something like that. No, not Tamar. Her stories are very complex and completely false, but with such detail that they sound believable. I have no idea where she got such an imagination, but it has caused problems for the entire family and they all try to avoid her as much as possible."

"What kind a stories?"

"The kind of stories that hurt people's reputation, that makes her look like a victim. Stories that cause people to gossip, point fingers, stare at you when you walk down the street, or avoid you because they think you're evil. Those kind of stories.

"She's always been like that," said Dorothy, "a liar, a pathological liar! Ever since she was a child, she had difficulty distinguishing between realities, the way things are, and the way she wanted them to be. She makes up lies in order to manipulate, to use, and bend the truth in order to get what she wants. She uses everything and everyone. It's been a nightmare."

Fauna was stilled by what Dorothy was saying about her daughter, a woman she'd been yearning to know and love since she first had heard about her. But Dorothy's expression of resignation, of failure and utter hopelessness, made it difficult to doubt what she was saying.

"Her father was so frustrated by her continued scandalous remarks that it virtually ruined his practice. He had to move out of the country to get away from her."

Fauna noticed that the old woman's lip was vibrating, her face was white and chalky with a small bead above her lip. Dorothy paused for a moment, then regained her composure and continued. "Well, as you can see, I don't like talking about her. There are too many unpleasant memories. I will let Tamar tell you what she did.

"Now, Fauna," concluded Dorothy, "what about you? What have you been doing with your life? I want to know everything."

Fauna accommodated her, but all the while protecting her family. She told her about her school and her job, and Jimmie and Homer, leaving out all of the unpleasant details and making herself sound as though she had a very normal childhood, deserving of being included in this illustrious family of which she was so proud.

They talked in small bits, allowing the other to comment politely, and trying to feel each other out. They parted after planning to meet again. Dorothy offered to take Fauna to meet the rest of her family on her next visit. Fauna left with a bundle of unanswered questions, feeling uneasy about the bitter Dorothy and the strange Tamar tales.

Bobby and Fauna drove back to Sparks. He felt put out at not being included in her meeting with Dorothy. She felt sorry for him and they talked about everything Dorothy had said. He was interested in the details but somehow didn't grasp the scope of what all this meant. She didn't either, not all of it. Dorothy was right; it was a private matter. Nor did she want Bobby to know how disappointed she was in what she was learning. They grew even more distant after that day.

During the next few weeks Fauna became noticeably dispirited. For her entire life she had wondered about her real family, who they were and what they were like. She only had her Momma's explanations. Now Tamar's mother, her maternal grandmother, had presented her with a far more complex puzzle with most of the pieces missing. And the pieces she had didn't quite fit. She was disheartened.

Her cousins and friends often nudged her to go out and meet new people, to do something other than work and be a housewife and mother. After much urging, Jean finally persuaded her to go to a local nightclub.

The Driftwood Lounge in Sparks was not a large place, but it did have a live band and catered primarily to whites. They were there no more than fifteen minutes when a well-dressed black man, sporting a wide, friendly smile, approached.

"Well, what do we have here?" he said smoothly. "Two of the most lovely ladies ever encountered in this quaint little town. Let me introduce myself. I am William Sharpstein, Jr. Perhaps you've heard of me," he said confidently with a flamboyant gesture.

"No," they answered in unison, giggling.

"No? Well then, let me be the first to take this opportunity to dispel any misinformation you may hear in the future from those jealous plebeians who would, without any justification, mind you, do harm to my good name and reputation.

"My friends, of which I now include you, call me Billy, and I am an engineer, engineer extraordinaire!"

He looked directly at Fauna, so she responded, "An engineer. Hmmm."

"Yes, as a matter of fact, and to be more specific, I am the Project Engineer for Bill Lear, responsible for establishing the design criteria for the steam turbine, among other things."

"I'm impressed," said Fauna.

"And what is your name, may I ask?"

She hesitated, and didn't say Pat as she normally would. "Fauna," she began.

He cut her off before she could say another word, "Fauna, what a wonderful name. Now that we have all that established, let's dance."

She didn't hesitate a second. His charming manner and eloquent speech captivated her at a time when she was most vulnerable. He wasn't the most handsome man she had ever met, certainly not. He wasn't even what you would consider good-looking. But he had magic, and it was the magic that made her tingle all over.

They danced, and talked, and drank, and had a wonderfully exciting time together. It took all of her energy to keep from screaming with joy. Jean felt the electricity between them, and told her later that it was the fastest move she had ever seen any girl make. Jean was glad, she said, that she didn't take Fauna along with her all the time.

The evening went by quickly. From that first moment, she knew she was in love with him; she knew also that he would fall in love with her. She understood that if she slept with him, her marriage, which was falling apart, would surely be over. When it was time to go, he walked her outside and asked for her phone number, which she was unwilling to give.

As he casually slid into his new Corvette, he said, "Here's my number. If you change your mind, give me a call."

"I already did. When can I see ya again?"

She was somewhat disappointed when he told her that he would be out of town on business for a week. She finally left, sizzling with excitement. She didn't sleep the entire night. For the next week, she counted the hours waiting for him to return to Reno. She had really enjoyed being with him. He was charming, witty, intelligent and educated. His manner of speech was worlds away from the slang expressions and garbled, ghetto drawl that she had grown up with.

Fauna wanted to improve her manners, speech, and education in order to live up to his expectations. She was not about to let him get away. He was someone special.

The following day, still floating on air, she told everyone at work what a wonderful time she had with this man called William Sharpstein, Jr. One of the girls thought that anyone who called himself William Sharpstein, Jr., was all bullshit and decided to prove it by calling Lear personnel to check him out. The only discrepancy she found was that there was no William Sharpstein, but there was a William Sharp, an engineer assigned to turbines.

That confirmation made her feel even more energized. Her mind went into overdrive. She contrived a plan to lure him in, not just for a short affair, but something much more. She enrolled in a correspondence course in order to qualify for a high school diploma and immediately became very conscious of the way she spoke, carefully and methodically pronouncing every word with the utmost propriety. Suddenly, *wut* became *what*, *gots* became *have to*, and *PO-lice* became *police*. *Y'all* was gone, too.

The most disastrous thing in this romance would be to have this urbane and charismatic man meet her capricious Jimmie. Knowing what a different world he came from, she assumed her uncultured background would repel him.

On the day he returned from his business trip, she was in a frenzy. More than a week of anticipation had passed, during which time she envisioned what it would be like to be married to a man with such culture and refinement, education and position. She imagined herself going to elaborate dinner parties, meeting exciting professional people, and, of course, being adored.

To meet his expectations, it was necessary to rehearse everything for their next encounter. But when the time was at hand, their conversation was short and to the point.

She called the number he had given her and asked, "How was your trip?"

"Very successful. When do you think we can get together?"

"I'm on my way."

Within twenty minutes she was at his apartment. He met her at the curb, paid the cab fare, and opened the door for her. When they walked into his apartment, she lost control and threw herself into his arms. Any formalities gave way to their lust. The entire afternoon was spent passionately making love. She knew that her marriage to Bobby was over.

Bobby was waiting in the kitchen, nervously. He moved from one chair to another, and then back to the counter where he stood with his arm folded. He turned and opened the refrigerator, stared at the meager contents and then closed it and sat down on one of the chairs, glancing up at the cat on the wall that stared back with the time, its tail wagging slowly. When she finally returned home more than two hours later than usual, disheveled, Bobby was standing again. He saw the fear and contempt in his wife's eyes. "Where you been?" he asked. After five years of marriage, he knew her well enough to know that something wasn't right. She answered sarcastically, "I was out, just like you is every other day."

"With who?"

She paused a moment and glared, "Somebody who treats me the way I deserve, with respect, not taken for granted."

The look in his eyes turned cold. "You've been out with someone, on a date?"

"What's the difference where I was? Our marriage is a joke anyway. I decided it's time for me to live my own life, not just exist." She watched callously as anger filled his face. "So there ain't no point in us staying together."

Before she could complete her carefully planned speech, he became enraged.

"You white bitch! Just who you think you are? Your old drunken mammy found you in a garbage can. No one knows what type of mess you're from. You bitch, if it weren't for me, you would still be in a dump!"

Bobby knew how confusing her life was, but he wanted his words to dig deep.

He rushed into the bedroom and threw her clothes into a suitcase. His anger was controlled, but it still infused fear in his wife. Within minutes, he forced both his daughter and his wife into the car, and then drove straight to momma's.

"Get out!" he shouted, "Go back to the shit where you belong. You ain't good enough for me." He opened the trunk and threw all of her belongings onto the front yard, then sped off.

Jimmie was on the stoop with her arms folded calmly. Fauna looked at Jimmie who appeared not too upset. She was humiliated in front of her momma, proving her right once more. She detested Bobby for it. She wanted to start a new life, leaving everything that was a reminder behind. She gave away all the belongings Bobby had thrown on the ground.

Fauna stayed with Jimmie for about a week, and then found a small apartment for Yvette and herself. Each evening, and whenever they were free, Billy and she were together, either in his plush apartment at Amesbury Place with its manicured grounds, or at her small cubbyhole. They talked at every opportunity. As quickly as they fell in love, so they planned to live together. Before her second month's rent was due she and Yvette moved into his apartment.

Fauna did her best to prevent her urbane lover from meeting her momma, but her momma had too much street sense to be outfoxed. It didn't take Jimmie long to maneuver Fauna into arranging for Billy to pick up Yvette, allowing the inevitable meeting between the past and the future to take place, whatever the consequences. She fretted most of the evening waiting for Billy to return.

She was embarrassed to look at him as he entered the apartment shaking his head, but he was so upset it was impossible not to. "That woman is crazy! When I knocked on her door," Billy told Fauna, "she opened it and said, 'Who the fuck are you?' I said, 'What?' Then she took me completely by surprise. I tried to be polite, charming in fact. I introduced myself, and she said, 'I don't give a shit wut ya friends call you. Y'all the one who's been screwin' that white bitch, my Patta, ain't you? Ain't you?' to which I finally said, 'Yeah, that's me!'"

"I told her that I came to pick up the baby. You know what she said to me?"

Fauna sunk back into the couch, her reddened face cringed with embarrassment.

"She said, 'You ain't the one who put the baby in, so you ain't the one who's gonna get her out!'

"Now what kind of a thing is that for a grown person to say? She's out of her mind! We argued back and forth, back and forth. Why does she hate me? She's never even met me before. I don't care if I ever see that crazy again!"

Billy had held up quite well in their first confrontation. Fauna expected him to walk into the apartment with at least a black eye, ready to dislodge her from the comfort and safety of his home. But he was gentle and understanding. He saw Fauna as a person, not as a "race." She began her transformation and Billy was the catalyst.

"I tried to tell you, my momma's set in her way, she either likes you or she don't," Fauna said.

"Oh really?"

"Yeah, she says what's on her mind. Straight out. She don't pull no punches."

"She *doesn't* pull any punches," Billy corrected her.

"Yeah, of course, I meant to say she doesn't pull any punches."

"Do you know what else she said to me?" Billy said. "She told me that she felt sorry for Bobby, that I got in the way of a perfectly good marriage, and that no high sadity nigger's gonna corrupt her daughter and take away her granddaughter. I don't know what high sadity means, but I got the gist."

Fauna dropped her head into her hands fearing that Billy was about to give up on their relationship and send her back to Momma's. Billy knelt down in front of Fauna and gently pulled her hands away. "Hey, I know this has nothing to do with me. Your momma's probably afraid of losing you to me. She's just jealous and that's the way she reacts."

"How do you know so much?" Fauna asked.

Billy just shrugged his shoulders and kissed her on the forehead, then said, "I don't know anything about any of this, other than the little you told me about her. But I want to know everything about you, about how you came to live with her in the first place."

She hesitated for a long while, deciding whether or not to empty her heart by unloading all the secrets she harbored about her race and her family. She guessed he would either freak and disappear forever, or stay and understand. In either case, her history was too heavy, too convoluted to keep private any longer. She gambled on his sincerity, and told him everything. He was fascinated by how she had come to live with a black family, and how she had done everything possible to make herself, and everyone else, believe she was black. Fauna told Billy all she had learned about Marion, Tamar, George, Dorothy, and the phone conversations, the letters. Billy was the first person Fauna told of her true identity. He was intrigued and excited. Billy encouraged her to continue, not to give up her search, and offered to help in any way possible. His enthusiasm was all she needed. His logical mind organized all of the incidents quickly. Together they decided to try to find some of the answers that had plagued her for so many years.

CHAPTER 21

I met a man
Who told me
I don't see you as white,
I only see
A sensitive soul.
Slowly, I started my entrance
Into a living world

Fauna felt the stability within her provincial reality slipping. She relinquished the security of the only lifestyle with which she was familiar, that of a poor female from a black quarter. It defined her insular existence since she was born, and now it was all a lie. She changed jobs and abandoned her husband and home to be entangled with a man that she barely knew, while avoiding the family that raised her. The anxiety only intensified when she learned that the clan who perpetrated this fraud and discarded her, concealed secrets that now engrossed her, the most haunting of which was that she was not black. In the past, when times were difficult, Homer was always there for her. But Fauna had stayed away from the Esquire far too long.

Six months had gone by since Fauna had last spoken with Homer. Although he tried to reach her many times, Fauna avoided him. She was no longer proud of her father who shined the shoes of strangers. Her embarrassment prevented her from telling Billy. Instead, she hurt

Homer, the kindliest person she had ever known, rather than harm her chances of moving upward to a better life.

Fauna's absence was far more distressing to Homer than it was to her. In her quest for something, Fauna became insensitive to Homer's tender feelings. He asked nothing of her, yet always attended to her welfare. Deep inside, she knew he was heartbroken.

When the guilt overwhelmed her soul, and she could no longer live this lie, Fauna went to the shoeshine stand and met with her beloved Homer. He was alone, sitting in the worn-out leather chair that Fauna had spent so much time on as a child, listening intently to a baseball game, unaware of her approach, just the way Fauna always remembered him.

"Homer," Fauna called.

He looked up at her with such saddened eyes that it hurt her to return the glance. "Pat! Pat! How yo' been?" He turned down the radio. "What a surprise this is. Let's take a look at you." He gave her a quick once over. They stared at each other for a moment and then, as if they both felt the same tender ache, threw their arms about each other in heartfelt embrace.

"I've missed you, Homer."

"How's comes you stayed away so long, Pat? Did I do something wrong?" His voice was weak and raspy.

"Oh no, it wasn't you, not at all. I just felt . . . well there were so many things that were going on."

"What kind of things?"

"You know, things, things with Bobby and Jimmie. You know how it is."

"Yeah, I know how she is" shaking his head in disgust.

"Homer," Fauna gently held his hand, "Why'd you stay with Jimmie so long?"

"That woman's sick, Pat. Mental. Oh, at first she was a good lookin' woman—the prettiest I'd ever see'd. But I should of know'd she got a temper—saw it right from the beginning. She got a mean streak a mile long. Jealous too! Imagine, that woman jealous a me, a crippled-up old nigger who's old enough to be her father. She was feisty, all right. Ooooweeee!

"Then you came along. If it weren't fo' you being such a delicate little thing, I would of left her a long time ago—maybe gone back to my own kids in California, I don't know. But she's too wild and much too dangerous to be taking care a little four-year-old, especially one that's as light-skinned as you.

"I couldn't leave y'all alone with that woman—somebody had to protect you, somebody gots to make sure that nothin' bad happened to you. I did the bests I could, Pat."

"I know you did, Homer," Fauna said as tears rolled from her cheeks, "You're the only one I can count on. The only one I really trust." He reached out and wiped her face with his thumb and she held his weathered hand close to her face.

"I'm gettin' tired, Pat. You're a grown woman now, with a family of ya own to take care of." He put his head down. "I can't stop her no more. I'm too old to be fightin' and I don't want to do it no more."

Fauna stayed with him for the remainder of the day, until closing time, and then they walked together just like when Fauna was a little girl. He limped along, listening to his radio, while Pat teased him. They reminisced about the many times he slyly intervened when Jimmie was about to lose her temper, and all the times he took her to school, and the PTA meetings, especially the first time he met her teacher—he loved to tell that story—and she listened again as if it were the first time.

"You remember that first day when the parents came to school?" he asked. "Your Momma didn't want to go, so she asked me to go for her—to meet your teachers and all. Well, I said okay, and off we went to school, just you and me. But when we got there, you just ran off ahead of me and left me in the dust. I felt so bad, I thought you was ashamed of me. That's the way we grew up in the South. No one was proud of a Negro. Specially no little girl looking as white as you did."

"I remember it like it was yesterday," Fauna said.

"Later on I found out that you ran ahead just to tell everyone that your poppa was coming and you was as proud as a peacock. I felt a lot better after that."

They laughed together out loud. But inside she cried, knowing how much she missed of life by not spending more time loving this wonderful man.

Fauna promised never to stay away so long, but her promise was short-lived. In less than ten days he was admitted to the hospital. A man who had never been ill in his entire life was now dying of lung cancer. Fauna vowed to make up for all the time she had wasted by staying at his side at every available moment.

———————

Jimmie received the news in her usual hysterical manner. Because of her brief stay in the hospital a year earlier, she regarded herself as the family medical expert, no matter what the illness.

Although the weather was unseasonably cold the day Jimmie visited Homer for the first time, she refused to not be noticed and wore a tight pink dress with large white polka dots the size of oranges. Her head was covered by a black silk headpiece with a wide brim and tall crown that had a long, bright, red ribbon. The ribbon wrapped around and tailed off to her left shoulder. The matching black patent leather shoes with red leatherette bows and she carried a small black purse that made her look out of place even in an era of disco. It was a noticeable contrast to the white uniforms of the hospital personnel. She entered the ward strutting like a movie star at a premiere. Jimmie halted her entrance and glanced around to the three other patients lying immobile in their hygienic beds, all too ill to even look up. She lifted her chin and marched over to Homer's bedside.

"Don't pretend you's sleeping," Jimmie said, "I've known you too long."

"Hey Jimmie, it's good you could come," Homer said.

"What's wrong which you? They won't tell me nothing downstairs."

Homer remained quiet. She never suspected that Homer had terminal cancer. "It must be that cough you been carrying around for years acting up again. This cold weather, you need to wear your heavy coat when you go out. I been telling you that, but you just don't listen. Now I got to take care of you. How I'm suppose to do that? You got any money to pay for the stuff you need? While you're in here, resting up, I'm trying to keep everything together and I need some money to pay the bills."

"Money, that's all you could think about's money?" Homer asked.

"If you didn't get yourself sick like this, then I won't be needing no money," she said.

Homer began to cough violently. Jimmie leaned over and stroked his forehead, "Take it down a bit, I'll get you fixed up and out of here in quick." Jimmie turned and strutted out to the nurse's station, where she began by giving orders to the nurses.

"Hey, girl, you got any Vicks back there?" she asked.

The nurse was heavyset with a young, light-skinned face. She peered over her glasses at Jimmie Lee, who was now leaning over with both elbows resting on the counter. "Hey girl? My name is Gomez, *Nurse* Gomez. What's Vicks?" she asked.

Jimmie snapped her head up and gave the nurse a leering eye. "You don't know what's Vicks? He's got that cough from a cold and Vicks is what makes it go away. No wonder people die in here."

"Who are you?" Nurse Gomez stopped what she was doing and looked Jimmie in the eye.

"That's my man in there and he needs some Vicks, that's who I am."

A second nurse entered from the back of the enclosed area and leaned over to Nurse Gomez. Jimmie watched carefully. "What's she about?" the second nurse asked Gomez.

"I don't know, some crank asking for cough medicine," said Nurse Gomez. She turned back to Jimmie and added, "You need the pharmacy. It's down on the first floor. That-a-way." She pointed toward the elevator.

Jimmie snapped to attention, turned with her nose in the air, and sauntered back into the ward.

"I got to do everything myself," Jimmie complained. Homer said nothing. "They won't give me no simple thing like the medicine, I got to buy it myself. I need some money. If it weren't for me taking care of everyone, then I'd have something left over. Instead, you get sick, now I got to take care of you. If it wasn't for you I'd have something today. But now look, I'm practically in the poor house." Jimmie huffed out of the room.

Homer knew that his condition was much worse then he was letting on. He sent for his daughter, Helen, who was not a big fan of Jimmie's. Immediately, the two headstrong women disagreed on everything. The real problem lay in the fact that Jimmie was constantly nagging Homer for money—a fact that didn't sit well with his daughter.

Jimmie paraded into the ward as Homer lay in bed watching the Giants in the World Series on TV, Helen sitting quietly nearby. "I talked to the boys over at the Esquire, they said you could go back anytime you feel up to it," Jimmie said.

Helen rose imposingly from her metal hospital chair. She was a stout woman with black shiny hair ironed flat to the middle of her neck. Her face was round with a soft complexion and brown eyes, the same as Homer's. But that's where the similarity ended. "He's a very sick man, he can't go back to work, what's the matter with you?"

"Well, he needs to go back to work, cause we got bills to pay," Jimmie said.

Helen walked around the other side of the bed inches from Jimmie Lee's face. "Money," said Helen, "that's all you want, you don't care one bit about my father. I told him long ago to leave you, but you wouldn't let him go. You took advantage of his good nature and used him any way you could. And now when he's dying, all you care about is his money. Well, you're not getting any more of his money. That's over with. When he's better, I'm taking him home with me. He's leaving you for good. Cause without him, you'll be in the street—where you belong."

Jimmie never even peeked at Helen, instead she placed her hands on her hips and looked right at Homer. "Homer," she said, "how much money you got? I need twenty dollars for the food store, I told him I'd be right back, and I need another thirty-three for the light company and twelve more for the phone. Now, how much you got?"

Helen's eyes popped wide, her arms opened in disbelief. "Didn't you hear a word I said? You ain't getting no more money from my father. All you're doing is getting him upset, and I want you out of here." She rushed out to the nurse's station and Jimmie was asked to leave the hospital. But that didn't stop her from harassing Homer. She continued to visit and argue with him during her visits.

———————

Just before noon on the third day, Helen made her early visit to her father's bedside. The World Series was starting, but Homer's condition worsened. He went from an alert, responsive man, to someone who had lost the will to live.

"How you feeling this morning, Poppa?" Helen said as she leaned to hold his hand. His eyes were sad and glassy. She noticed he was trying to tell her something, but his voice was too soft. "What is it, Pop?"

Homer cleared his throat and whispered, "She took my money."

"Who took your money?" Helen looked puzzled.

"Jimmie snuck in last night and took some money out of my pants. She thought I was asleep, but I know her smell," Homer coughed intensely.

"You get some rest," Helen said, "take it easy, just rest. I'll take care of this." After Homer fell asleep, Helen explained what happened to the nurses, the doctor, and security. Jimmie was barred from the hospital.

She was furious but didn't give up. She found her way in through a back door and continued to pester Homer, showing up at odd hours. When the nurses discovered her presence, a padlock was placed on the door, leaving only one entrance into the hospital. But Jimmie persisted and harassed him over the phone for not sticking up for her. Homer was too ill to argue and let matters rest.

———————

For a week or two things settled down. Billy was much more helpful, taking time out of his busy schedule to watch Yvette while Fauna made her way each day from work to the hospital, sometimes not getting home until late at night. Fauna avoided Jimmie completely. It took all of her energy and time to deal with just one sick member in the family.

The cancer eating away at Jimmie's liver was causing her only mild physical pain, far less than expected, but the aggressive treatment of both chemotherapy and radiation caused her to be sporadically ill. The side effects of losing her already thinning hair became more evident in her personality. Now that Homer occupied center stage and she was excluded from the spotlight, her jealousy raged. She refused to accept the gravity of Homer's illness.

For the past six months Sierra Wine & Liquor employed Fauna as a computer operator. The methodical work prevented her from reflecting on current family events. She made friends with a few of her co-workers, and enjoyed her work. She disclosed nothing about her personal life, a vivid contrast from the many years she waved her birth certificate and boasted of her blackness. But now, her life was in a flux and she could no longer afford to be confrontational.

Her boss was a big man, both in size and temperament. Even at fifty, his manner was loud and forceful, similar to a football coach preparing the team for second half. So when Mr. Barengo walked gingerly into the computer room and pulled up a chair next to her, looking rather apprehensive, almost frightened, she was confused.

"What's the matter?" Fauna asked, "You look like you saw a ghost."

He hesitated a moment, then said, "I've got some bad news, Fauna. I don't know how to tell you this, but," he vacillated again.

"What is it? What's wrong?" she asked.

"I just received a call, your mother was found dead on her front porch. I'm sorry, I really am. Why don't you go, just leave everything, don't worry. I'm sorry."

Fauna felt a chill envelop her skin when she accepted his earnestness. Her eyes became moist. Mechanically, she reached for the telephone to call Jimmie, but she caught a glimpse of Barengo's awed expression. She hesitated, and then her head began to wobble in disbelief. She replaced the receiver, stood tall, and hurried out of the warehouse to her car. As she zipped through the silent streets toward Jimmie Lee's apartment at the projects, she thought about the person who dominated her life so thoroughly. Fauna relived the unfulfilled dreams of her momma—the plans of being famous, of being free of poverty. All the concerns that Fauna planned to make right for her momma flashed through her mind. She now would have to live with her self-imposed guilt for preventing those dreams from becoming reality. But most importantly, it was too late to learn the secrets about her real family that Jimmie once promised. It was over; Jimmie Lee was dead.

Fauna reached her front door and pounded with her fist, frightened at what she would find. But the door was locked and her key was at home. She rushed next door only to discover that the neighbor knew nothing. She let her use her phone to call the hospital but to no avail. Fauna then called four different funeral homes, and the ambulance service, all with the same result.

They were sympathetic and polite. Her only choice left was to call the police. While she waited, she retrieved the master key from the superintendent. Perhaps, Jimmie Lee was inside her apartment, lying there dead. Fauna cowered as she entered the familiar room. It was empty—no sign of life, no sign of death. Fauna treaded lightly into the bathroom, threw water on her face, and cooled her dewy eyes. She glanced at her confused expression. What was all this strangeness? Where's the body? She shook her head and tiptoed back outside, without understanding why. It was only a minute before the police arrived. Fauna's heart began to beat faster.

A young policeman stepped out of the car and asked, "Did you phone the police?"

"Yes, my mother is dead—somewhere. But I don't know where."

She couldn't help but notice his eyebrows lurch upward. "What do you mean?" he asked.

"We got a call at work saying that my mother was found dead on her front porch. She lives here." Fauna pointed to the apartment. "But she's not there. I don't know what to do." She began to shiver and cry hauntingly, like a lost child.

The young cop consoled her. "It's OK. We'll find her. What's your name?"

"Fauna. Fauna Hodel."

"OK, Miss Hodel, why don't you sit down in the car. We'll take a look around."

As Fauna stepped off the stoop toward the car, a young boy from the projects stood nearby. "What's goin' on, Pat?"

Fauna looked up at him through misty eyes, but didn't recognize him as one of the neighbors. "I got a call at work. Someone said that Momma was found dead on the front porch."

She jerked her head back when she noticed his incredulous expression. "What? You mean Miss Jimmie? Yo' momma ain't dead," he said. He was so arrogant in the way he said it that the officer twisted around to pay closer attention. "Least she wasn't five minutes ago," he said as he pointed to the apartment on the far side. "I just see'd her in Reverend Mayfield's apartment."

"What?" Fauna asked, "You sure?"

"'Course I'm sure. They been there all afternoon."

Fauna said nothing, just stalked quickly toward Mayfield's. The two cops and the young black boy followed. As she approached his apartment, Fauna caught a glimpse of someone peeking through the blinds. She became anxious. Two raps on the door and immediately it opened up.

"Pat! What a surprise," Mayfield shouted. "Yo' momma's inside."

Fauna marched passed him, and sitting at his kitchen table with a drink in her hand and her legs crossed was her momma with a malicious look in her eye, and all too familiar smirk.

"Aha! I told ya!" She pointed to Mayfield, and then slapped her knee.

"You're right! You win," said Reverend Mayfield. "Miss Jimmie, I'm never gonna doubt you again. You said you could get her over here anytime you wanted and that's exactly what you did—jus' by picking up the phone."

Now they both laughed triumphantly, the two of them, together, drunk, having a good time at her expense; playing a joke as if they were two children. Fauna was enraged.

"What the hell do you think you're doing?" Fauna shrieked. "You think this is funny! Y'all think this is some kind a joke! You call the owner of the company where I work and tell him my mother is dead just for fun? What the hell is the matter with you?"

They giggled together as if they got caught with their hands in a cookie jar. Then Jimmie acted more serious.

"Don't you talk to you momma that way! And how dare you cuss at me. You been spendin' too much time over at the hospital with Homer. I'm the one who has cancer. I'm the one who is sick. You should be spendin' more time takin' care a you momma! And if it ain't Homer, it's that new nigger you been messin' with—that Billy goat or whatever his name is."

Fauna was too angry to answer. She slammed the door on the way out, still hearing their laughter as she walked away.

Over the years, Reverend Mayfield lost most of his congregation and saddled himself with debts that he could never pay back. He took up the bottle with Jimmie—a self-confirmed saint and the town sinner, now joined together as drinking partners and next-door neighbors.

On November first, Homer asked permission for Jimmie to visit one last time while he was in the hospital. Fauna watched tearfully as this old man, frail, beaten, now forty pounds lighter than when he went in, soulfully motioned for Jimmie to come closer so that he could whisper in her ear.

"Baby," he could barely speak, "Get me my shoes."

"You don't need no shoes," said Jimmie. "You're in bed."

"No Baby. I got to get my shoes on."

Jimmie just looked at him. She, too, was saddened at this pathetic man.

"I'm goin' on a long journey," he said. "Please, Baby, put my shoes on so I can walk along wit 'em."

Jimmie, solemn, genuinely heartbroken, moved closer and placed her ear near his mouth. Fauna watched his lips move but not a sound was heard. Then Jimmie held his hand, and placed a gentle kiss on his lips. Moments later, she took his old, worn-out shoes from beneath the bed and placed them gently on his feet for the last time.

Fauna gasped for breath, trying to hold back her mournful cries as she watched these two people together for the last time. There was so much between them, but there was very little either one could say.

Fauna walked Momma out while Homer rested. That evening he died, six weeks after he was admitted to the hospital. Fauna went home by herself and wrote in her diary:

He was a man
He was my father
He was my friend
I said . . .
I had no mother;
That's a lie.

He was that . . . and more
He shined shoes for a living
And when he left me
I was a polished lady

I loved that man
I respected him so.
To me he was . . .
HE WAS—a man.

I remember days
He gave me his last.

Oh, how he would fuss
He instilled in my heart
The joy of living
That man is away
But not far enough
for me to ever forget

He shined their shoes
To pay for my shoes
OH MY GOD
WHAT A MAN. . . .

Shoe shine man
Shoe shine man . . .
Gentle shoe shine man.
Gentle were your strokes
And to think,
me, a reflection
Of a shoe shine man

They buried Homer, and Fauna avoided Momma as much as possible. She prayed for answers, and hoped that Billy could help free her from this life of desperation.

It was more than a month after Homer's death when Fauna saw Momma again. She seemed to forget her outrage, and actually started treating her nicer. It was also noticeable that for the first time in years, she had cut down on her drinking. With the exception of Fauna, Reverend Mayfield, and Aunt Rosie, no one took an interest in the once "Pretty Jimmie."

Billy and Fauna became very close, and continued to plan a life together. His trips to San Diego were becoming more and more frequent. He was working on a project there, and he kept enticing her by dropping hints about how beautiful it was in San Diego and that it might be a good idea for them to move. The thought intrigued her.

"Fauna, my life has changed so drastically since I met you—and all for the better, too. It's good for us to start a family. It's time for me."

"We're not going through that again," Fauna said.

"No, it's something else. Before I met you, before I worked for Lear, I was just a technician not making enough money to survive. I had a part-time job as a clerk in a grocery store to make ends meet. Yeah, I got the position in engineering at Lear on my own, but since I've been with you, a whole other world has opened up."

Fauna was baffled. "What are you talking about? What other world?"

"Well, you know, things have been happening at work," he said reluctantly.

"What things?"

"People have been taking an interest in me—important people at the company. I'm a new guy; I've only been there about a year. I don't understand. Before I met you no one even noticed me. Now people are telling me that they have big plans for me. I just don't understand. I'm just one of a dozen other guys. Almost all of them have far more experience, too."

"What people?" His evasiveness peaked her curiosity.

"Well, one person in particular. John Scoffield. He's a Mormon from Utah—well established. He said he's got some things outside of Lear that I would fit into perfectly—setting up a new company to do work in Saudi Arabia. He told me he'd get us a brand new house, plenty of opportunity, new car. He's talking big money."

"When did this all happen?"

"That's just it. I've known him since I started—at least I knew of him. He hardly said two words to me before. Then, right after I met you, he acted like I was his long lost son. He keeps pumping me up."

"Why?"

"I don't know! It's just strange that it coincides with my meeting you."

"I've never heard of this man until just now."

"I know. It's just things you shouldn't know about."

"What? What things?"

Just then the telephone rang. Quickly, he picked up the receiver as if he were relieved by the interruption, giving him time to think of how not to tell her something.

But as Fauna watched him, his countenance changed. A frightened paleness overtook him as he removed his glasses, placing them on the table and holding his left hand up to his face, as though he were trying to hide the fear. "Oh God, no! It can't be." There was a long pause as he stood erect, hanging on to every word. "When did this happen?"

Fauna stood up from the couch, sensing something drastically wrong. "Billy, what is it? What's the matter?"

He motioned vigorously for her to be quiet with his hand, then returned it to his ear and squeezed his head as if to muscle out the pain emanating from the voice on the other end.

Fauna came closer and stood by his side, wanting desperately to share his agony.

"OK, OK. I understand. I'll get a flight out tonight—right away."

He dropped the receiver; his lips and forehead were covered with tiny beads of sweat. His reddened eyes fixed and empty.

"What is it? What's wrong?" There was no response, just cold fear. "Tell me. What is it?" Fauna rested her hand on his shoulder, trying to absorb the anguish.

"Its my mother. She had a stroke. They don't think she's gonna make it." He took a deep breath and blew through his mouth. "I've got to get a plane right away. I've got to pack a bag and make a reservation."

Within thirty minutes, Fauna was driving him to the airport, praying to God that his mother wouldn't die. Although Fauna had never met Billy's mother, she had good instincts about her.

It hurt her deeply to see him in so much pain; to know that the one person closest to him was dying. Fauna could still see the sorrow in his face long after he was gone.

As Fauna drove home alone, Fauna couldn't escape her vision of him the moment he heard the sad news; he was in sheer agony. Fauna coveted that special feeling he had for his mother, his own flesh and blood. From the time he was born, they had shared a mutual love that only comes through a lifetime of knowing that once they were one.

Fauna yearned for that special feeling that had evaded her all of her life and vowed, then and there, to know the one person in the world who could satisfy her hunger—Tamar, her real mother—before it was too late.

Fauna told Momma about Billy's mother. Jimmie instinctively knew what Fauna was trying to say.

"Patta, when you find you real momma, will you leave me and never see me again?"

Fauna cautiously answered, "Oh no, Momma, I would never leave you—not ever."

CHAPTER 22

A few days later, Fauna received a call from Billy relaying the sad news that his mother had died. Fauna was saddened. Having just lost Homer to cancer, she empathized with his grief, and her spirit drew closer to him. She knew his pain, and was upset that she couldn't be there to comfort him.

As she hung up the phone, an astonishing revelation flickered in her mind: Billy had lost an endearing figure in his life—his beloved mother. She had never even met hers. For two years Fauna avoided facing the unpleasant reminder of her bogus life as a woman of mixed race, a usurper of false traditions. Until this very moment, she put off the notion of meeting with the source of the monstrous lie—a lie that had been impossible to merge with her history, the reality of Tamar—face-to-face. The decision was made without hesitation; she knew the time was now. She was going to Hawaii before Billy returned.

She called Billy back. "This may not be a good time to tell you, but I decided it's time to meet my real mother."

"Well, when I get back, we can talk about it," Billy said.

"No, it can't wait. I've got to do it now. I have to find out who she is. My whole life has been a lie, I need the truth. I need to know why God put me in this situation."

There was silence on the phone, and then Billy said, "I understand how necessary it is. I don't have a reason for you not to go. I just wish I could be with you, if only just to see the your expression when you meet her."

"Billy, you've meant so much to me, you taught me so much about life, about love, about how to act and to be a lady. I wish you could be with me, too. I'd love to share it all with you, but this is a very personal encounter that I can only do alone."

"Are you going to leave Yvette with your mother," Billy hesitated, "I mean Jimmie?"

"No, I'm taking her with me."

Two days later, Fauna and Yvette were on their way without regrets or second thoughts. When they reached the airport, a delayed flight allowed her a few hours to mull over the events that led her to this point. It was then she realized that all these characters—Jimmie Lee, Marion, George, Dorothy, and Tamar—all had secrets. And, they distrusted one another. They were her real family, her lifeblood. But she was the center, the key to all of their sorrow. Deep inside Fauna felt the need to heal all the wounds that separated her new family from each other, and only then could she bring harmony to her life. She called Dorothy Barbe. Perhaps Dorothy wanted her to bring something back from Hawaii, a souvenir, a hula doll, but more importantly to bring Dorothy closer to Tamar.

"Where are you? You sound so close?"

"I'm close. I'm here at the airport. On my way to meet Tamar for the very first time in Hawaii and I wanted. . . ."

"Oh, no!" Dorothy cut her off, "You mustn't go there and meet with her! Oh, no! There are too many things you don't know about her. She'll fill your head with all sorts of unbelievable stories about everyone in our family. She'll never tell you the truth, just lies. She's been that way ever since she was a child. And I ought to know, I'm her mother."

"But Dorothy, she is my real mother—I've got to meet her. I've got to know who she is—who I am."

"You shouldn't go there. Not until we have a long talk together. She'll poison your mind. The woman is a pathological liar. She was put in a home for wayward children because of her outrageous stories, and caused all sorts of unbelievable problems for the entire family. Now she has those poor children, who are probably completely brainwashed. She is an outcast from society, a complete and unchangeable rebel who has no regard or respect for anyone or anything."

Fauna remained calm, "What sort of things will she say? I don't understand."

"She'll tell you terrible things—about her . . . and her father."

"But I want to know everything. That's why I'm going. I want to know why she gave me away. I want to know who my father really was, and why she. . . ."

"Never mind asking her that. I'll tell you why she gave you away. Why don't you come over here right now, and I'll tell you everything—the truth—only the truth!"

"No Dorothy, I really want to meet her, before it's too late. I've waited a long time and I've come this far. I'm not going to turn back."

"Well, at least tell me where you are. I'll try to come and meet with you there at the airport."

Fauna told her the flight number and departure time, but she felt uneasy. However, her maternal grandmother never showed. Fauna and Yvette boarded the plane and sat in their assigned seats.

Just as everyone settled down, a last-minute passenger came rushing into the plane, made a few thankful gestures to the stewardess and rushed to the seat next to Fauna. He smiled at her and winked at Yvette. He was in his early fifties.

"She's your daughter?" he asked.

"Yes," Fauna answered. His eyes widened as he reached for his seatbelt.

"Are you going to meet your husband in Hawaii?"

"No, I'm gonna meet my mother . . ." Fauna said, and then paused, "for the first time."

He turned slowly and peered at them with a look of concern. "You never met your mother?"

"No, she gave me away when I was born."

His reaction was the same as everyone else. After that, he kept asking her questions and she answered in detail. Finally, out of sheer exhaustion, she asked him what he did for a living, hoping that he would take over the conversation. He told her he was a detective. It took her only about six seconds before a helpless sense of paranoia overtook her. A detective! The only thing she could think of was that Dorothy somehow must have called George in the Orient to let him know that she was on her way to see Tamar. She could only believe that this man was sent by George to keep close tabs on her. She was afraid, and didn't answer any further questions about her personal life. She merely chatted politely about Hawaii, and the weather.

As they approached the islands in the early evening, the luminous clouds slowly melted to reveal deep green mountains that tapered sharply to the sea on one side, and graciously rolled to the lights on the other. Fauna was awed by the sight of such a contrast, and excited to be on the last leg of her life-long quest to find the woman of her dreams. She watched the look in Yvette's eyes, now wide with wonder, and knew that for her daughter this was a storybook adventure. As the plane touched down, Fauna speculated as to where Tamar would be and what she would say, how she would look, what she would wear—an evening dress, a muumuu, summer shorts or maybe a grass skirt. Her mind was fantasizing in all directions. Her steadfast emotions were now somewhere between nervous excitement and sheer terror. The detective spoke to her as the plane rolled slowly toward the terminal.

"Well, we're here. It won't be long now before you get to meet your real mother. Are you excited?"

"Excited? I'm very nervous."

"What's the first thing you're going to say to her?"

"I don't know. I've been thinking about that all the way over here. We've talked on the phone, and I've read her letters—over and over again. So it's not like we don't know each other—well, we really don't know each other. I don't know what I'm gonna do. I've thought of fifty different lines, but now they're all mixed up. I don't know what to say."

"I'd give anything to see the look on your faces when you first meet."

Fauna feigned a smiled, hoping he would go away. She felt uneasy ever since he told her he was a detective. When she led Yvette by the hand toward the door, she felt her own heart pounding loudly enough that she turned to her daughter and said, "Are you OK?" Not expecting an answer. Her senses were excited and the perspiration on her upper lip was annoying. With each slow step closer to the waiting crowd, she wiped the moisture off, but it kept coming back. It was hot and the whirling sound of machinery, people mumbling, and background music from overhead all seemed to make her entrance more obvious. She just knew that everyone there in the terminal was waiting for her, the long-lost daughter, coming to meet with Tamar.

She wanted to be right for the occasion. With just a few feet to go, a small bottleneck developed and everyone slowed down to a snail's pace. She took a deep breath, held it in, and then walked with her head high in search of the woman who gave her life more than twenty years ago.

There she was, just 30 feet away, waving her hand frantically. Fauna's heart began to beat louder and louder. She began to quicken her pace. The detective grabbed her arm, and held her back. "No, that's not her," he said. She squinted to get a better look. He was right, the woman didn't look anything like her mother's photo.

She glanced quickly at all the faces in front of her. None of the others were looking her way. It was easy to tell that they had other things on their minds. She felt relieved, less uncomfortable. Her pace slowed and she stretched her head to peer around a group of people who were placing strands of ginger leis around an elderly couple. Everyone was smiling and happy. There were other people with leis, too, all waiting for someone. She stopped near the end of the open area and turned to see where Tamar was. She looked at every person in that section of the terminal. Within five minutes almost everyone was gone, with the exception of some of the employees of the airline, a soldier, and a young couple who were still holding each other tightly.

She turned just in time to see the detective walk toward her with a woman by his side. At first she thought it was Tamar, but that notion quickly vanished. The woman looked nothing like the photo.

"Where is she?" he asked, "Don't worry, she probably got caught in traffic or something. She'll be here. Oh, this is my wife, Grace."

"Aloha, and welcome to Hawaii," Grace said.

"Hello," Fauna replied.

"Grace says there's been an accident that's blocking two lanes of traffic. Why don't we wait around a little just to make sure?"

"Oh no," said Fauna, "That won't be necessary. We can manage by ourselves."

"Nonsense, we don't mind at all. It's one of the great things about living here in Hawaii—the *aloha*. Besides, I'm sure it'll only be a few minutes, anyway."

She thanked him, and together they waited. They told her all about Hawaii. It was far different than what she imagined. Fauna phoned Tamar, and then paged her but both calls remained unanswered. Outside the air was sweet and damp. For an hour, they waited near the baggage terminal, surveying passengers departing in taxis and buses every few minutes, but no Tamar.

"I don't think she's gonna make it," the detective said, "Why don't you and your daughter come home with us? We have room. Or, if not, can we drop you off at one of the hotels?"

"No, that's OK, she'll be here," Fauna said.

The detective glanced at his wife, and then said, "Well, why don't you at least make a reservation to return home. You can always cancel it. Just to be on the safe side."

Fauna just smiled and nodded.

"Here, this is my phone number," the detective said, "call if you need anything. We really don't want to see you alone in Hawaii disappointed like this."

"I guess it would be a good idea to make a reservation and just go back home. It's a long way to travel for nothing," Fauna said.

As they talked in front of the baggage terminal, she noticed an old van, painted like a Peter Max poster, drag itself near the curb. It was noisy and fumes filled the air. Three children in the back seat slid the door open and jumped out first. They all had long hair, and were dressed in shorts and T-shirts. In the mercury vapor lights of the airport, their small faces glowed from their golden tans. Then a barefooted woman clothed in wraps of dazzling colors caressing a flower lei, stepped out and glimpsed toward them. Fauna's heart beat mercilessly. A chill cooled her skin, then suddenly changed to hot. The emerging hum of background noise was all she heard as her whole life flashed in front of her. The detective's wife was chatting on about something, but she might as well have been talking to a signpost. Fauna ignored her as her palpitations became louder and faster. Her mind focused on the lady with the leis.

The woman pointed to Fauna and slowly, as if it were a small band of hippies getting ready to embark on a long camping trip, they began to walk toward her. All of her years in Sparks and Los Angeles, dreaming thousands of dreams of her "vision," had never prepared her for the sight of this group of flower children. Her thoughts unraveled. Everything flowed in slow motion.

The three little boys acted shy, each trying not to be out front, but staring her way. Fauna barely noticed. Her eyes were fixed on the woman from the photo, only now it was real, and she was smiling. The barefooted boys, all handsome, walked ahead of the woman who advanced with robes billowing out to catch the light breeze. She stopped within a foot of Fauna and Yvette.

"Eieeeee," the woman screeched, "Ooooh, my God! I can't believe it's you!" She fell to her knees in front of them, shrieking.

"Tamar?" Fauna gasped, and her eyebrows lifted skyward as her head followed the motion of the figure on her knees. This woman was not the faceless image that she dreamed of each night as she cried herself to sleep. This was not Doris Day, nor her vision, nor her quest. But this was reality; and a twenty one-year odyssey played out.

"Hello? Tamar?" she said.

"Hello! Aloha! Oh, let me look at you!"

Fauna looked away, downward toward Yvette. "This is my daughter. Yvette, this is your grandmother!"

"Oh my! What a beauty!" Tamar arose and glanced back at Yvette.

The detective and his wife stood innocuously by revealing expressions of disbelief. Tamar seemed to be incoherent and overcome with emotion, but she acknowledged their presence. They were relieved that she had finally arrived, and left without good-byes.

Now she was alone with her real mother. "Oh my, how long I've waited," Tamar said, "When I saw your eyes, I knew it was you. I knew it was the same baby I held so many years ago. Even then, when I saw the expression on your face, it seemed to ask a question, like, 'what's going on?'" She unraveled some tissues and began to blow her nose. "And now, all this time has passed and you have that same puzzled look. I've held that memory of you—the only memory I had for so many years—and now you're back with me," she began to cry painfully, as if someone had strangled her heart from the inside.

Fauna stood passively, bewildered and silent. She couldn't bring herself to say she felt the same way. She didn't know what she felt. But soon, tears welled her eyes, not from love, but from compassion. She observed the emotional upheaval of a complete stranger, and blocked the strain and tension that should have dropped her to her knees. Fauna prayed for the strength to get through this ordeal.

The emotions quickly gave way to the present reality as Tamar introduced her sons: Peace, Joy, and the smallest, Love, only two years old. She talked incessantly, making excuses about why she was late, blaming friends with strange sounding names, and then apologizing for them. Fauna listened, with dispassionate comprehension, and in her thoughts began comparing Tamar with Jimmie Lee. But that quickly disappeared as Tamar moved everyone along toward the rainbow colored van.

Fauna settled in the front seat with Love and a friend of Tamar's who took the wheel, and whom Fauna presumed owned the van. His unshaven face had a few days' stubble that matched the unconventional appearance of his tie-dyed jeans and rumpled shirt. His movements were slow and his speech lazy, as if he were drunk. But it was a different type of intoxication, similar to the way her cousin Johnny acted around the time when Lucille died. The smell of marijuana permeated the vehicle. When he asked Fauna if she wanted some, she refused. He was silent the rest of the trip.

He parked the van in front of a house far larger than that which Fauna was used to in Sparks. It only confirmed the many tales Jimmie relayed about her wealthy family. Fauna was anxious to see the artwork and heirlooms similar to those that intrigued her at Dorothy's apartment. Once inside, however, she discovered large rooms sparsely equipped with a potpourri of time-worn furniture and accessories that reminded Fauna of the poor shanties from her early years. She felt the damp air meld with her skin and was drawn to the distinct scent of the salt water emerging from the rear of the house. As she ambled on through the rooms following Tamar, she was lured to the steady flap of wavelets rolling onto the shore. Through the screen on the lanai, just 50 yards from the back of the house, lie the white sandy beach and the ocean.

Fauna was unfazed as Tamar ordered her children outside to play. She recognized that Tamar, too, was anxious to talk about their separate histories. But Fauna required some breathing room, time to absorb the unfamiliar, and plan a strategy.

"Tamar," Fauna said, "this has been a long day. I'm OK, but Yvette is really over-tired. I want to get her ready for bed."

"But I don't want to go to bed," Yvette interrupted.

"You can't keep your eyes open. Besides it's a lot later than it looks, we're in a different time than at home." Fauna was insistent. Yvette shrugged her shoulders and yawned.

"Sure, let me show you where your room is, and then I'll put on some tea, it'll make you sleep," Tamar said, and then let them into the bedroom she prepared for the visit.

Fauna had been up since early morning, spending five hours at the San Francisco Airport, another five and a half on the plane, and then another two for the time change. Tamar was almost two hours late, and still another hour had gone by before she could sit down without being on edge. Her body slumped onto the cane-seated chair opposite Tamar to enjoy a relaxing cup of tea. She was fatigued, but her mind whirled furiously, trying to take in everything, especially Tamar.

Before her first sip, the children returned to the house with a young girl about twelve years old who Tamar introduced as Cynthia. The girl had a sensitive intelligence about her. She was polite and confident and everyone, including Tamar, offered her respect. Fauna enjoyed the small talk while the boys gathered around. They were inspecting their new sister as if she were a curious visitor from another world; a fact that didn't escape Fauna, because in many ways, it was true. They clung to her every word and carefully eyed all of her movements. Fauna felt as though she was auditioning for a stage play and became uncomfortable. She caught the eye of Cynthia who quickly sensed the angst and offered to take the boys Christmas shopping. Fauna realized Tamar was far too poor to afford even the barest necessities, let alone presents, and that if it weren't for this young lady, the children's Christmas would have been just another day off from school.

Cynthia left with Love, Peace and Joy, leaving just Tamar and Fauna finally alone. Tamar's eyes were glassy. Tamar reached over, held her hand and said softly, "It's so good to see you, to finally have you here with me. So many thousands of times I've sent my love to you. I never expected to ever see you. I'd given up hope so many times, but I knew that you were receiving my love, my feelings, my heart."

Her words relaxed Fauna. She could feel they were genuine. She really seemed to care, far different from what Dorothy had described. She just had to know why Tamar's own mother would say such things. "Tamar, before I left San Francisco, I called Dorothy to see if there was anything she wanted me to bring you. She insisted that I see her before I came here. She was adamant, almost desperate."

Tamar sat upright in her chair. "Oh. Yes, I'm sure she did. She despises me. This has been going on all of my life. We don't get along at all."

"Yes," Fauna said as she took another sip, "she really dislikes you. I was shocked at the things she said about you."

"She blames me for the trouble that happened. But it wasn't my fault. I was just a young girl, barely in my teens."

Fauna's glanced up from her tea, her eyebrows lifted.

"Didn't she tell you what it was all about?"

"Tell me what *what* was all about?"

"OK. You don't understand. Let me try to explain. It's not going to be easy to accept all of this, but I've been living with it my entire life."

Tamar paused for a long tme, staring into her cup. Fauna watched as Tamar's expressive face slowly recast itself. She became very serious. She took a deep breath and looked directly at Fauna. Her voice was willful and unruffled.

"Years ago, before you were born, I was involved in a nationally publicized incest trial . . . with my father."

"What kind of a trial?"

"It was actually a criminal trial having to do with incestuous relations between me and my father."

"What are you saying?" Fauna asked.

"My father made love to me. There was a trial and a jury acquitted him, so that means in the eyes of the law, he's not guilty. The whole thing was in all the newspapers and magazines across the country. Of course, at the time, I didn't realize it was being so heavily publicized because they kept me in Juvenile Hall in Los Angele,s during the whole thing— almost a year. When I came out . . ."

"I was in Juvenile Hall in Los Angeles, too," interrupted Fauna, "but only for ten days."

"You were! Then you know the place, what a coincidence. Anyway, during the trial, my mother sided with the defense and told everyone that I was a pathological liar. She said I made up the whole thing; claims I'd been making up stories all my life."

Fauna's mouth was open and stiff. She felt the electricity racing through her body. "Wait a minute, wait a minute. You mean to tell me that you actually went to bed with your father?"

"Let me start from the beginning," Tamar said, as she set her cup aside and folded her hands on the table. "My mother and father were never married."

Tamar's speech was very slow, deliberate, her memory excellent as she recalled every detail.

"They lived together for a while. He was in the process of a divorce from another wife. My earlier years as a baby were spent in Sam Francisco. When I was old enough, and I heard about my father, the fabulously wealthy doctor, who now lived in a magnificent Hollywood house designed by Lloyd Wright, Frank Lloyd Wright's son, called *Shangri La*, I wanted to go there. Who wouldn't? In my mind I immediately envisioned servants, fountains and statues, fancy limousines, swimming pools, everything. So my mother made arrangements to have me move down from San Francisco.

"When I arrived, it was almost like I was in a dream world. It took me a while to be able to see my father. He was always busy with something or another. Most of the time he'd send me off to his library to read books. But the interesting thing was that his library was filled with books that dealt with the fantasy world of gods and goddesses, all making love. A friend of mine who knew him called him the first avant-garde. He was very handsome and mysterious. In their home, the cinder part that covered the outside was where they lay naked in the sun. There was a whole bevy of servants; you didn't have to do anything. His whole life was dedicated to sex. At age eleven, this was very interesting to me.

"He began my sex education by giving me the whole library. It was a fairy-tale library, not erotic or violent like American pornography, but about gods and goddesses, and kings, and knights, and fair maidens. In these stories, if you arrived at the gate, you went to the gatekeeper and made love. After the gatekeeper you went to the housekeeper, and the other servants, before you got to see the mother and father. And that's the way I thought it was. I didn't know any better, this is the way the stories went. In his house it was like that, too—these lines of women waiting to see my father. I wasn't objective, but just wanted to see my father. Most of the time I was just shushed off to read books."

Fauna was fascinated at the way she unfolded this tale. She was a great storyteller, slow, deliberate, emphasizing the most dramatic points. But then, without even a change of tone or expression she said.

"My father did let me have oral sex with him when I was eleven. He told me it was a special privilege. I wasn't quite sure if this was OK, so I went to Mother and asked her. She then told my father, who turned to her and said, 'Dorothy, she's making the same accusations about you and Effy. She said the two of you fondle each other.' My grandmother said, 'How ridiculous!' He was clever. He just turned the cards around and blamed me. My grandmother was so concerned about her own reputation that she never investigated any further. She didn't know about this until later, so all that happened concerning my education was about giving him "head," and reading books. Then I went back to be with my mother in San Francisco.

"When I returned at twelve, the following summer, I wanted to put more of this back into practice. He promised that when I was sixteen he would give me the honor of making love to him and I would become a woman. I wanted to be a woman much faster, naturally. I was just right for the whole situation.

"Then one day, when I was to see my father, he had a whole bedroom full of people, and was about to hypnotize one of them.

"I sat down to join them and the next thing I knew, they were in an orgy. My father said, 'Everyone out of the room,' and he was with me—except one woman who was there for a while, and then she said, 'Oh, my God, this is dreadful.' And then she ran out. I think her name was Connie. Well, I became pregnant—immediately."

The words banged around inside Fauna's head like cannon fire on the Fourth of July. The rushing blood throughout her body stopped cold. *Could she be telling me that my father and her father are the same?* She was too terrified to ask. She waited, and prayed.

"My father said," Tamar continued, unaware of her daughter's paralysis, "'Well,' ever so amused, 'this is interesting.' But I didn't think it was interesting. I felt that all of a sudden everything was going to be a lot of trouble. So I told one of my girlfriends at Hollywood High, and she said that I should have an abortion. I didn't know what an abortion was, other than it would have made me not pregnant, and that seemed OK.

"So I asked my father for an abortion and he said that he didn't believe in them, and he was going to send me away to a home to have the baby. But I didn't want to go to a home. So, I begged everybody else for an abortion. And he was afraid of all the talk and finally arranged for my abortion. And when I got one, I hated it! No anesthetic, at age thirteen, screaming in the middle of it to stop. And then, the person who was driving me to the abortion, a friend of my father's, raped me in the car. I was just freaked out. I told my father what happened when I got back, and he became furious. Things became stranger."

It may have been strange for Tamar, but Fauna was so relieved that she had had an abortion. Tamar's story made Fauna want to vomit and pass out at the same time. But there was no letting up once Tamar had started.

"I went to my stepmother, Dorarro, that is, and she said, 'Enough! That's it!' And then she told me a story about a woman that my father dated, who was a nurse, who was very much in love with him.

"Dorarro was called in to get two manuscripts for books that the woman was writing about my father—one was a novel and the other factual—and burn them. The woman had committed suicide. She had taken pills, and my father was waiting for her to die. So, Dorarro burned the books. My father signed the death certificate, and everything was very suspicious. So I was afraid of that.

"I decided to run away to the house where some friends of mine lived, and hide. Their parents were away in Europe, so I went there. The servants kept an eye on everything.

"And I think my stepmother, Dorarro, called my mother and said something was going on. She immediately came down from San Francisco to see me—unannounced. And when I wasn't there, she filed a missing persons report. The next thing I knew was that the servants told me that the police were looking for me. I was scared. I had never even spoken to a policeman before, and I felt like a criminal.

"I didn't know what to do. I was on the run, and one boy after another began to hide me. It got to be a great drama.

"I was finally found by the police and they said that they already knew about my father. Years earlier, he had been investigated about the Black Dahlia murder."

Fauna thought to herself that what Tamar was telling her was so fantastic! It was a great drama! She couldn't help but to compare her to Momma, who told stories that were short and to the point, with very few details. After living with Jimmie's outrageous antics her entire life, and believing that no one could live a life more complicated, she was beginning to doubt all reality. Jimmie's life seemed almost normal after listening to Tamar. She exhausted all her sensibilities, and drained all of her energy. But still she wanted to know more. "The Black Dahlia murder? What's that?" she asked, hoping it would give her much more insight into her family.

"Well, when I was about ten or eleven, my father told me one day, that the police were coming to investigate them, and that they should keep their clothes on because they had spies looking for all kinds of things. So I said OK.

"There was a murder in the area at that time. A woman's body had been found dissected, apparently by someone very capable, who knew the workings of the human body, like a physician—like my father. His name was found in her little black book. So that is why they investigated him. And I don't know why—still, till this day—and I really don't care one way or another, but I would like to know if I'm safe with my father— and that's what I don't know."

"Are you worried about your father harming you?"

"Well, no, not exactly. George is a very powerful and persuasive man. If he hasn't done anything by now, after all I've put him through, at least what everybody thinks I've put him through, then I don't believe there is anything to worry about. Don't get me wrong, I love my father.

"Anyway, I had a baby doll at that time, that I brought from my mom's house. It was so pretty, curly hair, like a real baby. And I didn't know what to name her. So my father said, 'Oh, let me name her.' And he named her Elizabeth Ann. Now my father never picks ordinary names; he always picks exotic names. So Elizabeth Ann she was.

"As the Black Dahlia name kept coming up in movies constantly, I never thought much of it. Then, a few years ago, I was reading an article in a magazine about the Black Dahlia that someone had brought me, when suddenly, I got a frightening chill when I saw the victim's real name was Elizabeth Ann.

"Now I don't know, it may all be coincidence, and I'm not accusing anyone. I'd like to know, sure. But my father, above all, was a charming man. He could entertain. There were always beautiful people around him. He could do whatever he wanted, but he could be cruel, and he was—and is—a genius.

"So I didn't know what they knew. They were going to examine me. I assumed they knew about the abortion. I didn't know! So I told all. He forgot to tell me to lie.

"They arrested him, and they put me in Juvenile Hall to protect me, and told me to wait there—after they sprayed me with insecticide. It was horrible. They kept me there, and that was the worst.

"So, I turned to the only person who I knew could help me. I needed love. And I heard, on records, this wonderful person who could sing and play the guitar and tell stories. His name was Joshua Daniel White. And he sang and told stories, and played the guitar better than anyone—blues guitar. I later knew him. You could tell from his music and songs what a kind, compassionate man he was. So I asked him in spirit to be with me through this thing, because I had to go through a court trial.

"You understand that in 1949, sex was never discussed, let alone incest, or freedom, or oral sex, or being naked in your house in the sunshine. And to me it was totally natural, the whole thing, except when some of the radical things happened with my father.

"No one talked to me except to question me. As of this day, if some stranger comes up to me in the street and asks me an intimate personal question, I just answer because I'm so programmed from that.

"I never saw my family, my father, my brothers, my mothers. I was just led into the courtroom to testify and then was taken out. I'm sure that what they did was highly illegal; it was definitely immoral. So they told me what they wanted me to hear, and I told them what they wanted to hear.

"The way my father defended himself when he was arrested was to allow his attorney, Jerry Giesler, to say that this was just a young teenage girl who was in love with her father—which worked. The jury acquitted him on Christmas Eve.

"I didn't look like a victim, I didn't look like 'Oh poor me! Why is this happening to me?' That's not where I was coming from. I was a lady, I spoke well. I was calm on the witness stand. I was special—special lucky me was going to be with him.

"The publicity was very bad for him; he would have probably liked to have me just disappear. And let me assure you that that's what my father wanted to do to me, not because he hated me, but because he wanted the evidence suppressed. He was in such a terrible position. That's why he wanted me to stay as 'bad Tamar, the awful person, pathological liar.'

"Until this day, my mother, and aunts, and everyone think I made up this terrible lie and ruined everybody's lives. So, they have another perspective and only see it from one side, and not see what really did happen.

"I was held in this holding cell and there was nobody to talk to. I didn't get to go to school with the other kids. What I learned was that when I was allowed out with the other girls, I was told never to talk. There were, however, these real pretty black girls, real pretty. And when I talked with them, they didn't think they were pretty. I had no idea what it was like to be poor, or black, or come from underprivileged homes. When I told them they were beautiful, they thought I was weird. I'd draw them.

"Why . . . why this fascination with pretty black girls?"

"Well, my hero, the head of my tribe, was Josh White. And he was black, of course!"

"Of course," Fauna said. She still didn't understand everything. With each sentence Tamar spoke, more questions kept popping into her head, but she didn't know where to start, so she let it continue without interruption.

"When the court trial was over, the policeman and the policewoman who were investigators, and who pretended to be prospective adoptive parents, drove me to San Francisco. That was the end of it. They spent months questioning me and telling me that I had never known real love, and they were going to show me real love.

"I was transferred to San Francisco and saw my mother for the first time in many months. Outside of the newspaper reports, which I read daily, where she called me a 'pathological liar,' and something to the effect that I always made up stories, she didn't know anything.

"Well, the story she was referring to was the cover story my father gave me when I first told her what was going on, to which he said, 'Oh

Dorothy, she's saying the same thing about you.' That's what she was referring to, but she didn't know that. So I guess during the trial she was afraid I was going to say that too!

"I was shocked at what my mother said. Nobody ever asked my mother, 'Is this true?'—ever!

"When I found my mother, she treated me as if I did something very wrong, and she went out of her way to go to the Juvenile Hall to inform me that she had given away my savings bond and all the little things that I had. I didn't understand why, but somehow I knew I had really done a terrible thing.

"Now they told me that since I didn't commit a crime, they could transfer me to a half-way house for girls. Finally, my mother had to take me back. She didn't want to, but she had to."

"What about your father, where was he during all of this? He must have hated you!"

"No, I don't think he hated me. It was only in the later years that I found him to be really cold, even though there was this strange scene that happened.

"When I was still being held in San Francisco, at the home for bad girls, my mother took me out one day and drove me to the hills near Sausalito. My father and I met, him in one car and me in another; but always in the presence of others. We didn't say much. I was just thrilled to see my father. I loved him intensely. I didn't understand why he didn't rescue me because he could have told me to shut up, retract your statements. I would have done so. I wasn't out to get him. I didn't know how to lie. I didn't know any better. It could have changed.

"So, when I arrived at home, I went to see my friend David. We used to make ravioli with his mother, before the trial, that is. I walked across the street to where he lived as he was fixing his car. I said 'Hi', and just as he was getting up to say hi, too, while I was crossing the street, his mother came running down the stairs saying, 'You get away from my son, you whore! You whore!' He got up and went away. That's what shocked me—she was shocking enough, but him!

"So, later on, when I was going to the local delicatessen, I ran into Dave and he said, 'I'm sorry about how I acted, but my mother read everything in the papers and magazines.' He explained that he had to act like that. It was such a big scandal. His mother was having a fit. But then he said that someone wanted to meet me, his friend. And we'd meet at his apartment later that evening. But Dave never showed up, just his friend.

"I wasn't used to drinking and he gave me some kind of sweet liqueur. He reminded me of a hood in an Italian gangster movie. He was older, about twenty-four. I began to drink this sweet liqueur. It was ghastly, but I drank it down like soda pop. I got drunk and I got raped. I didn't get beaten-up raped. I was just too drunk to protest. And when I left I was so mad. I went home, and within a few weeks I knew I was pregnant. I never wanted to talk to this man again, so I didn't go back to him for help or anything.

"You mean you got pregnant again?!" Fauna said as she sat back in her chair her eyes widened.

"Yes, and he's your father, but don't ask me who he is. I've forgotten his name, blocked it right out after the incident."

Fauna was dumbfounded. She never thought much about who her real father was; just that he was black. Now she was learning how it all happened—how *she* happened—and somehow it still didn't seem important.

Tamar continued, "I went to my mother and I said I was pregnant. She said, 'Oh, no, I'm not going to help you. Look what you did to your father.' So I've got this script going on in my head about this thing I did to my father. So she wouldn't help me—and I had to take care of this on my own.

"I had been reaching for my roots. I identified with blacks by this time. So I went out in the black neighborhood looking for family. I hadn't found too much family yet, but I did run across a man whose name was Happy Feet. He was an entertainer, singer, and hustler. He said that he knew someone who could help me out. But I had to have $60 for this lady to give me a 'slippery elm' treatment—whatever that was. But $60 was hard to come by, so I spent the next month going through all kinds of schemes to get this money, but it never happened. So finally, I was gone from my home for a few days trying to arrange this and my mother reported me as a runaway to my probation officer. Now, I heard that the police were searching for me, again.

"This really nice man who was a bartender at the Fillmore Hotel, Charles White, noticed that I was too young to be in there, and said that I looked like I was in trouble. We talked a little, and I told him the problem. He suggested that I go to his apartment and wait. He'd talk with me after work. He was very nice. We did talk and I told him everything. Then he said the police had come in looking for me at the Fillmore Hotel.

"Anyway he said I'd have to ask permission from the court to get married so that I would be legally on my own and have my baby, which is what I wanted to do. Because when you're pregnant, that's what you usually want to do. I was having phone conversations with my probation officer all this time, and she said that the court would have a heart attack at the idea of my asking a black man to be married, but they wrote him down as the father. That's all they got out of the whole thing.

"Charles got me out of the hotel. It was a miracle, because they were in and out of the place, searching. It was pouring rain, and I had no umbrella, so he called a cab for me. Just as I was going out the front, the police were again at the desk asking questions, and I just walked past them.

"Some very nice people helped me go from place to place. I called my friend, Faith Petric Craig, who was very left wing. She was a matron at Juvenile Hall and we sang folk music together. She turned me on to someone else, who turned me on to someone else and off I went again. And finally, I was at someone's house and I was talking to the head of the Communist Party. Then I realized how many people I was getting in trouble. I decided to call my Probation Officer and turn myself in.

"So again, they transferred me to the Salvation Army Home for Unwed Mothers. Immediately, my best friend there was a black girl, who was pregnant. You have to understand that I identified with black, that's just the way it is. It caused uproar at that place.

"Major Cox, who was in charge of the place, called me in and said that she could hardly believe what she saw. I couldn't wait to see what she was talking about. On their days off, they used to go out into the world, wearing their scarlet letters, and what she saw was me walking and talking with this black girl.

"The next thing I knew, I was shipped off to St. Elizabeth's Home for Unwed Mothers, where the nuns were very kind, but everyone seemed to be treating pregnancy as if it were a disease. And I was told that I couldn't keep the baby, and my mother wasn't going to go through that, which meant that she wouldn't be responsible. But they told me that they found a wonderful wealthy couple to raise the baby. I remember being told that I would never be able to see my baby, but that my baby would be raised in a wonderful way with all the things that I couldn't have."

"Tamar, you mean you never met Jimmie when you were at St. Elizabeth's?" Fauna asked.

"Oh no, my duty in the nursery, we all had jobs there, was to take care of this little baby named Patricia."

"Patricia!" Fauna snapped straight in her chair staring at Tamar in disbelief.

"Patricia, yes Patricia. Why do you ask?"

"Oh, nothing, nothing at all." This was all getting too strange, too confusing. There were so many coincidences that she felt their lives were being manipulated by some higher cosmic order, but for reasons that were still very unclear.

"Well, Patricia's mother didn't want her. She was old enough to keep her, she just didn't want to, which I didn't understand. Patricia was my favorite. I think I transferred all my feelings I had for you into this little baby because I knew I had already accepted the fact that I couldn't have my baby.

"When you were born, it was a real hard birth. It was treated like it was a disease. The labor was long and they didn't tell me they were going to cut me and that I would have stitches. I didn't know at that time that it was a totally unnecessary surgery. After I could get up, hobbling around pouring water on my stitches every couple of hours from a cold silvery pitcher, they let me see you through a door that had a large window, and the expression on your face was 'What is going on?' And I didn't know what was going on; I didn't know how to explain it to you. I never got to relay to you my feelings other than that one time, because they figured that I would get too attached. I probably had rights I didn't know about.

"I named you Fauna because I loved Robinson Jeffers' poem about Flora and Fauna. I asked that they keep that name. I wanted only two things, I didn't think they'd let me have what I wanted, but one was that you be named Fauna, and the other was that you at least have on your birth certificate that your father was Negro. Because in my little world I believed that black people were made of far superior stuff than the whites I knew. All the great men that I knew, all the great girls that I knew were black: Paul Robeson, Marian Anderson, Josh White, and then there were those mystical Russian dancers in the Ballet Russe. But I was very unimpressed with my mother and my grandmother and my father and the entire white court system, and I was embarrassed to be white.

"The blacks had conscience. They spoke up about right and wrong; not in the moralistic bullshit way that white people did, who lied about right and wrong. They talked nobly and eloquently about kindness, love, and fair treatment. And they went through such terrible times. They suffered so much. The more I read and saw, and the more black people I met, the more impressed I was.

"If you knew Josh White, you would know why I loved him so much, even before I met him in the physical. When I did meet him, at the Apollo Theater in Harlem when I was about seventeen, he was the most beautiful man I had ever seen.

"Black people treated me so nice. That's why the greatest and only gift I could give was that I could at least give you the benefit of growing up in a black society and not a white society. And they treated me kindly like a beautiful person, not like an unwanted leper in my own society. I thought that in time, by setting an example and marrying a black man and having a mixed baby, and if enough of them did this, then there would be no separation of the races. My whole background was fairy-tales, noble people, and great people. And in those noble stories, that's how things were done—change the world by the way you live."

"Just after I was there, at St. Elizabeth's, I had a visitor, a beautiful lady, Lady Nada. I didn't know really who she was; I had no idea that she was an Ascended Lady Master, part of the Great Brotherhood of Life until many, many years later. She looked like the Mother of God, and told me that everything was beautiful and everything was going to be all right. The way she said it, it seemed okay. So I stopped being so upset. Later, after you were born, when I was depressed about losing you, my mother took me to Mexico City to forget. But I couldn't forget, because there were all these maids there with these little babies on their hips, wrapped up in their *serapes*. You can't just have a baby, have it taken away, and forget. But I wasn't worried about you. I knew from the combination of my mother saying that everything was taken care of, and what Lady Nada said, that you would be okay.

"I always sent love to you. I just sent this ray of light, like when I hold a picture of something, and I say I never give up. It was like an umbilical cord; I just never let go. I also believed that I would never see you in the physical sense because my mother said so. I just thought you were off in some mystical world, being raised by a good family.

"When I found out about where you were years later, sitting in Hawaii with my second daughter, her name is Deborah Elizabeth Wilson, who *is* half-black, and had the privilege of really being black, and is the daughter of Stan Wilson, I was shocked.

"When Deborah was about sixteen, she wanted to have a better name than Debbie, as everyone called her. She said that she would like to use the name Fauna. She knew how I felt about losing my baby, and she wanted to use that name. And I thought, well, that's all right, sure. I was trying to get used to calling her Fauna. It was really hard after calling her Deborah all of her life.

"And then, about two weeks later, sitting in my house, after I had just given birth to my youngest son, Love, Debbie, now Fauna, said to me, 'Fauna, your daughter, is on the phone.' I mean, the world dropped away from me. Get away! How could I relate to any of this? I never thought of this possibility.

"Now just prior to this, I had told George that Debbie was no longer Debbie. After trying to explain that to him, he said to me, 'How would you like to talk with the real Fauna?' I was stunned. He said that he had your address, and that he had been in touch with you. He never said that you had searched for him, or anything. He said that he would send it to me. I just thought that he had done research. I never heard from him again. George says things and sometimes never does them. He didn't follow up with it, so I just dismissed it from my mind."

"I know very well," said Fauna, "about George saying things and not meaning it."

"What do you mean?" Tamar asked.

Fauna told her about the time when Aunt Lucille died and George was supposed to meet her in Los Angeles. Tamar wasn't surprised. But then she did surprise Fauna.

"Would you like to speak to him?"

Before Fauna could say anything, Tamar was on the phone calling Manila or Tokyo or someplace. "Hello. It's Tamar. I have the real Fauna—here, with me—here in Hawaii. Would you like to speak with her?"

Fauna's heart was racing. Tamar handed the phone over to her daughter without a word, as if she were trying to get her to confirm everything she had said about George.

"Hello, Fauna?" he paused, then said, "Well, what do you think of Tamar?"

Fauna couldn't think fast enough; things were happening too quickly for her to understand any of this—all that had happened to Tamar, all that had happened to her as a result of their relationship. She was frightened, confused. And now he wanted to know what she thought of her real mother, the woman she had dreamed of ever since she could remember.

Fauna answered him with something stupid, like "she's very interesting." They didn't say much to each other. He must have sensed that Fauna was very uncomfortable. She was glad when he said good-bye.

After that phone conversation, Fauna was now at a point where she just wanted to go home. She wanted something familiar, something safe. She wanted Billy to hold her and get her away from all of this. It was late. Her eyes were burning from lack of sleep. She arose from the table and walked toward the screen door. She could hear the whooshing sound of the waves again, sounds that soothed her troubled heart.

Tamar appeared to be exhilarated from their meeting, but Fauna couldn't listen to any more. She was exhausted and needed to get some sleep. Tamar showed her into a bedroom that was even more sparsely furnished than the rest of the house. There was no bed, just a small mat on the floor, something that was as foreign to Fauna as everything else she encountered on this odyssey. But it didn't matter she needed the sleep and cried herself into her dreams.

Christmas Eve morning she awoke early to the laughter of her brothers, Peace and Joy, playing just outside the bedroom window. It was a beautiful, sunny day in Hawaii and the sunshine somehow made her feel much more content and relaxed than the night before.

Tamar was on the phone when Fauna entered the kitchen and she seemed to be arguing with someone over money that she owed. She lowered her voice when she saw Fauna. Fauna poured herself some tea and walked outside to view the clear blue waters of the ocean that stretched in a straight line to what seemed like the ends of the earth. It was a revitalizing sight. Fauna took a deep breath and returned to the kitchen.

"Well, good morning!" Tamar said with a big smile, "Did you sleep well?"

She shook her head. "It was a hard night. I must have fallen into a deep sleep, because I can't remember dreaming about anything. My body's not used to sleeping on the floor."

"Oh, everyone sleeps on them out here. By the way, Merry Christmas!"

"Merry Christmas to you, too! I never thought I'd be spending Christmas in Hawaii, and with you!"

They sat down together again. Tamar started telling her more details about her life, not once asking Fauna about hers. She kept telling her how grateful she should be to be raised by Jimmie, just because she was black, all the while justifying her actions. Fauna wasn't ready for another heavy discussion, but at the same time she wanted to know everything about Tamar.

Tamar said Fauna II had called and was coming over later on. Tamar prefaced her statements about Fauna II very carefully, indicating that Fauna I should not listen to everything that Fauna II might say, because she had a tendency to exaggerate.

It was difficult trying to discern who was telling the truth. Was Dorothy the troublemaker? Was Tamar a liar? And who was this sister with the same name that she so proudly owned? Fauna still needed time to breathe.

"Tamar, it is Christmas, and I need to call Billy at home. Can I use your phone—don't worry, I'll reverse the charges."

"Sure, go right ahead."

Tamar stood by and listened, although nonchalantly, to their conversation. Fauna was evasive, and Billy immediately sensed that she needed him with her. He could tell she was in trouble.

"Billy's coming out to Hawaii; he wants to spend the holidays with me," she shouted in excitement to Tamar.

"Oh, that's wonderful. Tell me all about him."

Fauna began to talk about Billy, but Tamar kept interrupting, asking specific questions that seemed to be out of nowhere and quickly bringing the conversation back to Tamar's tale. They spent the remainder of the morning talking about Tamar's beliefs, Tamar's life, and Tamar's story. With each episode, Fauna became drawn in further and further. Fauna's mind was again becoming clouded with suspicion. It was all too much for anyone to adjust to, yet she had no reason to doubt anything Tamar said.

Early in the evening, she finally got to meet her half-sister, Deborah, or now Fauna II, as everyone now had begun to call her. It was awkward for both of them having the same name. Fauna resented it. She had always believed that she was an original, but now there, in front of her, was a duplicate, at least with the same first name. She never once called her by Fauna, but addressed her as "sister." She was a beautiful girl, something of what she thought she should look like if she really were mixed. They got along very well together on that first meeting. Fauna II wanted to know all about her.

"Tamar talked about you a lot when I was little," she said, "I always felt that you were my bigger sister and I used to wonder what it'd be like if you were around, or what you would do in certain situations."

Fauna looked at her with a puzzled look. It was so strange to hear that coming from someone she hadn't even known existed. She quickly glanced over at Tamar, who was busy ordering Joy around, but gestured as if to say, "never mind."

"Let's go check out the beach," her sister said, changing the subject quickly, "Do you want to go?"

"Sure, that'd be great!"

"Wait. I'll go with you," said Tamar in a way that suggested she didn't want the two sisters alone, "Just let me get this done first."

Fauna suddenly felt a strange jealousy coming from Tamar and it made her uncomfortable.

"No way," said Fauna II, "The moon will be up by the time you're ready." Fauna II was not interested in having Tamar tag along. "She takes forever to do anything," she said, "Come on, let's go."

They strolled in the cool sand near the waterline. The sea was calm; the waves were almost invisible. There were other large houses, just like the one Tamar was renting, some set further back from the beach. Together they walked, splashing their feet in the water.

"You have to be careful with Tamar," the sister said.

"Whadaya mean, careful. In what way?" Fauna listened intently.

"Just careful. She's done some crazy things in her life," she turned around and glanced at Fauna, almost as if she wanted her to ask the obvious question.

She stared back for a moment. "Well?"

"My mother thrives on confusion. She never takes the easy way; everything in her life is complicated. She makes it that way. I don't know if she enjoys it, but—I don't know; maybe she just can't function any other way. She's intelligent—very intelligent! Don't get me wrong. It's just that she likes to play one person off of the other, and I still haven't figured out why. It's almost as though her life is the only thing that matters. Her story, that's all she lives for, that's how she gets by—by telling everyone her story. Sometimes I think its all nonsense."

Fauna was shocked, "Don't you believe her?"

"I don't know. I suppose so. No one could have made up such a ridiculous thing. Besides, what would she have gained from it?"

"Nothing! Absolutely nothing!"

"I guess I'm just tired of hearing it. And I'm tired of her manipulating people and dragging them into her problems. She doesn't do things normal; everything's a project—a major project. A lot of times she tries to put words in your mouth, just to add to the confusion. That's one of the reasons I don't live with her. The other, of course, is that I have a baby."

Now Fauna was really confused. They talked a little longer and Fauna II told some strange things about how much trouble Tamar seemed to attract, or cause. All of which ended with a warning for her to be careful.

Tamar finally found them, long after the sun had set, taking its warm rays with it. She brought them each a sweater. She was in a jovial mood and fun to be around.

"It gets chilly here on the beach at night. Sometimes when there's a storm, the waves come up almost all the way to the house, but we're kind of protected here. On the North Shore, it really gets bad, especially in the winter. Last year it took two houses right off their foundations."

"Oh mother, it did not. It moved them a little. Tell the truth."

"I am telling the truth," she giggled. "She thinks I make up everything I say."

"Was the baby all right?" asked Fauna II.

"Yeah, I told Joy to keep an eye out."

"Well, I'd better go and check."

She ran back to the house, leaving Tamar alone with Fauna on the beach. The moon was just above the horizon, safely peeking out from behind the clouds, its light glistening on the water.

"It's so beautiful out here, Tamar. If I were God, this is where I'd want to live."

"God does live here," she chuckled, "Just to the left of those clouds, and on the right is where the angels hang out."

She laughed at her silliness.

"I have an angel," Fauna said.

"So do I."

"That I talk to."

"So do I," Tamar said emphatically. "In fact, the first angel I ever communicated with was when I was pregnant with you. She said she would watch over you and that I shouldn't worry. I had trouble with the pregnancy with Deborah and again saw the angel and asked for help. I saw her as a bridge between two people. I asked the angel to oversee all of this.

"I had read, as a little girl, the teachings of the Ascended Masters. I read them as fairy-tales. The Ascended Masters are a giant brotherhood, all working together for Jesus Christ. Jesus is the Great Way-shower on this planet along with many others such as Buddha, etc. I read their stories about their retreats in the Himalayas, often referred to as Shangri La, and where they worked to raise the consciousness of mankind. They were in my library as a child. George and mother were both into metaphysics.

"I always knew about magic and transformation. I remember when I was little, I worked briefly at an orphanage and while I had to work, I never asked my father for anything, and he never offered. My mother wouldn't allow me to be baptized and receive Holy Communion. I wanted to go with the other girls to Mass, and she said I had to wait until I grew up. I wanted to do the candles, and the magic, and be part of that ceremony. I remember that I just had to sit and wait, and wait, and wait until I grew up, whenever that was. In the church, they had statues of angels, and that's where I first got to see what they really looked like, but just as a statue, of course."

They talked more of spiritual things, but just for a short time. It was getting chilly for Tamar and they decided to call it a night.

The following day, a woman who had worked for George when he lived in Hawaii came to see Tamar to wish her a happy holiday. Tamar introduced Fauna as the daughter she was forced to give away. They talked briefly about the only thing they had in common, her grandfather.

The woman relayed a strange incident that happened frequently while George employed her. She said that he was often known to do strange things and experiment with people in his attempt to find the meaning of life and love. "Sometimes he would go into the bathroom by himself and stay there for hours at a time." At first, she was frightened, not knowing if he had taken ill or what. But each time he would emerge, his eyes were filled with tears, as if he spent the entire time crying.

As she told Fauna this and other stories, she began to wonder what kind of people she was dealing with. She couldn't wait for Billy to rescue her.

When Billy arrived the following afternoon, Fauna was excited, not only because she needed his help to sort all of this out, but also because she missed being with him. She wanted him to make love to her.

They stayed away from the house for most of the day. She needed his strength and his support. She relayed to him some of the particulars of what Tamar had said to her, not nearly in as much detail, but enough to make him want to know more. He didn't say much about it, just listened and comforted her.

Billy was his usual charming self when he met Tamar. He acted as if he knew nothing about her life. But it wasn't long before the conversation turned to her story.

That evening and all the following day, she relayed all the events in her life to Billy. The atmosphere was charged with intense emotion for her. She succeeded in making Fauna feel sorry for her and almost guilty that the life she gave to her was ideal compared to what she went through.

Billy's reaction was conciliatory, but not overly sympathetic. As much as she tried to draw him into her life, to make him part of her story, he refused to budge, not giving way to her emotional and intellectual seduction. Fauna, again, however, clung to her every word, trying to know as much as possible about her life and why she gave her away. Although this time, she was not nearly as frightened knowing that Billy was there with her.

That evening, Billy and she sat alone and in complete silence on the beach while the golden sun sank slowly below the ocean. The air was salty from the sea breeze.

"What a magnificent sight," he finally said to her. It was beautiful, but her mind was still on Tamar. "How did she manage to find a place like this, right on the beach? I thought only millionaires could afford to live in this kind of a house?" she asked.

"Don't you see what kind of a woman she is?" Billy asked.

When she glanced at him, he knew she had no idea what he was talking about.

"She is a victim, a perpetual victim. Or at least she appears to be. Anyone who hears that story would believe that she has been carrying the weight of the world on her shoulders. And she tells it all so well. She's an amazing woman. She gets all the attention she needs, without having to ask. People want to make things right, so they give her what she needs at that time, for nothing, or at the very least what she can afford to pay. Does she work?"

"No, she's never worked . . . you mean like in a real job? No, never," Fauna said.

"Well, see," Billy continued, "She could have dropped the whole thing and went on to be anything she wanted to be. She's very intelligent, witty, with good verbal skills. She just chose to do things the hard way."

"The hard way! What do you mean the hard way? Look where she lives!" Fauna said.

"Yeah, but she has to fight off bill collectors, making up excuses all the time, moving from one place to another, she won't be here long. When they get tired of getting dragged into her world, she'll just find someone else to help her get her life together. It isn't ever going to change."

"But . . . it's not her fault; she didn't start this whole thing," Fauna said

"How do you know? She got her father arrested and brought him to trial, right? The jury acquitted him. As far as the law is concerned, the man is innocent. He didn't do it," Billy said.

"Yeah, but what if they were wrong. What if he did cause this whole thing?"

"It doesn't matter. Justice sometimes has nothing to do with the law. Once a man is innocent—he's innocent, that's it. The only two people who will ever know the truth are Tamar and George. And sure as hell, he's not going to say nothing. And she knows that, so why don't she bury it and get on with a normal life?"

"I feel so badly for her. I feel like I want to make it right," Fauna said.

"That's exactly what she wants; that's how she lives. She tells this great story for effect, and it works. It's working with you. You're getting sucked in deeper and deeper. Soon you'll be in so deep, you won't be able to breath. And then what are ya gonna do?" Billy said peering down at her.

"I said I feel like I want to make it right, not that I was going to. At the same time, I feel like I don't want to be around her; it's too intense. I've already got enough to handle dealing with Momma. I couldn't take on another one."

She sat on the beach going over everything that was happening. Billy kept analyzing Tamar, a process that he was very capable of without getting too involved, but she didn't listen to what he was saying. She made up her mind that the best thing for her to do was to go home— immediately. She couldn't deal with Tamar's complex personality any further. All of it was much too much. The next day, over Tamar's strong objections, they left for home.

CHAPTER 23

Fauna was utterly confused about Tamar. She wanted to scream loud and long until she became unconscious, hoping that when she awoke, it would all be just a bad nightmare. Her dreams of the faceless woman, who would liberate her from a life of uncertainty, had become her purpose in life. Realizing that dream was the one thing above all else for which she yearned. Through all the fears of living with Jimmie, and trying to find her rightful place in life, it was her vision of Tamar that kept her lucid. Now those dreams had evaporated and the vision spoiled. From now on all that she needed would have to come from within her own heart. Fauna wrote in her diary.

The sea,
The beautiful sea;
Sometimes I wonder
Who
Has more turbulence,
The sea or me.

my head is ringing;
my heart is sinking;
my time is slipping.
I chew on my lips,

I bite my nails,
And I claim . . .
I'm sane!

A couple of weeks passed since her return from Hawaii. Fauna's thoughts weighed heavy with all that Tamar unloaded on her. But she maintained direction, believing that there were valid reasons behind her family's peculiarity. She was in the middle of a transformation, emerging from a black soul in a white body, raised in ignorance, superstition, and poverty, to an apprentice of Billy Sharp, dining at elegant restaurants and mingling with the elite of Reno. He taught her how to survive in the middle class, the basic elements of proper etiquette and English grammar. Her mannerisms and outlook changed. There would be no going back to a life of poverty and frustration.

Over the next few months, Billy's challenging career at Lear was on the upswing, and Fauna matured at his side. They debated marriage; it was time for a new lifestyle. He already knew everything about her. He knew about Momma, Dorothy, George; and he had experienced Tamar. They kept all of this to themselves, not revealing anything to Momma, who now became more attached to Fauna, almost childlike in her dependence.

After her trip to Hawaii, Fauna felt the need to be free of her snarled background and create her own life. But the tugging stretched her heart in two directions: Billy wanting her to be his wife and move to San Diego, and Jimmie trying to control Fauna's life from Sparks. Fauna desperately wanted Billy, but she could never leave her momma, the only one she had ever needed to please. Her interference was the biggest obstacle Billy and she faced and ultimately, it affected their relationship.

It was at this time that Billy decided to accept an offer from a company in San Diego. He gave Fauna an ultimatum: "Either go with me to California and be my wife, or stay here."

"The choice isn't simple," she told him, "I want to be with you more than anything, but what about Momma?"

"Just tell her the truth: you're starting a new life with me and we're moving to San Diego."

For days she agonized over it, trying to visualize Jimmie Lee's reaction, but the only certainty was Jimmie's unpredictable response. Fauna lacked the courage to face her. Instead, she wrote her a note and asked a girlfriend to deliver it to Jimmie after she left. Billy and Fauna were married on the day they left Reno for San Diego.

The guilt enveloped Fauna's soul. Leaving Jimmie in such ill health and sneaking away almost in the dead of night created havoc within her conscience, not allowing her a moment's rest. It was more than a month before Fauna mustered the courage to call. Long enough, she hoped, for Jimmie's hurt to subside.

"Patta, how could you leave me?" Jimmie said in a whispery voice, "I've been so sick with this cancer. It's eating away at me more every day. I ain't got much time to live. I'd like to see you just one last time before I die. You got to come back to Reno to let me die in peace."

Fauna's body sank, humbled by her conscious. Her momma sounded so frail, a woman who would scrap with anyone and come out on top, was now fragile and weak. Without forethought, Fauna left Yvette with Billy and drove the car from San Diego to Sparks. She worried that she might be too late. She couldn't let her momma die—there was nothing worse.

When she arrived at the house, only Roxy was there, sitting at the kitchen table with a drink in her hand. "Pat, what are you doin' here? I thought you moved to San Diego."

"Where's Momma?" she asked.

"She's in the john takin' a pee, where you think she is?"

"Is she all right?"

"Honey, that woman's never been all right!" Roxy paused and took a sip from her drink, "Know where she dragged me off to today?"

Fauna shook her head and sat down, "What do you mean?"

"We went to a funeral parlor," Roxy began to laugh wildly, "She walked in there just as if she owned the place; started telling the undertaker that his caskets were cheap looking."

"Why? What for?"

"I got no idea. Then she tells him that she wants the best and prettiest box he's got. The man thought she'd just lost her husband or her mother or something. I thought she'd lost her mind!" she took another sip from her glass and giggled again.

"Tell me. Tell me, what did she want?" Fauna said, waiting for Roxy to put down her drink.

"He takes us to another room with these high-priced caskets, you know, and she spots one, real fancy with all white satin and lace all around the inside, and brass handles, and two doors, and a real fluffy pillow. Her eyes lit up when she saw that one!

"Well, the man started leading her the other way, but she acted like he wasn't even in the room. I'm following the guy, cause I don't know what's going on, and she. . . ." Roxy snorted, tears filled her eyes, and she then hammered her hand lightly on the table, and then continues, "she climbs in to the casket and lays down on this fluffy pillow, fixes her dress and folds her arms as if she's dead." Roxy then sipped her drink and said, "Aha—but she got this big, shit-eatin' grin a mile wide. And then she says, 'How'd I look? Is this box pretty enough for me?'"

Jimmie came out from the bathroom; Fauna's back was to her.

"Hey guys, what's you all giggling at?"

Fauna turned and startled Jimmie, who smirked and then got serious. "Patta, when did you get here?"

"Just now," Fauna said, "I thought you were dying."

"I recovered."

"In twelve hours?"

"Yeah, you know. It was one a those twenty-four-hour things, but I guess it only went halfway."

Roxy hammered the table again laughing loudly. Jimmie did her best to hold in her amusement, but Roxy's laugh was contagious.

Fauna's eyes pierced through their silliness.

"But I was sick . . ." Jimmie said, "real sick. That's why I tried out the coffin." She started to snicker, knowing Fauna was furious. Roxy held both hands over her mouth and put her head between her legs in a foolish attempt at disguising her giggling.

"Momma. You ain't gonna die."

"I know that now, but I didn't know it before."

"Then why did you make me come all the way up here? Don't you realize what I had to do to get here? I stopped everything just for you, because I thought you were dying. I left Yvette, the apartment, Billy—I was in a panic."

"I was dyin'—didn't you hear me?" Jimmie said.

Roxy could no longer contain herself, and neither could Fauna. She spent the night and returned to San Diego the following morning.

Billy and Fauna worked hard to forge a higher standard of living. Business opportunities seemed to appear out of nowhere. A magnanimous offer to work overseas quickly became suspiciously realistic. For months there was persistent pressure from business associates to move to Saudi Arabia. Although Fauna didn't understand the details, she knew that a move would leave Jimmie behind. They felt their lives were being scrutinized—little things that you couldn't put your finger on: a clicking sound on the telephone, the same car parked near their house, or their work, or near a store with a man sitting behind the wheel. Billy and Fauna began to pay closer attention to their private lives.

At the same time, Jimmie begged Fauna to return to Sparks. She threatened, cajoled, cried, cursed, and encouraged Fauna's guilt for what she believed was her abandonment. The more Fauna tried to explain that she had to live her own life, the less Jimmie wanted to hear.

A few days later, Rosie called and said that Jimmie had been rushed to the hospital. Fauna packed a bag and flew to Sparks with Yvette. Rosie met them at the hospital.

"What happened?" Fauna asked.

"Oh, child, it's the same thing," Rosie said, "only this time she overdid it. Roxy called an ambulance when she found Jimmie rolled up in a ball on the bathroom floor." Rosie motioned for them to follow her to the ward where Jimmie was resting. "A normal person would have just asked for help, but not your momma. She started cussing and fighting with Roxy, but Roxy paid no attention and got her brought over here."

As they entered the ward, Jimmie's now gravelly voice could be heard barking at one of the nurse's aides.

"She'd been on a steady diet of gin for a month," Rosie whispered, "and it don't look good, least that's what her doctor said."

"Hi, Momma, how you feeling?"

Jimmie's demeanor shifted quickly when she heard her daughter's voice. "Oh, Patta, is that you?" she moaned, "They been doing such god-awful things to me, I'm so glad you're here. I thought I was gonna leave this earthly place without seeing you one last time."

Rosie rolled her eyes and shook her head, "Well, she's all yours now, I got lots to do today."

"They been poking and prying and shoving pills down my throat and giving needles," Jimmie said in a weakened voice, "now that you're here, you can get them to stop."

"Momma, I don't want them to stop. You need to get treatment for this stuff," Fauna said.

"But, Patta, I'm dying. I don't want to die with all these tubes and bottles. I wants to die in my own bed," Jimmie said, "with you at my side. I don't want you to leave me."

Her acting skills remained intact while Fauna was there, playing the dying victim for an audience of one. To everyone else, Jimmie appeared belligerent. It took a week before Fauna discovered the pattern in Jimmie's behavior that was being used in an attempt to separate her from Billy. Jimmie's condition eventually improved and Yvette was out of school far too long and Fauna had to get back to her life in San Diego.

A few weeks later, Fauna treated Yvette to some of the sights in Sea World. Afterward they had lunch at a restaurant near the waterfront. While they were eating, ogling the expansive harbor stocked with elegant yachts parading in and out, Fauna noticed two men, an Asian and a Caucasian, both eyeing her. She nervously tried to ignore their intermittent stares. When Yvette finished eating, she begged her mother to look over the yachts up close. As they walked across the street and headed casually toward their car, Fauna noticed a limousine parked just ahead. From the distance it looked like the same Asian was standing near the car. Without alarming Yvette, she slowed her pace to an easy stroll, and then stopped in front of a large sailboat to give her time to think about the next move. "Oh, look Yvette. Look at how big this one is. Isn't it beautiful!" She stopped and glanced back at the limo for only a moment.

"I like this one better," Yvette said, pointing to the one right next to it.

"Oh yeah, that one's even better."

Suddenly, the Asian opened the limo door, and out stepped a tall man, thin, and fastidiously dressed in a white suit. Fauna held tightly to Yvette's hand as she watched him slowly walked toward them with a confident stride. Fauna tried to ignore him but he was staring directly at her. He stopped only a few feet in front of them, and just stood there, watching. She stared back into his eyes. His mustache was thin, his white hair neatly layered over a golden tanned face. This elegant image scratched onto her memory. Then just as suddenly, he turned and walked back to the limo where the Asian held the rear door open for him, and they drove off. She watched as they sped by, hoping to see if anyone else was in the car, but the windows were darkened.

Later, over dinner, she told Billy about it.

"Well, who was he?" Billy asked.

She shrugged her shoulders.

"Didn't you ask?"

"No. It's not the first time I felt like I was being watched. It's happened before." She thought for a second. "In fact, it reminded me of a time a few years ago when I went to Aunt Lucille's funeral. There was a man in a car. I saw him three or four times over the next few days while I was in Los Angeles. And before I went to Hawaii, too, now that I think about it."

"Was it the same man?" Billy asked.

"I don't know, I never got to see him up close, but there was just something that made me think of that again," Fauna said.

"You mean someone's spying on you."

"I think so. And I noticed someone else, just last week, when I dropped Yvette off at school. I saw the same car three times during the day."

"It's probably just a coincidence. Why would anyone follow you?"

She looked at Billy and could easily tell that his concern was genuine, and that he had no idea who this man could be or why he wanted to take a good look at her.

———————

Deborah, Fauna's half-sister, married a soldier who was being transferred from Hawaii. She called Fauna and asked if it was all right if she spent some time with her in San Diego while he got things settled at his new base in Kentucky. Fauna happily agreed, and picked Deborah up at the airport and drove back to the house, where she made her new guest feel comfortable. They sat down in the living room with some iced tea. Deborah wore shorts and a tropical print top and sat up straight, confidently. Her legs crossed right over left, and she balanced the napkin-wrapped, cold glass delicately on her knee.

"Where's your son, Starr?" Fauna asked.

"Oh, he's gone on with my husband to get things going at our new home. I thought it would be a good idea just for the two of us to be together," Deborah said.

"I'm glad you called me," Fauna said, "even though I don't know much about you or Tamar. I felt when we met in Hawaii you were following a different path and were more grounded than Tamar. It was such a trip for me; I was in shock for most of the time."

"I know what you mean," Deborah said, "I grew up with all of that stuff, so I was very used to it and it doesn't bother me anymore. I can't be caught up in someone else's drama, even my mother's. I've got my own life to live."

"Still, it's a nice place to grow up in, right there on the beach. . . ." Fauna started to say.

"Wait, we weren't always on the beach. That house you were in belonged to a friend of my mother's, excuse me, our mother, Tamar. In fact, since you've been gone, she already moved to another place. We were always changing houses, changing schools," Deborah said.

Fauna could not help but notice the eloquent mannerisms of her half-sister. She was poised, articulate, straightforward, and she really was half-black, everything Fauna struggled to be in her own life.

"But I thought the family was very wealthy? I met Dorothy in San Francisco, and she told me about this illustrious heritage. . . ." Fauna said, but Deborah cut her off.

"Wait, there may be some heritage, but we never saw any of it. It probably went to the other side of the family. We were all born and raised in California. When Tamar moved us to Hawaii, she only had a knapsack and $140, and no place to live. She gets by on her wits, and with the help of some friends, always new, and always on the outermost fringe of society."

"I guess I was mistaken about Doris Day," Fauna said.

"You mean the old actress? Who said anything about her?"

"Oh, nothing. It was just something I was thinking of," Fauna said.

They meshed as if they were on the same oar, rowing across their history together. Deborah filled in much of the lost years, mostly with stories of Tamar, not all kind, and Fauna had no reason to doubt her. She began to understand why.

A few days after Deborah's arrival, she asked Fauna if she would like to meet the rest of her long-lost family. Elated at the prospect of getting yet another point of view, Fauna quickly agreed. That weekend, they drove to Venice to spend the night with Tamar's brother, Kelly. Fauna was not happy at Kelly's beach apartment, but notably impressed with her very fine-looking uncle. He wore his golden brown hair shoulder length and dressed the part of a stylish hippie, appropriate for the times and place. He wasn't very tall, only about five eight or nine. His sociable persona and bright smile made up for the unconventional accommodations.

The following day, Fauna was nervous and uncomfortable at the thought of having brunch and meeting more of the Hodel clan. Knowing Tamar, Dorothy, and George, she was on guard and ready for almost anything. They went to a more elegant condominium in Santa Monica that was owned by George's ex-wife, Dorothy. Deborah, who everyone referred to as Fauna II, introduced Fauna to Steve, a detective with the Los Angeles Police Department, and much taller and distinguished looking than Kelly. He was medium in build and dressed conservatively in a sport jacket. The third brother was Michael, more studious looking than the other two and quieter. Dorothy, an attractive woman in her late fifties, spoke first, "Fauna, you're finally here. Welcome back into our lives."

She was surprised at the warm greeting and said, "Thank you. What do you mean 'back into your lives'?"

"Well, you've been gone for such a long time. Since when, well, in fact, since you were born. I'm surprised Jimmie didn't tell you . . . on second thought, it was made very clear to Jimmie not to say anything— that is, until you were older," Dorothy said.

"Tell me what? What is it that everyone seems to know but me?" Fauna asked.

"I was with George around the time you were born," Dorothy continued. "In fact, I was married to him. I tried to keep in touch with Jimmie, sending her letters, explaining things and the like, making sure everything was okay for George. He always wanted to know what was going on—very curious."

"Wait a minute. Is that how Momma used to know so much about my grandfather, I mean George?" Fauna said.

"He is your grandfather, of course," Dorothy said.

"She used to tell me all the time that whenever she wanted to get hold of him, she'd just have to pick up the phone and call Dorarro," Fauna said.

"Yes, I'm Dorarro!"

"Dorarro? I thought my sister said you were Dorothy."

"Well, yes, that's true. But before I married your grandfather, I was married to a man named John Huston. . . ."

"That name sounds familiar," Fauna said.

"Yes . . . he's well-known. He gave me the name Dorarro, which is Spanish for Dorothy. I used it for a long time. Later on, when I left John to marry George, he called me Dorarro, too, so as not to confuse me with Dorothy, your real grandmother.

"John and George were very close friends during those days, partying and playing all over Hollywood, Mexico, and San Francisco. That is before George got arrested for the incident with Tamar. After that, John didn't want to be associated with the publicity. It would have been a disaster for his film career. So he couldn't take a chance. In those days, any bad publicity would stop an actor or director in mid-stride, adversely affecting his films. George tried to disappear, which he did. I, in turn, kept in touch with Jimmie to make sure that everything was all right with you. But then, early on, she somehow seemed to have disappeared, vanished. I guess you were only about two or three at the time."

"When I was in Hawaii, Tamar told me who you were, but I didn't put it all together until now," Fauna said.

"That's right," Michael interrupted, "Wait, you met with Tamar. What did you think of her?"

"That's exactly the same thing George asked me!" said Fauna.

"You spoke with George?" Kelly asked.

"Yeah, Tamar just picked up the phone while I was there and called him. She passed the phone to me, and he asked me what I thought of Tamar, too. Why? Is that unusual?"

"Unusual! That's putting it very mildly," said Kelly, "George is not an easy person to get hold of. He's very mysterious."

"And extremely private," Steve added.

"Yeah," agreed Kelly, "usually you have to make an appointment just to call him, and if he doesn't want to talk with you there's nothing you can do."

"The last time he was here—in fact, each time he comes here, it's usually for medical reasons," said Steve. "He doesn't trust any foreign hospitals or doctors. That's the only time we see him.

"He always makes an appointment for us to see him. He doesn't just drop in like most fathers," Steve continued mimicking loftiness, "No, not the mysterious Dr. Hodel. He'll meet us, all together, at the most posh restaurant, in one of their private dining rooms."

"Yeah," said Kelly, "and he always travels with his entourage."

"What are you talking about?" Fauna asked, now on the edge of her seat.

Kelly said, "George is exceedingly rich. He's never without his bodyguards, and chauffeur, and a bevy of beautiful women—some Asian, some black—all beautiful, and dressed in the most fantastic clothes and jewelry. It's unbelievable!"

"We only get to see him for about two hours over these dinners. No one ever gets close to him. But he's always been like that," said Steve.

"You mean even when you were little?" Fauna had to know.

"Oh sure," said Kelly, "My father was always into erotica—not pornography, the more exotic stuff. He had very little time for us. He was ever-so-charming. We were always in awe of him, everyone was, you can't help it, he's just so mysterious."

Even as they talked about him—their own father, she noticed how clearly fascinated they were. It was as if they were discussing a supernatural being who occasionally paid a visit.

"What does he look like?" Fauna asked, "You make him sound so powerful."

"He is powerful! I'll get a picture," Kelly said. "Wait." He got up and left the room.

"George is," Michael thought for a moment. "Charming, very sophisticated, and handsome. He's brilliant, a real intellectual who knows how to manage people with his charisma." He glanced at his brother for approval.

"Yes!" Steve added, "He's an enigma to everyone, and everyone considers him an absolute genius, if there is such a thing, particularly when it comes to dealing with the occult, paranormal psychology, medicine, psychiatry, and anything else you can think of." He shook his head and they all chuckled.

"What about Tamar?" Fauna asked, "Is that where she got all her ideas?"

"Probably, said Michael, "When you grow up in an environment dedicated to the exotic and the supernatural, it's difficult to keep your feet planted firmly on the ground."

"Well," asked Fauna, "what about this incest thing? Do you think it's all true?"

They all looked at one another. It was obvious that they had discussed this subject many times. "We really don't know," said Steve, "In twenty-five years, neither one has changed their stories. Tamar has everything to gain by saying that she made the whole thing up. I mean my father would probably give her a trust fund—if she changed her mind.

"On the other hand, they went to court and everyone heard all of the evidence. The psychiatrists, my mother, my grandmother, everyone said she was trouble, a liar, a storyteller. The jury acquitted him. So even if he did do it, and admitted it, he wouldn't get into any trouble with the police. He can't be tried twice for the same crime, right? Double jeopardy and all that stuff."

Kelly finally came back into the room. "I've got 'em . . . take a look at these." He showed them to Michael and Steve and Dorarro. "Do you remember when this was taken?"

They passed them around. Fauna looked at some of the old black-and-white photographs of Tamar and the rest of the family. As she was going through them, wondering who these people were, she suddenly came across one that really startled her. It was a photo of the same man who had approached her while she was with Yvette at the marina—it was George!

Fauna told them what had happened, and they just looked at each other as if it were the most natural thing in the world. They all knew how curious George was. No one offered an explanation.

When she and Deborah left the following day, Fauna had a much more relaxed attitude toward this newfound family. But from what they had told her, she still didn't want to get any further involved with Tamar or George unless it was absolutely necessary. She had more important things to do with her life.

Yvette was in school on a trimester program that allowed her three weeks off every other month. Jimmie discovered the school schedule and each time a vacation neared, she put pressure on Fauna, feigning illness, begging her to come to Nevada to take care of her. At first, Fauna dropped everything and flew to Reno. By the time Yvette was due to go back to school, Jimmie would recover. After the pattern of Yvette's time off and Jimmie's illness became obvious, Fauna balked and Jimmie added an inducement by offering to provide Fauna with crucial information about her real family. However, when the time came to reveal the secrets, Jimmie reneged, trying to hold on to as much history as possible. When that effort lost its varnish, Jimmie would have someone else call Fauna and plead with her to come home because it looked like "the end." The manipulation and travel played havoc with Fauna's marriage.

There was added pressure. It was time for Billy to make a decision regarding the negotiations on the Saudi project and he was reluctant to commit. "I just don't understand how this whole thing came about," he told her, "There are probably a dozen other people more qualified than me to do this. I just don't understand."

"Don't you feel you deserve it?" She asked.

"It's not that," he said, "There are just too many unanswered questions."

"Like what?"

"Like the echo when I talk on the phone—and the clicking sound, too."

"Yeah, I hear the same thing—almost as if someone is listening in on their phone."

They looked at each other.

"You don't think the phone's being tapped," said Fauna. "do you?"

"I don't know," said Billy, "What for? Who'd bother listening in on our conversations? It doesn't make any sense."

"It could be the Saudi thing," she said.

"Yeah, it could be. But . . ."

"But what?"

"I don't know. They already know everything about me. Besides— nah, it can't be them. This has been going on before I even knew anything about that project."

"How 'bout George?" She knew George had spied on her in San Diego. Billy looked at her and said nothing. But his eyes showed fear.

———————

That Saturday, she was home alone. Billy was away on business. When the phone rang, she was expecting his call, but instead of Billy it was her cousin, Johnny, who she hadn't spoken to in four years.

"Wuts happenin', Baby?" his voice was sluggish.

"Johnny, is this you? You sound different. How you been? I haven't seen you in such a long time."

There was a long pause before he spoke again. "Yeah . . . I'm fine . . . real fine . . . but . . . not . . . as fine as my fine looking' cousin . . . heh, heh. Ya still as fine . . . and foxy . . . as ever?" his tone was insincere.

"Yeah, Johnny . . . just the same."

"I ain't seen ya in a loooong time, Sugar. I forgot wut it feels like ta feast my eyes on a sexy thang like ya'self. Where ya been hidin' out at?"

"I ain't been hiding out. Since I moved to San Diego, I hadn't had a chance to see anybody. You don't sound too good . . . what's the matter?"

"Nothin'! Nothin's wrong. You know how it is, Sugar. I just miss seeing ya, that's all."

"You're talking . . . funny . . . not like I remember."

There was silence for a few seconds, then Johnny began to slur his words.

"Ya 'member when we was little . . . and played at Big Momma's? we . . . we . . . we used to play together, we used to be together . . . all the time . . . 'member that?"

"Of course, we were always together."

"We used to play under the bed . . . ya 'member that?"

"Yeah, I was just a baby . . . and you weren't much older."

"They was the good ol' days. I sure miss 'em." Again, he paused, then said, "Hey Pat . . . I was thinkin' 'bout coming down by you . . . for a visit . . . maybe next weekend. Ya got room for me?"

"Always got room for you. Just call me when you get in town and I'll give you directions."

"Ok, sugar; I'll do that," Johnny hung up abruptly. A second later, Fauna heard the clicking sound on the phone. She listened for a moment longer, but only to silence.

The week cruised by quickly. Although Fauna was anxious at first to see her cousin, that soon evaporated, as the daily routine of work, helping Yvette with a school project, and creating new excuses not to visit Reno took precedence. Billy checked in each day by phone, always trying to dissuade Fauna from succumbing to Jimmie's plea. Each conversation ended with the same clicking sound, distracting but not disconcerting. The clicks were heard not just with Billy's calls but with everyone she spoke with on the home phone. The last thing she thought about was Johnny's upcoming visit; her thoughts were occupied with Tamar and her mysterious grandfather.

On the day he was scheduled to arrive, instead of a visit, Fauna received a call from Barbara, Johnny's sister. Her voice sounded disconnected from what Fauna remembered as familiar. She was sobbing, "Pat, what am I gonna do?"

"What's the matter? You don't sound good at all."

"Oh God! I don't know what's happening. It's my brother . . ." Barbara said and then silence.

"Johnny? What is it? What about Johnny?"

"He's dead . . . Johnny's dead!"

There was silence from Fauna. Barbara continued, "he was found in the water . . . drowned."

"That's impossible, Johnny is a good swimmer. I don't understand. How could this happen?"

Barbara screamed, "He was murdered!"

"Who? Who killed your brother? Who was it?" Fauna asked, but there was no response, only incoherent squeals that turned into uncontrollable wailing. She tried to get her to calm down, but instead Barbara screamed, "NO! He was MURDERED! They killed my brother. Don't you understand?" Her voice blasted through the phone, shocking Fauna into a deeper reality, into the core of her being. Someone very close to her was brutalized. She held the phone in silence not understanding another word. She could only think that Johnny was supposed to be here—today. Johnny had been murdered the night before. She needed Billy near her more than ever.

Later that evening when Billy called, she gave him the salient points and heard the frustration in his voice. She felt his anger, but knew it wasn't with her, but with all that was going on around her. He wanted peace in his life, a comfortable lifestyle, and a happy marriage—Fauna and her family were anything but. She knew he'd be on the next flight for San Diego so they could drive together up to the funeral in Los Angeles.

———————

The casket was closed and she wondered why. She searched the room and recognized most of the mourners, many of whom she hadn't seen since she was a child. They looked the same as she remembered. But as she looked closer, she sensed something was wrong. Jimmie was off to one corner, unusually quiet. Fauna moved slowly toward her but was intercepted by Roxy, who always seemed to have her finger on the family pulse. "Pat, I'm so sorry; this is so awful."

"I can't believe this. It's just not real. I just spoke to him last week."

"You did? You spoke to Johnny?" Roxy looked surprised.

"Yeah, why is the casket closed?"

Roxy turned to look toward the end of the room, "We'll it's the way he died; don't you know? They didn't want to show his face." Pat was puzzled. "When they found his body," Roxy looked around and then came closer to Pat and whispered, "he was mutilated. His penis was hacked off and shoved in his mouth."

"What?! Who the hell would do such a horrible thing?"

"He must have made some really powerful enemies."

"But why would they do that? It doesn't make any sense!?"

"Sense? None of this makes any sense. But from what I was told it means that he made some sexual advances to the wrong somebody and that was their idea of teaching him a lesson."

"What? Johnny never made sexual advances to anyone."

"Honey, you ain't been around this family much, have you?"

"Well, but I know him."

"You knew him. What'd you two talk about when you talked last?"

Her mind wandered back to the prior week when she last spoke to Johnny, trying to recall every word he said, "Nothing important. Just hello, what's going on, like that."

"Oh."

The wake and subsequent funeral felt tense to her; everyone spoke in short, guarded phrases, more nervous chatter than actual conversations, and no one spoke of the details of Johnny's death, Fauna included. She didn't tell anyone, except Billy, that Johnny was supposed to visit her that weekend, and she never mentioned to anyone other than Roxy that he talked to her on the phone. She just let him and his memory rest in peace. Fauna kept the same cautious feelings about why he was killed to herself.

On the return trip to San Diego, Billy broached the subject gently. He knew Fauna was in a fragile state. "Listen, I know this is a touchy subject and it may sound crass, and we've talked around it for a long time, but we need to talk about it."

"What is it?" she asked, "about Johnny?"

"Well, that's a part of it. What exactly did he say when you spoke last time?"

"Just that he was coming to San Diego for a visit and he wanted to stay with me, with us."

"And this was on the phone, right?"

"Yeah, of course."

"In the house?"

"Yeah, why?"

"Did you hear that clicking sound?"

Fauna hesitated and looked over at Billy, "Sure, how did you know?"

"Well, it's been happening right along. So somebody is listening to our conversations on the phone. Now who do you think would do something like that?"

Fauna felt the chill run through her shoulders, but kept her cool, even temper. "My grandfather. Do you think he had Johnny killed?"

"No, that's a mystery for the police to unravel," he said.

"But why? All Johnny said to me that he was coming down for a visit and that he missed our times together when we were kids." Fauna thought for a moment, "And then he asked me if I remembered when we used to sleep together?"

"What? What are you talking about?"

"Well, nothing. We were little kids. I was about four years old. He wasn't much older. I don't think he meant anything by it."

Billy stared through the windshield of the car, not uttering another sound.

The weeks passed slowly. Billy and Fauna talked about Johnny over and over again, trying to piece together everything that they alone knew concerning his last phone conversation with her. They suspected that his death was drug-related, but there were so many unanswered questions. It was impossible for them to know for sure who killed him and why he was so demonstratively mutilated. After one such conversation, Billy changed the subject.

"I want to know how do you do it?" Fauna didn't answer. "I mean how do you deal with all of this stuff. I mean, you got Jimmie Lee, your grandfather, that mother who gave you away. . . . I was raised black, I am black, and I work with the whites, and I know that there is no difference between people, and I think you know that by now."

"Yes, you taught me the difference by introducing me to all your friends," she said, "your educated friends, and knowing them as little as I do, they seem to look at things from another perspective."

"Right, I know that, but I want to know how you feel about your family, because, frankly, they exhaust me. Granted, you grew up with these people and I can understand that, but there's a barrier that exists, a wall that keeps you at a distance. I see it, I feel it."

Fauna remained silent, staring out the passenger window at the landscape floating by. Her mind wandered to the many bus trips with Momma, in another world so far in the past. She thought of her first trip to meet Big Momma, and Aunt Lucille, and Homer, especially Homer.

"And there's your momma," Billy started to say.

"I don't feel a wall," Fauna answered. "I knew I was different; I knew my family was not my blood, but they took care of me and raised me with love."

"Love?" Billy said, "Your momma has love for no one but herself."

"That's not true. She does care; she does love me." Fauna paused and again glanced out the window, and then said, "She had dreams, and I interrupted those dreams. She has a right to have some resentment, but it isn't against me, it's against the white people who put her in this position."

"But you're white," Billy said, "and I'm not, and she resents me, too, and she resented Bobby, and everybody else who tries to get in her way."

"Like I said, she had dreams," Fauna said.

"What about your dreams?"

Fauna turned from the side and faced forward watching the array of taillights in front of her. "My dreams were always the same—to find the fairy-tale princess, my real mother, to find where I came from and why I was given away, to live happily ever after, and to make Momma's dreams to be somebody come true. I wanted to bring them both together: the fairy-tale princess in the dream world and Momma in the real world."

"Your real mother is not a fairy-tale, it's another reality that is just as bizarre as this one."

"But how was I to know this? I had to find out."

"I'm sorry," Billy said.

"Sorry for what? Sorry because I couldn't make it happen?

"Yes," Billy said, "and I'm sorry because your real mother believed that growing up in poverty, prejudice, hatred, and racism, that no white person could ever understand, was somehow a noble gesture. And because of her twisted vision, you become a part of. . . ."

"Of what . . . ?" Fauna said, "Of a sick conspiracy, or a poor woman who's dreams I destroyed? I understand what prejudice and hatred is cause I grappled with it from both sides. The blacks resented me because I was white, even though we lived the same life, even though we lived through the same ordeals, time after time. The whites hated me with a fervor because I was living with and loving the blacks, but that doesn't change who I am."

"I don't get you. You still feel like you owe your momma something. You don't owe her anything. She made that decision a long time ago. That was the life she chose. She didn't have to say 'yeah, I'll take the baby'."

"God chose her. There was a reason, she was the one," Fauna said.

"And what reason was that?"

"Big Momma told me that God doesn't tell why He does things or chooses people for certain things, He just does, that's all. And Momma was chosen to raise me."

"So, now you're saying that Momma is the victim for going through the trouble of raising you," Billy said.

"There is no victim. If there is anything I learned from all of this is that no matter what we start out with, we can make it into whatever we want. If she had chosen another path, who knows where I'd be."

"And if Tamar hadn't said that your father was 'Negro', where would you be?"

"That's really the thing that hurts the most—to be lied to all these years. My whole life was a lie," Fauna said as placed her fingers on her temples and squeezed trying to erase it from memory. "I wanted a better life, but the one I got showed me how to love unconditionally. In that sense, Tamar was right."

CHAPTER 24

A few weeks later, Fauna's life was interrupted by a panic call from Reno. Momma had again been rushed to the hospital—and this time it was very serious. Immediately she took Yvette out of school and boarded the next flight from San Diego, arriving at the hospital late afternoon.

The atmosphere was different this time. She gasped at the sight of Jimmie. She looked so different, so gray, so small, and so helpless. Her hair was almost gone. Her eyes were sunken into her skull making them appear larger than normal. Across her face, leading into her nose, was a long, flesh-colored tube that stretched down the side of the bed. The sight of it made Fauna take a deep breath and her eyes filled. It had only been a little over a month since she last saw Jimmie, but so much had changed.

Here, in front of her, lying helpless was her momma, a sickly old black woman. In spite of it all, Fauna loved her—loved her so deeply that only now, as her once-stony body crumbled before Fauna's eyes, could she feel the pain that only love brings.

Jimmie was asleep, and breathing quietly. Fauna sat at the edge of her bed delicately, not wanting to disturb her peace, nor bother the other silent old woman in the next bed. She placed her hand on Jimmie's, and with the other gently stroked her leathery forehead. It was cool and dry, unlike the normal warmth that had caressed her since she was a baby.

Later, she took Yvette, who had sat patiently nearby, over to Aunt Rosie's house, and again she returned to her momma's side. She spent the next twelve hours awake and alone, with only the souls of two tired old bodies resting in their respective cradles—Jimmie and the elderly woman who died in her sleep that very night. Seeing death made Fauna more determined to make Momma live so that she could give her the good life.

Before Jimmie awoke, the attendants had removed the remains of the old woman. Fauna couldn't help but notice the surprised expression when she saw Fauna sitting.

"Patta! When did you get here?" she asked, "I didn't know you was even coming. I had a dream 'bout you, though. It was when you was a little girl. You and Inez, both of you." She paused and slowly turned her head toward the window. Then she continued. "'Member when you and Inez stole those little footies from the store. You both told me that someone bought them for you. I didn't believe that, not for a minute. You just had to have those footies—with the little red balls on the toes," With much difficulty, she began to chuckle.

"I remember," said Fauna."

"You thought you could pull a fast one on me. Ha! The day ain't never came that you could get one past me. Uh, uh. Wished you could a see'd the look on your little faces when I told you I called the store and the man told me two little girls stole them footies." She tried to laugh, but began coughing instead, "You believed that story. And we didn't even have a phone, we was so poor, and you two little goddamn shits were so dumb. You fell for it and confessed."

"I know. We were so stupid. That was a long time ago."

"Yeah, sure was. Lots happened since then. And there's lots more you don't know about."

Fauna was curious. Jimmie had said that so many times to her and never told her what she was talking about. She asked again, "Like what Momma? What is it that you've been promising to tell me?"

"Never you mind. One a these days, before I die, I'll tell you the real reason why you could never change your name. There's a whole lot you don't understand. It involves you inheriting a lot of money," she paused a moment to swallow, "All my life I wanted to be somebody. Here I am at the end, and I'm still a nobody."

"You are somebody! You're a very important somebody—you're my Momma."

"Yeah, but that didn't make me the good life. I could've been just like any of those famous people who had money. Like that Dorothy Dandridge, I was prettier than her, too."

"You're still pretty, Momma. That's never gonna change."

"I could never figure out how they did it. Having you around, a little pinky-skinned baby—should've let them white folks know a little more. But it was too dangerous. They would've taken you away, real quick like. If it wasn't for the chauffeur, you'd been out of my life long ago."

"The chauffeur? What chauffeur?"

Jimmie looked up at Fauna, "The one you almost met a few years ago. He hadn't been a chauffeur for a long, long time, but every once in a while he'd like to pretend he was. He was always trying to be young again and doing something different." She paused a moment, and then added, "He liked me, too—cause I was different."

"I don't know any chauffeur."

"Well, he knows you; been watching you all your life. Keeping an eye out, too. If someone bothered you, he'd know about it. And if something ever happened to you, well God help the poor soul who did it."

"Who is he? Why haven't I met him?"

"Well, when you was a baby, he had to leave the country. Somehow he knew something about some white girl getting hacked up in California or some place. But when he came back, he didn't want nothing to do with me, but he was always knowing about you."

As she talked, she seemed to be getting weaker. It wasn't much, just the way she moved her head. There was slightly less quiver in her voice.

Over the next week, she did improve—considerably. In fact, enough so that she thought it was safe for Fauna to return to San Diego and get Yvette back in school. So, with Momma recovering, she returned home to Billy, who was becoming more frustrated at her sudden departures.

On Friday afternoon, Jimmie called from the hospital. Her voice was very weak. She said the doctors didn't give her much chance. Fauna panicked and again dashed to Reno to be at her side. Just the thought of

Momma dying put her in a state of sheer terror. However, she discovered to her relief that Jimmie was no worse off then when she had left her a week earlier.

Jimmie continued her deceptive tactics, trying unmercifully to separate Fauna from Billy. Her jealousy never waned for a moment. She wanted Fauna with her always, and dreaded the thought of Patta not being forever at her side even more so than death itself. Fauna made dozens of urgent trips back and forth between San Diego and Reno. Billy and she argued each time.

"Why do you keep falling for that crazy woman's story?" he screamed. "You know what she's trying to do. She's trying to destroy our marriage. And you can't let her do that. You're the only one who can stop her. Just tell her! 'No, you crazy old nigger, you ain't dying, and I ain't coming!' Just tell her, tell her!"

"I can't. She's my momma! What if I don't go, and she dies? What do you think I'll be like then?"

He turned away from her and she could see that he was angry and frustrated. He turned to her and said, "It's a game with her. She's fuckin' with your mind; can't you see that? Look, just don't go this time. Just tell her you have other things to do."

Fauna was apprehensive and scared. Billy was probably right, but she didn't know, she just didn't know. That night, Jimmie called again. Fauna answered the phone and Billy glared at her. He knew who was on the other end before she even said hello.

"Hi, Momma, how are you feeling?" she turned away from Billy. His stare was making her uncomfortable.

"Oh, Patta," she sounded so weak and old, "I thought you'd be here by now. Oh my God! Why you still there? Why ain't you with your poor old Momma? You've got to come. There's something I got to tell you before I go."

She felt so guilty, "Momma what is it? What do you want to say to me?" Before Momma could answer, she glanced up at Billy. "I can't come this time, Momma. I was just there. Why didn't you tell me then?"

"Oh, Patta, you just got to come."

Fauna began to cry. Billy rose from his chair and knelt next to her. His hand gently touched her shoulder.

"Good-bye, Momma, I'll talk to you tomorrow." She hung up the phone, left Billy alone on his knees, and cried herself to sleep.

The night was restless. She tossed and turned. The next morning she told Billy about it.

"Last night, I had this dream, over and over again. Momma was there with me, alive! It was real, I swear. She looked at me, almost as if she could see into my soul, she said in a very sweet tone, 'Patta, I'm gonna die.' I said, 'No Momma, you're not gonna die, you're gonna get better, you'll see.' She said, 'Patta, I'm gonna die—before Christmas.'"

Billy was annoyed. He took a deep breath and said, "Well, what do you think it means? Is she gonna die?"

"Oh no," said Fauna, "I think it means just the opposite. I think she's gonna live. I don't accept it for its face value. She's gonna live. But I'm still gonna go to Reno to see her."

"What? I thought we went all through this shit last night! I thought for once, you were going to use a little reason, a little common sense. Now you have a dream that you believe is telling you that she's gonna live, and you're going to fly up to her again! What the hell is wrong with you?"

"There's nothing wrong with me! She's my mother. What's wrong with you? Can't you understand that?"

"Fauna, you're not going up there. You've been in Reno more than you've been with me. I'm your husband—remember? What the hell kind of a marriage is this?"

"Our marriage has nothing to do with this!"

"Fauna, I've had it! It's finished! If you get on that plane, I won't be here when you get back."

Her face went cold and stiff. She felt the shock and anger. He was willing to abandon her at a time like this, a time when she needed his support and understanding the most. She shot back coldly, without reservation, "I can always get a new husband, but I've only got one mother."

He stared blankly, almost as if paralyzed. She left for Reno that day.

When Fauna arrived at the hospital, she was upset. She felt very strongly that Momma would recover. She wouldn't allow anything to happen to her—there were too many things left incomplete. She hadn't given her the best that life has to offer—she hadn't given her a nice home, or plenty of clothes, or vacations, or the best medical attention.

The situation with Billy, however, was another story. It was true that she was neglecting their relationship. She was too involved with Momma. Still, Billy's reaction had surprised her and she was upset.

She went directly to Jimmie's room without bothering to check in at the desk. Everyone was used to seeing her around, anyway. But the bed where Momma had stayed over the past weeks was empty. Stunned, she walked closer to make sure that it was the same room. It was. Everything was exactly as she left it the last time, except Momma wasn't there. The worst of thoughts raced through her mind. Quickly, she rushed to the nurse's station, demanding, "Where've you taken her mother? She's not in her bed! Is something wrong?"

The nurse was startled, "Oh, Mrs. Sharp. They had to move your mother. She's downstairs, on the basement level."

"What? Oh my God!" She didn't wait to find out why. She rushed down the hallway toward the stairway exit. Her emotions were scrambled; her heart was pounding. When she reached the bottom floor, she searched frantically from room to room, not waiting to ask a nurse where they had taken her momma. In the fourth room she entered, she saw Momma, so fragile, so tiny, unconscious. But Fauna's eyes were immediately drawn to the opposite side of the room. The small window near the top of the wall cast a light across the face and shoulders of a beautiful black woman who was sitting up in her bed, wearing the customary green hospital gown. Fauna glanced back at her momma, but only for a moment. Her eyes were drawn back to the other woman, and this time she looked more carefully. The woman's reddened eyes were full of hatred. The tense muscles in her face cast shadows. Her arms were bound with straps to the steel frames of the bed railings. As Fauna stared, the woman became even more irate, and with a burst of energy quickly lunged forward, only to have the restraints frustrate her movement. Fauna stepped back closer to the head of Jimmie's bed, and kept a cautious eye on the woman.

Jimmie was asleep, or in a coma; she didn't know which. Her hair, once thick, black and wavy, was now sparse, stringy and full of scabs. The color was gone and through the dull gray Fauna could see her blotchy brown scalp. Jimmie was frail, and bedsores covered her body. Slowly she moved, just a wee bit, almost as though she felt Fauna's presence. Fauna held her small, delicate body in her arms. She feared a hug would break a bone. She rocked her very gently, and stroked her soft cheeks, whispering, "I love you, Momma."

She stayed with her for over an hour, trying to ignore the hostile woman in the other bed, who was now a bit calmer, but still staring and still angry, yet not saying a word.

Fauna left Jimmie's side crying and went into the small bathroom in the room. There, she closed the door and fell to her knees begging God and her angels to save her momma. She prayed with all of her heart, offering her own life for Momma's, letting God know that she would sacrifice anything for Momma.

A half-hour of continuous and fervent prayer changed nothing; Momma was still the same. Throughout the evening and all the next day, Fauna was in and out of Momma's room. She prayed with all her strength. She only left for the most necessary tasks—to go check with the doctor, or to check on Yvette, or to call Billy, or get something to eat. At no time did she ever reach Billy at home. She was worried and at the same time felt resentment toward Billy for insisting that she stay in San Diego this last time when Momma needed her most. In a way, she was glad that he didn't answer the phone.

When she entered Jimmie's room on the third day, the mad woman was exceptionally militant. She was screaming, cursing, throwing a temper tantrum, hampered only by the restraints, or maybe because of them, she didn't care which. But Fauna felt the hostility and it frightened her. Jimmie was sick enough without having to deal with a half-crazed patient. When she could take no more, Fauna went to the nurse's station and demanded that something be done with that woman.

A middle-aged nurse, with brown hair and big hips, walked back with Fauna to the room and confronted the screaming woman trying to calm her down with a soft but firm tone. Fauna returned to Momma's side and held her hand, keeping a vigilant eye on the disruptive scene. Within about five minutes the woman was more relaxed—still harnessed, but less emotional.

Suddenly, Jimmie reached up from her bed with both hands outstretched. Fauna was startled and elated. Jimmie's eyes were half-opened, looking directly into her daughter's. The nurse noticed Jimmie, who had not moved since she was moved into this room, and quickly came to the foot of her bed. Fauna raised her and held her frail body in an upright but slouched position. Jimmie stared at Fauna and tried to speak. Her dry mouth could barely utter a sound. Momma wouldn't take her eyes from Fauna's.

Fauna was filled to the bursting point with emotion.

"Momma," she said softly, "what is it?"

She again tried to speak, but the words would not come, only a slight "puhh" could be heard from the awkward motion of her cracked lips.

"She loves you," the nurse whispered.

Fauna whispered to her Momma, "What did you say?"

The nurse's eyes were glassy. She stood holding onto the edge of the bed. "She said she loves you. I can tell by the look in her eyes. She really loves you. She wants your forgiveness."

"Oh Momma, I love you. And I forgive you. Please forgive me. Please."

Tears streamed down Fauna's face as she held her close, kissed her forehead, and then placed her gently down on the pillow. "I promise you, Momma, I will make the good life for you. I will make you famous. I will make you a star. Everyone will know Pretty Jimmie Lee, everyone."

Slowly Jimmie's eyelids opened, radiating just the slightest hint of life. She coughed again and closed her eyes.

Fauna stood at her Momma's bedside with her head down. She watched the rise and fall of her mother's breath. She cried for her momma's life. She thought of nothing else but of God allowing her momma to get better, not worse. She couldn't bear the thought of her momma leaving this world.

Fauna was overwrought. Her knees began to quiver, signaling the need for her to sit down. She again went into the tiny bathroom and prayed to God for Momma's salvation. She knew now, from looking deep into those once fearsome yet loving eyes that her momma was going to die and there was nothing she could do. It was time.

She knelt down on the hard tile floor. Her knees were raw, but she couldn't move. Fauna wept aloud, letting all of her pent-up feelings burst forth; it seemed like every shred of anger and frustration. All of her muscles melted into a flaccid heap. And when she thought it was finally over, and there was nothing left in her reservoir of tears, she again exploded in a shower of grief, reliving all the pain of losing her momma. Her body ached from the convulsions and she fell to the floor.

Finally, after what seemed an eternity, she heard the harrowing screams of the other black woman; this time more frightening than before. Quickly, she calmed herself and washed the mascara and eye makeup from her face, trying to look composed. She left the bathroom and glanced at Momma, she was limp, just as before. The kind nurse was gone. Fauna turned to the nightmarish sounds of the mad woman and watched her, just for a moment, lurching and twitching in her useless quest for freedom. Fauna could no longer stay in that room with either one of them, she left them both to their fate.

At about two in the morning, the same nurse found Fauna sitting silently, staring at a single candle that glowed in the dimly lit chapel. "Mrs. Sharp," whispered the nurse, "It's your mother. She passed away a few minutes ago. I'm sorry."

Fauna didn't look up. She nodded. The nurse stayed with her a couple of minutes, then vanished in silence. Patta said a final prayer for her mother, without tears, without emotion. In her mind, she heard the nurse say the hospital would no longer take care of Jimmie.

There were so many things to be done. Momma needed a new dress, everyone had to be called and told of the news, funeral arrangements had to be made, limousines had to be reserved, someone had to take care of Yvette. The casket! Momma had the good sense to take care of that on her own; she needed to find Roxy to find out which one. There were so many details to be taken care of. Who would give her eulogy? What would they say? What about food? I'll have to call Aunt Dolly and Aunt Rosie. Her mind raced, trying to decide what to do first.

She rushed from the chapel and found the nearest phone. She searched frantically through the Yellow Pages for the mortician. "There! There he is! Rodgers Funeral Home." She called and let the phone ring until someone finally answered.

"Hello?" the voice on the other end sounded very groggy. She knew it was late, but this was too important. It had to be done—now!

"Hello. I'm sorry to call so late. . . ."

"Who is this?"

"This is Mrs. Sharp, Fauna Sharp. My mother is Jimmie Lee Faison. I'm here at the hospital. I want to know if you picked her up yet."

"Picked her up? What are you talking about?"

"My mother. She died. I want to know if you picked up her body."

"I'm sorry, but I don't know who she is."

"She's black. And very, very pretty, but she's lost a lot of weight recently. . . ."

Suddenly, someone jerked the phone out of Fauna's hand. She was startled and confused. She thought she was alone. Quickly she turned. It was the nurse, who held the phone close to her breast.

It's O.K., I'll take care of this," said the nurse, as Fauna began to cry. "Why don't you go home and try to get some sleep."

"But there's so much to do!" she said.

"Don't worry. Just go home. There's nothing you can do now."

When she realized the time and where she was, Fauna felt foolish. She apologized and left the hospital.

It was November 12, 1976. A phone call from Aunt Rosie woke her early. The hospital had called Rosie and she phoned everyone. She was on her way over, she told Fauna. Jimmie had been dead only a few hours. Fauna put on the coffee and took a shower, trying to invigorate herself for the long emotional ordeal that lay ahead of her. Alone for the first time without Momma, she prayed for the strength to go on.

Aunt Rosie entered with tears in her eyes and threw her arms around Fauna. Then she said, "I'm sorry, Patta. She's with the Lord now; she's finally at peace."

Rosie stepped back, "Her remains are at the funeral home. I spoke with them this morning. They want you to go down sometime later on today to sign some papers and make sure she looks okay."

"Oh God," Fauna said dreadfully.

"Don't worry, you'll be all right. Take her favorite dress with you, and the wig—don't forget the wig. You know she'd never want to be seen unless she was as pretty as she could be."

"I want to call Reverend Mayfield for the eulogy."

"But I've already spoken with Reverend Webb!" Rosie said.

"That's okay. He'll understand. Mayfield and Momma are two of a kind. It's better that way."

During the rest of the morning and most of the afternoon, relatives and close friends stopped by. They brought food and liquor and sat somberly, occasionally telling anecdotes that often turned into outrageous stories about Jimmie. Fauna knew most of them, but there were some stories about her early childhood that made her love Momma even more.

About eight o'clock that evening, she left everyone to go down to the mortician's. They were expecting her. They talked for a while and then they brought her into where Jimmie was, lying peacefully in her favorite casket. Her body looked so scrawny, yet somehow her persona was larger in death than it had been in life. Fauna stepped before the casket and placed Momma's wig on her brown head, fixing it so that she could look beautiful for her public. She was still Pretty Jimmie. She kissed her softly on the forehead, waiting ever so patiently for her to move, or perhaps smile at her, but all was motionless. She placed a single red rose in the cold, clasped hands and stood silently meditating, hoping that wherever Momma was, she would hear her prayers and she would know that she loved her.

When she returned to the house an hour or so later, she went directly to her room and opened her diary for the last time. She wrote:

Flowers of Remembrance
A Rose for your hand
A Flower for your heart
When we meet again
Will you
Remember it was
I who cherished you . . .

The Rose I placed
With you
Will wither
And fade with you —
But when you rise
The message of
The Rose will
Direct you to me.

On the day that Jimmie's body was to be viewed for the last time, the church was only half-filled with close friends and relatives. Reverend Mayfield escorted Fauna in and took his place at the pulpit. He was Jimmie's close friend and as he spoke, Fauna's mind wandered off, remembering all the sad times and good times. The service was short, but Reverend Mayfield preached from his heart.

He was her friend; he was her companion. He told all who were there to "be not quick to judge, for all have sinned. She was mocked for her drink, but don't be too quick—for sin is sin—and only God can judge whose sin is worse."

There were cries from mourners, some of whom only knew her as a kindly and generous pretty black lady. Afterward, outside, there were again condolences. An hour later, her body was taken to Mountain View Cemetery. Aunt Rosie suggested that Fauna go back to the house rather than stand outside the church. Fauna agreed, and the driver took her home, leaving everyone to go on to the cemetery without her. She would meet them later.

She walked into Jimmie's house for the last time and looked over Momma's few meager possessions. Not much to account for in a life that had lasted more than fifty-seven years. In a few weeks, no one will remember her, Fauna thought. No one will care that she even lived, no one except me. She sat down at the table and opened the guest book from the funeral home where Jimmie's friends had entered their names. She looked over them one at a time, picturing each face and each voice.

At the end of the small book there was a page titled "Biographical Notes." She picked up a pen and wrote the last note:

> *To Jimmie,*
> *My Precious Mother —*
> *Oh how I love you! Though we battled, and yes, even cried together, I know you're my mother, and that has made it all worthwhile.*
> *Momma, I'll meet you again when times are bliss. And oh, how we'll rejoice! Because God will have given us eternal peace.*
> *I sent you roses while you still lived. I bid you off to a final resting place. You look so contented. At last you've found a place where you fit.*
> *Your Pat*
> *Fauna Nov. 14, 1976*

She hadn't realized how much time had gone by until she heard a knock on the door. When she opened it, there stood the tall, distinguished chauffeur dressed in a black suit, with his cap pulled down covering his eyes, ready to escort her to the waiting limousine. "It's time to go, Mrs. Sharp," he said. His voice sounded familiar. She looked up at him and for just a second, thought she recognized something familiar in his face. She gently closed the book and said, "Yes, I'm ready."

The End

EPILOGUE

by Fauna Hodel

My biological mother chose to have me raised by African-Americans, or Negroes, as they were called in the early 1950s. It was unusual and dangerous for my momma to be in the custody of a white child. The thing is—I didn't know I was white; I believed what was printed on my birth certificate—that my father was a Negro. I defended my black existence with that important piece of paper. It was what defined me when I was younger. Though I soon began to realize that I was caught between two worlds. I lived in a constant struggle to balance between these worlds. In reality, I was balancing four worlds, the two worlds of black and white and two of my own worlds. My own worlds were those of my real life with my momma, and that secret and imaginary world that had me meeting, loving, and knowing my natural mother. However, my real world dominated my life. A world where I was being raised in a life of poverty, settled in the African American culture, and surrounded by people such as Big Momma, my aunts, the church, and other family and friends who embraced me and loved me even though I was white. A world where prejudice was a part of my daily life. . . . A world where I was being raised by a woman who complained about bigotry yet had learned to be prejudiced herself. . . . A world where the question of who I really was haunted me daily.

From about the age of eight, I had a mission. It all started with a film I saw with Momma in 1959, *Imitation of Life*, which still haunts me to this day. I found the anger expressed by the main character, Sarah Jane, because she was black, unbearable. She separated herself from her mother and denied her heritage. She had broken her mother's heart. As Mahalia Jackson sang during the mother's funeral, I vowed I would grow up and do something about the cruelty people heaped on one another because of the color of another's skin. I clearly remember the dirty looks given to me by the theatergoers when I called my mama 'Momma.' After the movie, I noticed that even the mean-faced people were sobbing. It was evident that their hearts had been touched. Yes, I thought, I would one day grow up and make a picture that would soften cruel people's hearts. I remember my Momma and I sitting in our seats for a long while after the movie—just taking in the message. When we both stopped crying, Momma looked at me and asked if I would ever leave her. I replied, "Momma I will never leave you."

Since the time my momma took me in, my momma knew I was not a mixed child and told me so. She would say, "You ain't mixed, child." Yet, people would say that she just needed to wait awhile for my skin to darken to show that I did, indeed, possess black blood. However, that was never to happen. While it certainly can be said that Jimmie Lee made mistakes as a mother, she loved me as best she could, sacrificed for me, protected me, and always did what she thought was best on my behalf. I loved her. However, my presence added to her experiences in the prejudiced world and served to help her bitterness thrive.

My momma really died from a crushed heart; her rage was her destruction. She resented the prejudice she experienced due to her color. It had all started in Mississippi after the death of her father. She was no longer pretty Jimmie, her daddy's pride and joy, but merely the white folks' slave. She had deep anger pent up and spilling out on a daily basis. Anyone and everyone in her path could be a target of her misplaced ire.

At a young age, I was aware; I understood my momma's soul even before I understood her rages. I wanted to make Momma a princess and give her a castle so she could be a prima donna. I did not get that chance.

My momma died in 1976, and I can honestly say that I have never abandoned her or my childhood mission. She is still just as much a part of my life as she was all those years ago. Her dying would take me many years to process. This personal tragedy was the hardest thing I have ever experienced. Momma's reaching out to me on her deathbed while I held her fragile body absolutely devastated me. She died a broken woman. It was immediately after her passing that I faced my biggest failure—she had died before I could fix her. From childhood, I had committed myself to her well-being. I made it my job to make her happy, keep her from drinking, and have her accept my love. A job, sadly, I could not totally fulfill. For over a year after her death, I suffered insomnia.

For as long as I can remember, I was writing my feelings in journals mostly through poems. I saved these scraps of paper, carried them with me, and told people one day I would publish a book and make a film that would touch the hearts of others.

Years later, as I stood on the corner of Virginia Street, in Reno, Nevada watching the filming of the movie about my life, in my mind's eye I saw my momma dancing up and down that street. I also saw my precious Homer grinning from ear to ear. My momma was finally somebody special. But she had always been special to me. While I lived with her fire and ice . . . she loved me and sacrificed for me. I feel blessed to also have been surrounded by extended family who shared their love. Plus, I had a few strong romantic relationships that also gave me the love I so desired. As I grew into my teens, I became more independent and perpetuated the cycle of generational teen pregnancy with the birth of my precious daughter, Yvette. From the time I was a little girl, I had dreamed of finding my real mother and learning where I came from. Now, as a young mother, with a very sick momma and mortality becoming a daily thought, I had to chase that dream into reality. This, I did.

Yet, words cannot even begin to explain the intensity of my first encounter with my natural mother, Tamar, in 1974. The revelations uncovered at that meeting still unnerve me. Momma had raised me to have compassion for my real 'mom.' She always made sure I understood that Tamar had been forced to give me away because of my 'supposed' mixed blood. She made Tamar's parents the villains. While I truly had empathy for Tamar, nothing would shield me from the shock of what she told me about her life, her father, and her mother.

My earlier meetings with Tamar's mother, Dorothy, sowed seeds of distrust toward Tamar. It would take me over twenty years before I would allow her into my heart. Because Momma had put me through so much, I felt I had to handle Tamar with kid gloves. The contrast between bizarre stories told to me by Tamar, and the fantasies I created about my 'real' mother would confuse me. Yet somehow, I managed to accept them for what they were, in their time and in their place.

I have to say that at times I identified with the real and unreal. For example, sometimes I felt like the fictional Nancy Drew, uncovering clues and facts about my real family, yet at other times I felt like Erin Brockovich, stumbling onto a much bigger and scarier picture than I imagined . . . a picture that threatened the very essence of my being. As I gathered more facts, and as the drama surrounding my conception, birth family, and subsequent life continued to unfold, I just knew I had to create a film. I felt it must be done if only to blow everyone up larger than life, dissect, and remodel them in order to attempt to figure out what this all meant to my purpose in life.

One important milestone I reached was that during my years with Bill Sharp, I let go of my need to be accepted as black. Billy reached deep into my psyche and helped me remove the color barriers in my head—it was about then I started to identify with the human race. It was then I also started to really think about the future. I felt a great need to spread the message of kindness.

When Yvette and I met Tamar in 1974, I fell in love with Hawaii. I loved the way we were embraced and bathed in the Aloha spirit. Hawaii was just the place for my daughter and I. It felt like a good fit. So, I moved to Hawaii while pregnant with my second child to ensure that my baby would not be raised in the racial strife of the continental United States.

Tamar's brother, my uncle, Steve Hodel, a homicide detective, chronicled his investigation into the mysterious mutilation and murder of Angeleno, Elizabeth Short, in his best selling book, *The Black Dahlia Avenger*. He not only confirms what Tamar had told me years earlier, that my grandfather was capable of anything, but also uncovers how powerful a man he was; powerful enough to prevent the completion and release of the film I had created that would have further blackened his reputation.

I will release a film and documentary based on my life. I am also interested in helping people in other ways. My big dream is to start a philanthropy center in Los Angeles and Hawaii that can help those in need, especially abused children. In the meantime, I pray that the release of this book will strike hope in the hearts of the readers who have encountered prejudice, bigotry, or racial strife. I further pray that my book has a strong impact on the reader and can serve as a learning tool on how to deal with cruelty and the injustice of racial prejudice. My ultimate goal through all of my endeavors is to point people to oneness and remind them that we are all one human family and to emphasize the importance of kindness. I have learned that my inner compass guides me in my belief of angels and points me in the direction of kindness and love for all I encounter. Life is precious and we are here to be the best person we can be and to live life fully. My daughters, Yvette and Rasha represent the color of love and are my driving force and . . . indeed . . . I am so blessed.

FULFILLING OUR DESTINY

by Tamar Hodel

When you were taken from me in 1951 . . . The beautiful Lady Nada visited me at St. Elizabeth's Home for Unwed Mothers telling me "that you would be watched over and taken care of" . . . and even though I wasn't even allowed to hold you, plus being told by my mother that "I must never try to find you or contact you in any way " . . . I sensed that you were being watched over by Angels

All that was to unfold in our future however was erased from my conscious mind. When we were reunited in 1972 . . . (how astounding and miraculous that was!). On the way to the Honolulu Airport to meet your plane I felt that something very big and intense was about to happen . . . and of course, indeed it was. :-)

At the house in Lanikai you asked me why you were given away and I revealed the events so familiar to me, but of course shocking to you (and most others)—the saga of "Dr. George Hill Hodel," "The Incest Trial in 1949," our family and the consequences of telling the truth.

From that moment on many mysteries surfaced, some bizarre connections and a *large* story began to unfold.

I speak up for those of us
Who walk the middle road
I speak up for those of us
Who have no place to fit.

We are not white, or black,
brown, red or yellow,
We are of the wandering tribe . . .
searching for humankind

— Fauna Hodel

ABOUT THE AUTHOR

Fauna Hodel, the white daughter of a prominent California family, was given away at birth to a young black woman who worked as a restroom attendant in a Nevada casino. Fauna grew up believing she was of mixed race, encountering prejudice from both blacks and whites. When she sought out her birth mother, Tamar, years later, she uncovered her family link to the prime suspect in the Black Dahlia murder mystery. Fauna's early life is the inspiration for the TNT series *I Am the Night*, which Fauna also produced.

After being born in San Francisco and raised in Reno, Fauna moved to Hawaii and became an author and a motivational speaker. She committed her life to breaking down racial barriers by sharing her own incredible experiences and encouraging others to pursue their dreams. In 2017, Fauna passed away from breast cancer. She was mother to daughters, Yvette Gentile and Rasha Pecoraro, who continue her legacy.